PRAISE FOR *THE WRITING REVOLUTION*

"The writing strategies discussed in this book are life-changing for students who are exposed to them. A must-read for educational leaders, teachers, and parents . . . giving students the power of the pen to write their way to a successful future."

—**Deirdre A. DeAngelis-D'Alessio**,
principal, New Dorp High School

"This program has the power to illuminate and make big ideas and big content move into the minds of our young people. Hear my plea . . . do not dismiss the work of *The Writing Revolution*. It represents the highest art of teaching."

—**David Coleman**, president and chief executive officer,
The College Board

"*The Writing Revolution*, true to its name, is a truly revolutionary resource for educators. This revolution is an awakening of consciousness firmly based in research, strong and easy-to-implement practices, and most importantly, refreshingly rational thought about writing instruction in particular, and literacy in general."

—**David Abel**, chief academic officer, ELA, of UnboundEd

"Every once in a while, you find an outstanding method that is clear, makes sense, and is embraced by teachers and students alike, and what's most important, works! This is how I would describe *The Writing Revolution*. I have observed it in action, and I have been encouraging teachers to learn about it and use it. Students who are engaged in this find that not only their writing skills but also their thinking and reading skills improve as well."

—**Sally E. Shaywitz**, author of *Overcoming Dyslexia* (Knopf);
Yale University School of Medicine, The Audrey G. Ratner Professor in Learning
Development; co-director, Yale Center for Dyslexia & Creativity

"As someone who has dedicated his life to writing and reading, I enthusiastically endorse the method so lucidly presented in *The Writing Revolution*. This book will give our nation's students a solid writing foundation because it shows teachers how to teach, not just assign, writing."

—**Peter Travers**, *Rolling Stone*, senior writer and film critic

"*The Writing Revolution* offers teachers across the content areas ground-breaking guidance on how to develop *all* students into clear, coherent young writers."

—**Jessica Matthews-Meth**, former director of secondary literacy for DC Public Schools,
instructional coach in the District of Columbia

"As an author, I am deeply concerned about the vast number of students who cannot express themselves with clarity in their writing. *The Writing Revolution* is grounded in research, has been proven effective by decades of classroom application, and is impeccable in its logistics."

—**Mary Higgins Clark**, best-selling author

"*The Writing Revolution* offers a clear, practical, research-based methodology for instruction. From teacher to administrator, all educators will benefit from this book. The authors demystify the teaching of writing so that we may better fill the world with strong writers."

—**Esther Klein Friedman**, executive director,
Literacy and Academic Intervention Services,
New York City Department of Education

"The practices and approach laid out within these covers work. We had the good fortune to discover Dr. Hochman's approach in 1988 through our son, who was her student at Windward. Since then, we've taught writing using the Hochman Method to elementary school reluctant writers in Harlem, adolescents studying the trades in Vermont, community college students struggling to put words to paper, and to hundreds of teachers baffled by how to improve their students' writing. We celebrate the arrival of this lucid guide to making every student an articulate, confident writer."

—**David and Meredith Liben**,
Student Achievement Partners and ReadingDoneRight.org

"*The Writing Revolution* provides concrete, evidence-based strategies for building writing fluency. It's a godsend for classroom teachers who are intent on giving their students the tools to communicate in a rich and engaging way."

—**Barbara Davidson**, executive director,
Knowledge Matters Campaign

"*The Writing Revolution* provides an excellent framework for teaching writing to all students. Elementary, middle, high school, and college educators can improve their instruction by applying strategies set forth in this book. This book clearly demonstrates how to use spoken language to support writing, in turn, supporting critical thinking by students across *all* content areas. It's a great tool for supporting college and career readiness standards outlined in the Common Core State Standards, a timely and important need for all educators."

—**Anthony D. Koutsoftas**, associate professor,
Department of Speech Language Pathology,
School of Health and Medical Sciences,
Seton Hall University

The Writing Revolution

A Guide to Advancing Thinking Through Writing in All Subjects and Grades

Judith C. Hochman and Natalie Wexler

Foreword by Doug Lemov

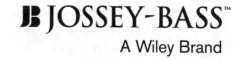

A Wiley Brand

Published by Jossey-Bass
A Wiley Brand
One Montgomery Street, Suite 1000, San Francisco, CA 94104-4594—www.josseybass.com

Jossey-Bass books and products are available through most bookstores. To contact Jossey-Bass directly call our Customer Care Department within the U.S. at 800-956-7739, outside the U.S. at 317-572-3986, or fax 317-572-4002.

Wiley publishes in a variety of print and electronic formats and by print-on-demand. Some material included with standard print versions of this book may not be included in e-books or in print-on-demand. For this title you may find those resources on the author site at http://twr-resources .thewritingrevolution.org/.

For more information about Wiley products, visit www.wiley.com.

Library of Congress Cataloging-in-Publication Data

Names: Hochman, Judith, author. | Wexler, Natalie, author. | Lemov, Doug, 1967- writer of foreword.
Title: The writing revolution : a guide to advancing thinking through writing in all subjects and grades / Judith C. Hochman and Natalie Wexler ; foreword by Doug Lemov.
Description: San Francisco, CA : Jossey-Bass, 2017. | Includes bibliographical references and index.
Identifiers: LCCN 2017026363 (print) | LCCN 2017010697 (ebook) | ISBN 9781119364948 (pdf) | ISBN 9781119364979 (epub) | ISBN 9781119364917 (pbk.)
Subjects: LCSH: Academic writing. | Critical thinking.
Classification: LCC LB1047.3 (print) | LCC LB1047.3 .H63 2017 (ebook) | DDC 808/.0427—dc23
LC record available at https://lccn.loc.gov/2017026363

Cover Design by Wiley
Cover Image: © chrupka/Shutterstock

Printed in the United States of America

FIRST EDITION

SKY10057439_101123

Contents

Acknowledgments

So many people have played a part in bringing this book to publication that it is nearly impossible to name them all—but we will do our best. First and foremost, we want to thank The Writing Revolution (TWR) team, led by Jacki Kelly, our executive director, and especially our senior faculty members Dina Zoleo and Toni-Ann Vroom. They each read the manuscript multiple times, displaying endless patience, making excellent suggestions, and providing much-needed editing.

The faculty and staff members at New Dorp High School on Staten Island, New York, under the outstanding leadership of Deirdre DeAngelis, provided us with an unforgettable experience. When Principal DeAngelis adopted the writing method in 2008, she began a partnership between TWR and the school's faculty that proved life-changing for all of us—and for many of New Dorp's students. The school, once failing, has now been honored as a New York City Department of Education Showcase School.

The teachers and administrators of the District of Columbia Public School system, which undertook a multiyear pilot project with us beginning in 2013, taught us much about implementing the method in a large school district. We were welcomed into many wonderful classrooms and saw some amazing teaching. Every school visit was a learning experience. We would like to thank, in particular, the following district- and school-level administrators and instructional coaches for their support and encouragement: Lauren Castillo, Corinne Colgan, Kimberly Douglas, Louise Fairley, Lauren Johnson, Jessica Matthews Meth, Gwendolyn Payton, Brian Pick, Mary Anne Stinson, and Lauren Weaver.

We are grateful to the Edwin Gould Foundation and its president and CEO, Cynthia Rivera Weissblum, for incubating our organization in its early days. We are also deeply indebted to Peg Tyre, an award-winning journalist who also serves as director of strategy at the Gould Foundation. Peg wrote a widely acclaimed article about the adoption of our writing method at New Dorp High School, which appeared in *The Atlantic* in 2012. The article sparked so much interest that we were obliged to start an organization to respond to it.

Our editor at Jossey-Bass, Kate Gagnon, was a supportive and steadying presence throughout the writing process and gave us excellent suggestions. Hannah Levy and Connor O'Brien also provided valuable guidance. Doug Lemov and Erica Woolway were generous enough to read the manuscript in its early stages and give us encouragement and perceptive feedback.

We are also grateful to the many administrators and teachers who have implemented our method in their schools and classrooms throughout the country and given thousands of students the opportunity to express themselves more effectively.

Last, but definitely not least, we appreciate the support of our families and friends and their recognition that our mission is an important one. In particular, we owe a deep debt of thanks to our husbands, Stephen Hochman and Jim Feldman, for their technical, legal, moral, and emotional support, without which this book might never have seen the light of day.

About the Authors

Judith C. Hochman is the founder and chief academic officer of The Writing Revolution, a not-for-profit organization. She was the superintendent of the Greenburgh Graham Union Free School District; head of The Windward School in White Plains, New York; and the founder of the Windward Teacher Training Institute. Dr. Hochman has taught in mainstream and special education settings and has master's degrees in special education and psychology as well as a doctorate of education in curriculum and instruction, all from Teachers College, Columbia University. Dr. Hochman lectures and presents workshops and courses for educational organizations, colleges and universities, and public and independent schools throughout the United States. She is the author of two books and several articles on writing instruction.

Natalie Wexler is an education journalist who serves on the board of trustees of The Writing Revolution. Her articles and essays have appeared in a number of publications, including the *New York Times* and the *Washington Post,* and for several years she was the education editor of Greater Greater Washington, a news website and communal blog in Washington, DC. She has also been a volunteer reading and writing tutor in high-poverty DC schools. Before turning to education journalism, Wexler worked as a lawyer, a legal historian, and a freelance writer and essayist on a number of topics. She is the author of three novels and holds a BA in English history and literature from Harvard University, an MA in English history from the University of Sussex, and a JD from the University of Pennsylvania Law School.

To Toni-Ann Vroom and Dina Zoleo,

for believing in the method

and for being invaluable partners in bringing it to others

Foreword

A few years ago our family spent a couple of months in London. My kids were 13, 11, and 6 at the time, and I had work there so we decided to take the once-in-a-lifetime opportunity to live in one of the world's great capitals. We paid regular visits to the British Museum, combed through the food stalls at Borough Market, and traced on foot the remains of the city's medieval wall. There were day trips to Bath and Cambridge. We even had a *local*—pub, that is, which really should go without saying.

It was an incredible experience, thanks in no small part to what I learned at a lunch I had with one of the authors of this book before we left. I'd read an article about Judith Hochman's work at New Dorp High School in *The Atlantic* a year or two before, and it had stayed with me. Hochman espoused embedding writing instruction in content. She thought sentences were overlooked and rarely taught. She thought syntax—"syntactic control"—was the link to unlock the connection between better writing and better reading. She believed in the power of deliberate practice to build reading skills. Her work was technical and granular. And the results were hard to ignore. It was the kind of thing I was drawn to.

A friend had connected us and I drove down to meet her—with what soon revealed itself as typical graciousness she had invited me to her home near New York City—and the result was one of the most memorable days of my working life. I remember scratching notes furiously on page after page of my notebook, trying to capture everything she observed—about writing, its connection to reading and thinking, and about why so many kids struggled to learn it. Over and over Hochman would hit on an idea that had been swirling in my head in inchoate wisps and put it into a clear, logical formulation of practice. Here was the idea you were fumbling with, described perfectly; here was how you'd make it work.

I couldn't write fast enough, but I remember thinking that when I got home, I would read everything she'd written. This, however, turned out to be the only disappointment. There wasn't, until now, any place where the ideas Hochman had talked about were written down in one cohesive place for a reader like me. I was left with the observations in my notebook, the hope that Hochman would someday write the book you are now holding, and her sentence-expansion activities.

It was these activities that were the gift that transformed our trip to London. Hochman had spent about 20 minutes riffing on the idea the day we met. The sentence was the building block of writing and thinking, the "complete thought," we agreed, but if you looked at the complete thoughts students produced in their writing, they were too often wooden, repetitive, inflexible. If the task of wrestling ideas into written words was to memorialize thinking, students—at least most of them—did not often have control of a sufficient number of syntactic forms and tools to capture and express complex thoughts. They could not express two ideas happening at once, with one predominating over the other. They could not express a thought interrupted by a sudden alternative thesis. Their ideas were poor on paper because their sentences could not capture, connect, and, ultimately, develop them. That last part was the most damning of all. One way to generate complex ideas is to write them into being—often slowly adding and reworking and refining, as I find myself doing now as I draft and revise this foreword for the 10th or 20th or 100th time. Because students could not say what they meant, and because, as a result, they did not practice capturing and connecting complex ideas with precision in writing, they had fewer complex ideas. Or they had ideas like the sentences they wrote: predictable, neither compound nor complex. What might have been a skein of thought was instead a litter of short broken threads, each with a subject-verb-object construction.

Hochman's solution was regular intentional exercises to expand students' syntactic range. You could ask them to practice expanding their sentences in specific and methodical ways and they'd get better at it. Crucially, she pointed out, this must be done in a content-rich environment because "the content drives the rigor." Sentences needed ideas pressing outward from inside them to stretch and expand their limits. Only rich content gave them a reason to seek and achieve nuance.

One example of a Hochman sentence expansion exercise was called *because, but, so.* The idea was deceptively simple: You gave students a sentence stem and then asked them to expand it three different ways—with the common conjunctions *because, but,* and *so.* This would help them to see each sentence as constantly expandable. And it would, as Hochman writes in this book, "prod them to think critically and deeply about the content they were studying—far more so than if you simply asked them to write a sentence in answer to an open-ended question." It would build their ability to conjoin ideas with fluidity. It would help them to understand, through constant theme and variation, the broader concepts of subordination and coordination.

I want to pause here to digress on the seemingly underwhelming concepts of coordination and subordination. I will ask you to stifle your yawn as I acknowledge that they are easy to dismiss—ancient, faintly risible, uttered once long ago by acolytes of sentence diagramming in the era of chalk dust. They smack of grammar-for-grammar's sake, and almost nobody cares about that. Teachers instead seek mostly to simply make sure the sentences work and dispense with the parsing of parts. It is so much simpler to tell kids to go with "sounds right" (an idea that inherently discriminates against those for whom the sounds of language are not happily ingrained by luck or privilege) or to make the odd episodic correction and not worry about the principle at work.

But coordination and subordination are in fact deeply powerful principles worth mastering. They describe the ways that ideas are connected, the nuances that yoke disparate thoughts together. It is the connections as much as the ideas that make meaning. To master conjunctions is to be able to express that two ideas are connected but that one is more important than the other, that one is dependent on the other, that one is contingent on the other, that the two ideas exist in contrast or conflict. Mastering that skill is immensely important not just to writing but to reading. Students who struggle with complex text can usually understand the words and clauses of a sentence; it is the piecing together of the interrelationships among them that most often poses the problem. They understand the first half of the sentence but miss the cue that questions its veracity in the second half. And so without mastery of the syntax of relationships—which is what coordination and subordination are—the sentence devolves—for weak readers—into meaninglessness.

For weeks I reflected on the power of these simple activities for teachers and students, but my reflections were not limited to my role as an educator. As a father I was intrigued as well, and I suppose this is the truest test of an educational idea.

Fast forward to London some months later, where I found myself for three months essentially homeschooling the Lemov children, those regular and long-suffering subjects of a thousand of their father's teaching ideas. To keep them writing and thinking I had them keep journals, and in those journals I found myself using and adapting Hochman's exercises. They were the perfect tidy-wrap summation to a long day out exploring.

Here are some early *because, but, so* exercises I rediscovered a few weeks ago in my then-11-year-old daughter's journal.

I gave her the sentence stem: "The Great Fire of London burned 4/5 of the city . . ."

She wrote:

The Great Fire of London burned 4/5 of the city, because *at the time, citizens didn't have the knowledge or equipment to stop the fire before it spread.*

The Great Fire of London burned 4/5 of the city, but *London survived and thrived.*

The Great Fire of London burned 4/5 of the city, so *many people had to live in temporary homes until the city was rebuilt.*

After a visit to the Museum of Natural History she wrote for the sentence stem, "The length of T-Rex's arms is surprising . . .":

The length of T-Rex's arms is surprising, but *this may have been a mid-evolutionary stage and had they lived for another million years their arms might have disappeared altogether.*

A few weeks later I gave her this sentence stem: "Farleigh Hungerford Castle is now in ruins . . ."

She wrote:

Farleigh Hungerford Castle is now in ruins because *of weathering and age.*

Farleigh Hungerford Castle is now in ruins, but *it is arguably even more interesting now (while in ruins) than ever before.*

Farleigh Hungerford Castle is now in ruins, so *you are able to use some imagination when envisioning the castle at its peak.*

We made these exercises a part of our daily lives, and as we did so their confidence and the range of syntactical forms my kids used in expanding their sentences grew, as did the ideas they developed and encoded in memory.

Another sentence-expansion activity Hochman proposed to me in her living room—and describes at long last in this outstanding book—is deliberate practice using appositives, brief, sometimes parenthetical phrases that, like the phrase you are reading, rename or elaborate on a noun in a sentence, and which can be surprisingly complex. Mastering this idea enables students to expand ideas within a sentence, adding detail, specificity, or nuance in a manner that subordinates the additional information to the overall idea of the sentence. With appositives mastered, students can link more things into the dance of interrelationships within a sentence, reducing the redundancy and disconnectedness of multiple repetitive sentences, and the Lemov kids reflected on their travels through the music of appositives as well.

After a visit to Cambridge and its historic university I asked them to use Hochman's appositive exercise with the sentence: "In Cambridge the 'backs' are in fact the 'fronts.'" You may not understand that sentence at all—it refers to the fact that when you punt down the River Cam, you face what are called the backs of the historic colleges, but this name is ironic because the buildings were mostly built to be seen from the river sides—the backs. My daughter's sentence expansion captures this with a smooth elegance that supersedes the laborious description you just read . She wrote:

> In Cambridge, *a small town with a world-renowned university,* the backs, *the sides of the colleges that face away from the street and therefore onto the river,* are in fact *the elaborate entrances,* the fronts.

I put the appositives she added in italics. Note here a few things that are interesting about this sentence from a teaching and learning perspective:

1. It includes three different appositives, which my daughter used to expand her description of Cambridge, turning it from a sentence whose meaning was locked in code—what the "backs" and "fronts" meant is very specific to Cambridge—and unlocked it for readers less familiar with the subject. This form of explication is common to papers written in academic discourse and is a key academic skill. But even so the three appositives are surprisingly complex.

2. The second appositive, which explains what the phrase "the backs" means, is in fact a compound appositive. First she includes the idea

that the backs are the sides of Cambridge's colleges that face away from the street. The phrase stands up as an appositive by itself, but then she adds—via subordination—a second appositive explaining that the backs are also the sides of the buildings that face the river. Necessity is the mother of invention. In her effort to explain what she knows and enrich the sentence sufficiently she's expanded her range, experimenting with a doubly complex form of appositive.

3. The third example is even more interesting. In it, my daughter has reversed the common order of appositive formation. Usually the noun in a sentence is followed by an appositive phrase that expands on it. But here she has instead put the appositive in front of the noun: the sides of the colleges that face away from the street and therefore onto the river, are in fact *the elaborate entrances, the fronts*. She has flipped the form and is again experimenting with her growing proficiency. No grammar lesson in the world could socialize her to understand and apply compound appositives and inverted appositives, but there she was within just a few weeks crafting carefully wrought sentences.

As our time in London went on I began experimenting with new sentence-expansion activities, and they became a bit of an adventure for my kids—could they express an idea that mattered and also meet the challenges of construction I set for them?

Could they, after visiting Kew Gardens, write a sentence about medicinal plants, starting with *surprisingly* and another sentence using the word *medicinal* and some form of the word *extract* (i.e., extracting, extraction)? Could they write a one-sentence description of the view from Primrose Hill starting *standing atop* but *not* using the name Primrose Hill?

In this sense our time in London was an exploration of the power of several themes that you will find constantly referred to in this book. Hochman and Wexler's study of these themes will be immensely useful to you as an educator, I believe.

The first theme is the idea that if we want students to be great writers we have to be willing to sometimes teach writing through intentional exercises. Writing responds to deliberate practice, and this concept is demonstrably different from mere repetition of an activity, which, as Hochman explains, is how many schools attempt to teach writing. Let me restate that in the plainest terms: Merely repeating an activity is insufficient to get you better at it. This is why you are still as poor a driver today as you were when you were 24. You drive to work every morning without intentional focus on a specific aspect of your craft. You don't get feedback. You don't even know what the skills of driving are really. And so you never get better. You get worse, in fact.

Research—particularly that of psychologist Anders Ericsson—tells us that for practice to improve skills, it has to have a specific and focused goal and must gradually link together a series of smaller goals to created linked skills. It must also be structured in awareness of cognitive load theory—it has to be difficult, to pose a real challenge but not be so difficult that learners engage in random, non-productive guessing to solve problems and not so difficult that the brain shuts down. As cognitive scientist Daniel Willingham points out, the brain learns best when it is challenged in a manageable amount. Finally deliberate practice requires all-in focus, and that is maximized in a short and intense burst. This book's proposal of sequences of adaptable high-quality exercises that can allow for deliberate practice should be adopted immediately by nearly every school.

Second is the idea that writing, thinking, and reading are indelibly linked. They are the three tasks of idea formation and so there is far-reaching power for all of these domains in focusing on the craft of formation. "I write," Joan Didion famously observed, "to know what I think." Related then is the idea that revision is not especially separable from writing. This much I know as a professional writer: As soon as this sentence emerges on your laptop screen you are planning its revision, and helping students to master this hidden phase of writing is necessary to ensuring that students develop refined ideas, not just hasty first-blush ones. This book's study of revision's wherefores and whys will be invaluable to schools.

Third is the idea that there is a scope and sequence to all this. The numinous task of writing can in fact be taught step-by-step with a bit of intentionality if you have Hochman's wisdom and knowledge to guide you. Now you don't have to invent it. The tasks and activities are outlined and organized for you here. You can move directly to execution.

Fourth is the idea of *embedded in content*. Writing is a learning activity as much or more than a discrete subject. It operates in synergy with ideas—the need to express them is after all the reason for being for what is otherwise an unnatural and artificial activity. This book will help you to make every classroom in your school "writing intensive" and therefore learning intensive. If I could wave a magic wand over America's schools and cause one change that would drive the most demonstrable improvement to learning and achievement I would almost certainly wave that wand and conjure up small bursts of intense, reflective, high-quality writing in every class period or every hour across America's schools.

Perhaps last is my own lesson from London. That writing, when taught well, is a joy. You build something real and enduring every time, and this is a source of pleasure. As is the unexpected form it takes. Successful writing gives its practitioner the mystery and satisfaction of constant invention and construction. When you look at the page and wonder, "Now where did that idea come from?" you know you are doing it right; you know your mastery of the craft itself is now guiding you. In that sense this is a magical book, one that can help you achieve a sea change in the minds of the students in your classrooms.

Doug Lemov

Doug Lemov trains educators at Uncommon Schools, the nonprofit school management organization he helped found. He has also authored *Teach Like a Champion* (now in its 2.0 version) and has coauthored the companion *Field Guide, Reading Reconsidered,* and *Practice Perfect.*

Throughout the book we've included student writing samples. Some of these samples are from actual students (under pseudonyms or first names only), and others were created by The Writing Revolution staff members. Some educator and student names have been changed, and in other cases, and where noted, we've used real names with the individual's blessing. Some anecdotes and classroom examples, although based on actual experience, incorporate invented characters and events.

Introduction

How to Lead a Writing Revolution in Your Classroom—and Why You Need One

When Monica entered high school, her writing skills were minimal. After repeating first grade and getting more than 100 hours of tutoring in elementary school, she'd managed to learn to read well enough to get by, and she was comfortable with math. But writing seemed beyond her reach.

During her freshman year at New Dorp, a historically low-performing high school on Staten Island, Monica's history teacher asked her to write an essay on Alexander the Great. "I think Alexander the Great was one of the best military leaders," Monica wrote. Her entire response consisted of six simple sentences, one of which didn't make sense.

An actual essay, Monica said later, "wasn't going to happen. It was like, well, I got a sentence down. What now?"

Monica's mother, who had spent many frustrating years trying to help her daughter improve her academic performance, was equally skeptical about Monica's ability to write an essay. "It just didn't seem like something Monica could ever do."[1]

Unfortunately, Monica is far from alone. Across the country—and especially in schools serving students from low-income families and English language learners—countless students have similar problems expressing themselves clearly and coherently in writing. On nationwide tests, only about 25% of students are able to score at a proficient level in writing.[2]

And yet expository writing—the kind of writing that explains and informs—is essential for success in school and the workplace. Students who can't write at a competent level struggle in college. With the advent of e-mail and the Internet, an increasing number of jobs require solid writing skills. That's true even of many jobs—such as being a paramedic—that people may not think of as involving writing. No matter what path students choose in life, the ability to communicate their thoughts in writing in a way that others can easily understand is crucial.

The Problem: Assigning Writing but Not Teaching It

The problem is not that students like Monica are incapable of learning to write well. Rather, the problem is that American schools haven't been teaching students how to write. Teachers may have assigned writing, but they haven't explicitly taught it in a careful sequence of logical steps, beginning at the sentence level.

That's not the fault of the teachers: In the vast majority of cases, their training didn't include instruction in how to teach writing. The assumption has been that if students read enough, they'll simply pick up writing skills, through a kind of osmosis. But writing is the hardest thing we ask students to do, and the evidence is clear that very few students become good writers on their own. Many students—even at the college level—have difficulty constructing a coherent sentence, let alone a fluid, cohesive **essay**. If you're reading this book, chances are that at least some of your students, and perhaps most, fall into that category.

To be effective, writing instruction should start in elementary school. But when students do get a chance to write in elementary school, they're often encouraged to write at length too soon, sometimes at a furious pace. They don't learn how to construct interesting and grammatically correct sentences first, and they aren't encouraged to plan or outline before they write. The idea is that later on they'll refine their writing, under the teacher's guidance, bringing coherence and—perhaps—correct grammar and punctuation to what they've produced. But after getting feedback, students may be reluctant to rewrite a multipage essay that they've already worked on for hours. And teachers, confronted by page after page of incoherent, error-riddled writing, may not know where to begin.

When students get to middle school or high school, it's assumed that they've already learned the basics of writing. As many secondary teachers know, that assumption has little to do with reality. But rather than beginning with teaching the fundamental skills their students lack—by, say, guiding students through the process of writing well-crafted sentences—teachers feel pressured to have their students meet grade-level expectations and produce multi-paragraph essays.

High school teachers are also likely to ask students to write analytically about the content of the courses they're taking. But many students have written nothing except narratives in elementary and middle school, often about their personal experiences. That kind of writing doesn't prepare them for the demands of high school, college, or the workforce.

In recent years, with the advent of the Common Core and the revamping of many states' standards, teachers at almost all grade levels have been expected to have students write not just narratives but also informative and argumentative essays. But there's been little reliable guidance on how to teach students those skills.[3] The writing standards tell teachers where their students should end up. But what teachers need is a road map that tells them how to get there.

The Writing Revolution (TWR) offers just such a road map. It provides a clear, coherent, evidence-based method of instruction that you can use no matter what subject or grade level you teach. The method has demonstrated, over and over, that it can turn weak writers like Monica into strong ones by focusing students' writing practice on specific techniques that match their needs and providing them with prompt and clear feedback. Insurmountable as the writing challenges faced by many students may seem, TWR can make a dramatic difference.

Beyond Writing: How Writing Instruction Improves Students' Reading, Speaking, and Thinking

As important as it is for students to learn to write well, it's not the only reason to teach writing. When teachers embed explicit writing instruction in the content of the curriculum—no matter the subject area—they see their students' academic abilities blossom. When students have the opportunity to learn TWR strategies and practice them through carefully scaffolded activities, they become better at understanding what they read, expressing themselves orally, and thinking critically.

Explicit writing instruction will help you and your students in the following ways:

- *Identifying comprehension gaps.* When you ask your students to write about what they're learning, you may uncover significant gaps in their knowledge and comprehension—before it's too late to do anything about them.

- *Boosting reading comprehension.* When students learn to use more sophisticated syntax in their own writing, they become better able to understand it when they encounter it in their reading.[4]

- *Enhancing speaking abilities.* As students begin to use more complex terms and sentence constructions in their written language, they begin to incorporate those features into their spoken language as well.

- *Improving organizational and study skills.* TWR activities teach students to paraphrase, take notes, summarize, and make **outlines**. These techniques help them absorb and retain crucial information.

- *Developing analytical capabilities.* The process of writing requires even young students to organize their ideas and sequence information. As they move through the grades they have to sift through a mass of material, deciding for themselves what's important, which facts and ideas are connected to one another, and how to organize their thoughts into a logical progression. When done in a systematic and sequenced way, teaching students to write is equivalent to teaching them how to think.

A Brief History: The Origins of The Writing Revolution

TWR's model, also known as the *Hochman Method,* is now being implemented at a broad range of schools, spanning all grade levels. Teachers from around the country—in fact, from around the world—have been using the method for 25 years, learning it through teacher-training courses held in or near New York City. More recently, TWR has partnered with schools and school districts in New York, Washington, DC, Louisiana, Texas, and elsewhere to provide more intensive and hands-on training and coaching.

But how did this method originate? Years ago, like most classroom teachers, I would assign writing activities that focused on my students' perceptions and feelings: a visit to an imaginary country, a meaningful moment in their lives. My undergraduate and graduate training hadn't included any preparation for teaching writing, as far as I can recall, nor had I been assigned to read any research on effective writing instruction. (Although this book has two authors, the pronoun *I* refers to Judith Hochman.)

Later, as an administrator, I observed many lessons in a similar vein. In the higher grades, when teachers assigned compositions, they assumed that students would intuitively know how to sequence and organize information, relate it to a reader with clarity and coherence, and develop sound introductions and conclusions. The results consistently and dramatically disproved these assumptions.

I was struck by the difference in how we taught writing as opposed to reading. When I taught reading, I didn't just give my students a book and say, "Read this." I used a well-researched method, providing explicit instruction in decoding and using carefully sequenced activities that scaffolded skills until students read fluently and accurately. But when it came to writing, arguably a far more difficult task, I had no way to give students the tools they needed. If their writing fell short, as it often did, we simply told them to "make it better" or "add more details." Clearly, that wasn't enough.

I tried consulting the research, but at the time academic researchers were paying far more attention to reading than writing. So I began to experiment. I was fortunate to be at Windward, an independent school for students with learning and language disabilities in first grade through high school. The Windward staff members and I were able to try varying approaches to writing instruction.

We stopped teaching the mechanics of writing in isolation as a set of rules and definitions. Instead we asked students to write about the content they were learning and then used their writing to give specific guidance. The feedback might be, "use an appositive in your topic sentence," "put your strongest argument last," "use transitions when presenting your points," or "try starting your thesis statement with a subordinating conjunction." Because we had explicitly taught them how to do these things, they were able to respond.

As we saw that these techniques were working for our students, we noticed that researchers who were looking into best practices for teaching writing were finding evidence that supported what we were doing. And our techniques weren't just turning our students into better writers. We also saw improvements in their analytical thinking, reading comprehension, and oral communication.

Seeing such dramatic gains in students who had been functioning poorly in mainstream classes, we decided to share what we were learning with teachers who, like myself, had no proper training in writing instruction. To that end, we founded the Windward Teacher Training Institute.

At first, those who came to the Windward institute were largely special education teachers and tutors, speech and language therapists, and teachers of students learning English as a second language. But as students at Windward benefited from the remediation they received and reentered mainstream schools, teachers at those schools began to notice their excellent writing skills. As a result, teachers of general education classes began enrolling at the institute to learn about the method.

Then, in 2012, an article appeared in *The Atlantic* magazine about how the method we developed at Windward had produced dramatic results at a low-performing public high school with 3,000 students on Staten Island—New Dorp, where Monica started as a freshman in 2009. The article detailed the New Dorp faculty members' discovery that many of their students didn't know how to construct sentences using conjunctions such as *but* and *so*—not to mention words such as *although* and *despite*. The principal of New Dorp, Deirdre DeAngelis, heard about Windward from a friend, went to visit, and decided she wanted to bring that approach to writing instruction to her school.

After New Dorp had been implementing what was then known as the Hochman Method for a couple of years, the article reported, pass rates on state exams that included essay questions rose sharply—in the case of English, from 67% to 89%—as did the graduation rate, from 63% to near 80%. The article spurred a tremendous amount of interest in the method, and in response I founded a nonprofit that used the title of *The Atlantic* article: The Writing Revolution.

Currently most of the requests we get for training, either through our courses or school partnerships, come from mainstream teachers. Most teach in schools primarily serving low-income students, some with high proportions of English language learners and students with learning disabilities. Many of these teachers have found that their students benefit greatly from TWR's explicit, scaffolded writing instructions, just as students at Windward have. But the method—and the principles that underlie it—can benefit any student in any school.

What Makes The Writing Revolution Revolutionary: Deliberate Practice

TWR is as much a method of teaching content as it is a method of teaching writing. There's no separate writing block and no separate writing curriculum. Instead, teachers of all subjects adapt TWR's strategies and activities to their preexisting curriculum and weave them into their content instruction.

But perhaps what's most revolutionary about TWR's method is that it takes the mystery out of learning to write well. In other approaches to writing instruction, a teacher might give students a description of the elements of a good paragraph or essay, or perhaps present a model piece of writing and have them try to emulate it. But for many students, that's not enough. They may be able to read and appreciate writing that flows well and uses varied sentence structure, but that doesn't mean they can figure out how to write that way themselves. For them, the techniques of good writing are a secret code they just can't crack.

TWR's method lets them in on the secret. It breaks the writing process down into manageable chunks and then has students practice the chunks they need, repeatedly, while also learning content. For example, if you want your students to make their sentences more informative and varied, you won't just ask them to do that and leave it up to them to figure out how. Instead, you'll introduce them to specific ways of creating more complex sentences—for example, by using appositives. But you won't just give them the definition of an appositive—"a noun or noun phrase placed next to another noun to explain it more fully"—and ask them to start using appositives in their writing.

Instead, you'll show them examples of appositives and then have them underline appositives in sentences you provide. For example, you might give them "George Washington, the first president of the United States, is often called the father of our country." In that sentence, they would underline "the first president of the United States." Then you'll give them a list of nouns—related to the content they've been studying—along with a list of appositives, and ask them to make the appropriate matches. After that, students will add appositives to sentences you provide or construct sentences around appositives you give them. After a while, you'll ask your students to create their own sentences using appositives—and eventually, they'll simply do that spontaneously.

This kind of practice—*deliberate practice*, as some cognitive scientists call it[5]—is quite different from having students practice writing by giving them, say, half an hour to write and simply turning them loose. Merely doing the same thing over and over is unlikely to improve their performance. To make their writing better, they need a series of exercises that specifically target the skills they haven't yet mastered, while building on the skills they already have, in a gradual, step-by-step process. They also need clear, direct feedback that helps them identify their mistakes and monitor their progress.

Although you will be the ultimate judge of exactly what your students need and when they need it, TWR provides activities that will enable them to engage in deliberate writing practice—along with vocabulary that you can use to give them prompt, effective feedback.

The Six TWR Principles

TWR's method rests on six basic principles:

1. Students need explicit instruction in writing, beginning in the early elementary grades.

2. Sentences are the building blocks of all writing.

3. When embedded in the content of the curriculum, writing instruction is a powerful teaching tool.

4. The content of the curriculum drives the rigor of the writing activities.

5. Grammar is best taught in the context of student writing.

6. The two most important phases of the writing process are planning and revising.

Principle 1: Students Need Explicit Instruction in Writing, Beginning in the Early Elementary Grades

Students won't pick up writing skills just by reading, and they need to learn how the conventions of written language differ from those of spoken language. Many students who are good readers struggle when it comes to writing. Unlike reading, writing involves deciding what to say, which words to use, how to spell them, perhaps how to form the letters, and what order to place the words in—and that's just at the sentence level. Writing a paragraph or an entire essay requires even more decision making, planning, and analysis.

Just as good readers aren't necessarily good writers, students who can speak coherently often write incoherently. Far too many students write the way they speak, using simple or rambling sentences or fragments. That kind of communication may work when we're speaking to someone in front of us: the listeners' facial expressions and gestures indicate whether they're following what we're saying, and we may already be aware of how much they know about the subject we're discussing.

But when we write, we don't have visual cues to draw on, and we often don't know exactly who the audience is. We need to express ourselves with far more precision and clarity, anticipating the facts and details a reader will require to grasp our meaning. We also need to rely on words and punctuation rather than intonation and pauses to indicate nuances in meaning or breaks in the narrative. We have to abide by conventions of spelling and grammar to ensure that mistakes don't distract a reader from the content.

Although good writing should be clear and direct, it often involves more complex sentence structures and a more varied and precise vocabulary than spoken language. When we speak, we rarely begin sentences with words such as *despite* or *although*, but they can be extremely useful in written language. And connecting our thoughts with phrases like *as a result* or *for example*, although unnecessary in most conversational speech, can be vital in creating a fluid piece of writing.

More generally, when we write, our words are preserved on paper—or perhaps on a screen—making not just grammatical and syntactical errors but also logical flaws far more glaring than in spoken language. And we rarely sustain spoken language for the equivalent length of a paragraph, let alone an essay, unless we're delivering a speech or participating in a formal debate. Shaping a logical, unbroken narrative or argument in writing requires far more thought and planning than having a conversation or making a contribution to class discussion.

The elementary grades are the ideal time to begin writing instruction. If we assign only stories, journal entries, and poems in the early grades—as I did as a young teacher—we're wasting precious time. Although it's certainly possible to teach expository writing skills to older students, it's much easier to begin the process in elementary school. Elementary students can practice their spelling and vocabulary words by writing original sentences, and they can acquire knowledge by developing questions about what they're reading. At the same time, they can hone their handwriting skills. (We'll address the importance of teaching handwriting in a later chapter.)

Of course we want children to enjoy writing and use it as a means of self-expression. But many students produce writing so incoherent that readers are unable to respond. We need to equip children with the tools that will give them confidence as writers and enable them to express themselves in a way that others can understand. And far from feeling that practicing the mechanics of writing is drudgery, students often gain a sense of pride and mastery from learning to craft well-constructed sentences and logically sequenced paragraphs.

Principle 2: Sentences Are the Building Blocks of All Writing

In many schools, the quantity of writing has long been valued over its quality. The Common Core and other standards have only increased the pressure on teachers to assign essay-length writing. But if students haven't learned how to write an effective sentence, that is where instruction needs to begin—no matter what the student's age or grade level.

Of course students must learn to write at length, and TWR includes strategies and activities designed to guide them through that process. But a writer who can't compose a decent sentence will never produce a decent essay—or even a decent paragraph. And if students are still struggling to write sentences, they have less brain power available to do the careful planning that writing a good paragraph or composition requires.

A sentence-level assignment is manageable for students who are still grappling with grammar, syntax, spelling, and punctuation—and for their teachers. It can be overwhelming for a teacher to correct an essay full of mechanical errors, especially if it also contains substantive misunderstandings.

Sentence-level writing shouldn't be dismissed as something that's too basic for older students to engage in. As Bruce Saddler has observed, sentences "are literally miniature compositions."[6] Producing even a single sentence can impose major cognitive demands on students, especially if it requires them to explain, paraphrase, or summarize sophisticated content.

Even at the sentence level, however, students need appropriate guidance if their writing skills are to improve. TWR gives teachers an array of activities that guide students to use complete sentences, vary their structure, and use complex syntax and vocabulary—while at the same time ensuring that students master content.

Once students have acquired basic sentence-level skills, TWR also provides structured support for lengthier writing. But crafting an effective sentence is a useful and important exercise, no matter the skill level of the student, and teachers should continue to assign sentence-level activities even after students have moved on to writing paragraphs and compositions.

Principle 3: When Embedded in the Content of the Curriculum, Writing Instruction Is a Powerful Teaching Tool

When schools do focus on expository writing, the assignments are often on topics that draw only on students' personal experiences or opinions rather than on the content of what they are actually studying in English, history, science, or other subjects. Students may, for example, practice persuasive writing by taking pro or con positions on school uniforms or an extended school day or year. They may learn to write a compare-and-contrast essay by weighing the benefits and disadvantages of being famous.

Such general topics can be useful for introducing students to a particular aspect of writing—say, creating topic sentences. But to maximize the benefits of writing instruction, students should start practicing their writing skills on topics embedded in content as soon as possible. At Windward, we saw that when writing assignments were embedded in content, students from the earliest grades through high school were better able to express themselves orally and in writing.

In addition, until students have had quite a bit of systematic and targeted instruction, the writing skills they develop with regard to one subject are unlikely to transfer to another. Even if a student learns to write a decent persuasive essay on why she should have a bigger allowance, she probably won't be able to apply those skills to an essay arguing that the Civil War was fundamentally about slavery.

Beyond that, having students write about topics unrelated to content represents a huge wasted opportunity to boost their learning. Writing isn't merely a skill; it's also a powerful teaching tool. When students write, they—and their teachers—figure out what they don't understand and what further information they need. And, as we observed at Windward, when students write about the content they're studying, they learn to synthesize information and produce their own interpretations. That process helps them absorb and retain the substance of what they're writing about and the vocabulary that goes with it.

So, if students are learning about Ancient Egypt or about tornadoes and hurricanes, part of the instruction in those subjects should include having students write about them. Writing and content knowledge are intimately related. *You can't write well about something you don't know well.* The more students know about a topic before they begin to write, the better they'll be able to write about it. At the same time, the process of writing will deepen their understanding of a topic and help cement that understanding in their memory.

A corollary of this principle is that *all* teachers, no matter their subject area, must be writing teachers. At our partner schools, teachers of history, science, foreign languages, math, and even music, art, and PE have learned to incorporate TWR activities into their instruction. And although schools can exercise some flexibility in deciding which classes will adopt TWR, the more teachers who use it within a given school, the better the results.

Teachers of subjects other than English may be apprehensive about incorporating the teaching of writing into their curricula. They may feel that they never signed up to be writing teachers. However, in our experience most of them find that, rather than detracting from their instruction, implementing TWR actually enhances their ability to teach and boosts their students' performance. And although the strategies should be practiced daily, they may take only 5 to 15 minutes of class time. The strategies can be used as quick comprehension checks, **do-now activities**, and **exit tickets**.

ASK THE EXPERTS

How Writing Boosts Retention and Knowledge

Researchers have found that giving students frequent quizzes strengthens their memories of the material they were quizzed on for two reasons. First, a quiz shows students what they don't know and where they need to focus their studying. Second, a quiz forces their brains to reconsolidate the memory, strengthening the connections between the new material and their prior knowledge and making it easier for them to recall the information in the future.

Asking students to write frequently about what they're learning has the same effect. This approach, sometimes called *writing to learn,* was tested in a college introductory psychology course with more than 800 students. After discussing certain key concepts, the professor asked students to write their own summaries, restating the concepts in their own words and giving examples. For other concepts, the professor merely showed the students slides summarizing the concepts and providing examples, and students copied the information from the slides. The study found that on exams, students scored significantly better on concepts they had summarized in their own words.

Beginning or nonexpert writers may simply put down whatever comes into their heads about a given topic. Here, for example, is how one sixth-grader explained his strategy in writing an essay:

> *I have a whole bunch of ideas and write down till my supply of ideas is gone . Then I might try to think of more ideas up to the point where you can't get any more ideas that are worth putting down on paper and then I would end it.*

Expert writers, on the other hand, decide on their purpose before they begin to write: who their audience is, what they want a reader to learn, and what ideas they want to introduce. They make a plan, sketching out the points they will touch on and deciding in what order to present them. They may show an outline or draft to a reader and find that they need to modify it because the reader doesn't understand it. As they try to make their explanations clearer, they may come up with new insights and make new connections between their ideas.

TWR's method, which has students writing frequently about content they're learning across the curriculum, works much the same way that the experiment in the psychology course did—at the same time giving students the tools to express themselves clearly in writing. The method also emphasizes planning and revising, which helps guide students toward the kind of writing that expert writers are able to do.[7]

Principle 4: The Content of the Curriculum Drives the Rigor of the Writing Activities

If you follow Principle 3 and connect your students' writing activities with the subject matter that you're teaching, you'll find that you can use the same activities for any grade level or content area and still challenge your students. The form of the activity will stay the same, but the content is what makes it more or less rigorous.

For example, one of TWR's sentence-level strategies uses the conjunctions *because, but,* and *so* to encourage extended responses. The teacher gives students a sentence stem, an independent clause ending with one of the conjunctions, and asks them to finish it in three different ways, using each of the three conjunctions.

If you're teaching elementary students, you might give them this stem:

Rocket learned to read _____.

You'll ask the students to complete the stem with a phrase beginning with *because, but, and,* or *so.* They might respond:

Rocket learned to read because *the yellow bird taught him*.

Rocket learned to read, but *at first he was bored*.

Rocket learned to read, so *he was proud of himself*.

In math, instead of asking, "What is a fraction?" you can give your students this stem:

Fractions are like decimals _____.

They might complete it like this:

Fractions are like decimals because *they are all parts of wholes*.

Fractions are like decimals, but *they are written differently*.

Fractions are like decimals, so *they can be used interchangeably*.

If you're teaching a high school American history class, you might give your students this stem:

Andrew Jackson was a popular president _____.

Then you can ask them to finish it with the same three conjunctions. Their answers might look like this:

Andrew Jackson was a popular president because _he was a champion of the common people_.

Andrew Jackson was a popular president, but _there were many critics of his "kitchen cabinet" and the "spoils system."_

Andrew Jackson was a popular president, so _he won the election of 1832 easily_.

If you're teaching science, you could give them this stem:

Aerobic respiration is similar to anaerobic respiration _____.

Here's what they might say:

Aerobic respiration is similar to anaerobic respiration because _both start with glucose and make ATP_.

Aerobic respiration is similar to anaerobic respiration, but _anaerobic respiration does not require oxygen_.

Aerobic respiration is similar to anaerobic respiration, so _both autotrophs and heterotrophs use aerobic and anaerobic respiration_.

In each of these cases, students need to return to the material they have been studying and mine it carefully for information to complete the stems.

No matter what content you use with these kinds of activities, the specificity of the prompts makes them far more powerful than an open-ended question such as, "Why was Andrew Jackson a popular president?" The conjunction _but_, for example, demands that students hold two contrasting ideas in their minds and find evidence to support one of them. Your students will be exercising their own judgment independently but in a way that gives them the structure they need.

Principle 5: Grammar Is Best Taught in the Context of Student Writing

Research has consistently found that teaching grammar rules in isolation doesn't work. But that doesn't mean teachers can't, or shouldn't, teach grammar. As we've seen over the years, what does work is to teach writing conventions and grammar in the context of students' own writing.[8]

Just as skills developed in writing about one subject may not transfer to another, many students won't be able to apply rules they've learned in the abstract to their own writing. Although it's useful for students to have a general familiarity with basic concepts such as "noun" and "verb," that won't necessarily prevent them from writing "sentences" that lack one or the other.

Some people swear by sentence diagramming—often, those who feel that they themselves learned to write by using the technique. And it may work for some students. But for many, and especially those who struggle with language, breaking sentences into their component parts, labeling them as parts of speech, and plotting them on a diagram just adds to the confusion.

An alternative technique for teaching grammar that has been shown to produce excellent results in numerous studies—and that is incorporated into TWR activities—is sentence combining. Rather than breaking down a preexisting sentence, students create their own complex sentences by combining two or more simple sentences in a variety of ways. Perhaps they'll use a conjunction, a pronoun, or an appositive or subordinate clause. Students often find this approach more engaging than diagramming, and it eliminates the need to devote mental energy to memorizing and remembering grammatical terms.

Using simple language to minimize confusion, teachers can guide students to correct usage by pointing out errors in the writing they themselves produce through sentence combining or other activities. For example, if a student's writing is repetitive or fragmented, you can point out that combining ideas will make the writing clearer and easier to read. As your students learn to combine sentences, they will learn that there are many ways to craft sentences and convey meaning more effectively and fluidly.

Principle 6: The Two Most Important Phases of the Writing Process Are Planning and Revising

When students are ready to tackle longer pieces of writing—paragraphs and compositions—they'll need to go through four steps before producing a final copy: planning, drafting, revising, and editing. But the critical phases are planning and revising.

All students need to plan before they write. Although experienced writers may be able to turn out a well-developed paragraph or essay on the fly, most of the students we work with find it overwhelming to organize their thoughts at the same time that they're choosing words and figuring out the best way to structure their sentences.

That's why we provide two basic outline templates: one for planning paragraphs and the other for planning multi-paragraph writing. The lion's share of the work of writing occurs at the planning stage, as students identify the main idea or theme of their writing, the points they will make, and the order they will make them in. As they do this work, students are discovering what further information or clarification they need, making the necessary connections between ideas or claims and relevant details or evidence and ensuring that they don't wander off into irrelevancy or repetition.

Once students have a well-organized outline, it's a fairly simple matter to translate it into a rudimentary draft. Then comes the next major phase of writing: revising the draft so that it reads smoothly and coherently. This is where students will draw on the sentence-level skills they've acquired: using subordinating conjunctions, appositives, and other techniques to vary their sentence structure and inserting transition words and phrases between sentences and paragraphs to make them flow.

Because teachers embed TWR activities in the content of their own curricula, the approach doesn't look exactly the same in every school or even in every classroom that uses it. But across the board, teachers who adhere to these six principles while implementing TWR method have found it to be a powerful way not only of teaching writing skills but also of ensuring their students are grasping content and thinking analytically. They've learned to give students clear, explicit writing instruction and feedback, using sentence-level activities regardless of what grade they're teaching. They ground the TWR strategies in whatever substance the class is learning, forcing students to grapple with text and using the complexity of the content to ratchet up the activities' rigor. They use students' own writing to guide them to the correct use of grammar, punctuation, capitalization, and other conventions. And they break the writing process into manageable steps, with particular attention to planning and revising, so that students don't become overwhelmed by all the factors that writing requires them to juggle.

How to Use This Book

The Writing Revolution will guide you through a carefully scaffolded sequence of strategies and accompanying activities that you can adapt to any content area, grade level, or ability level. Whether you're teaching large classes, small groups, or tutorials, you'll be able to find many ways to use them. The activities also easily lend themselves to differentiation, enabling you to modify them for a range of ability levels within your classroom.

This book provides you with numerous examples of how the strategies can be implemented. You'll also find additional resources—rubrics, sample pacing guides, interactive templates, and checklists—online at http://twr-resources.thewritingrevolution.org/.

Key Points to Keep in Mind

Before we describe the organization of the book, we'd like to highlight some points that you should keep in mind as you read it.

- We use the term *strategy* to refer to an overarching technique and the word *activity* to refer to scaffolds that support instruction in the strategy. For example, "summarizing" is a strategy, whereas showing students a painting or political cartoon and having them write a sentence that summarizes it is an activity that supports it.

- Although this book presents the strategies one after another in a linear fashion, in practice you'll be using *several different strategies at the same time*. You'll want to follow the sequence we suggest in introducing new strategies, but continue having students practice previous strategies as you go along. In particular, the sentence-level activities continue to be important when students move on to revising paragraphs and compositions. You can also combine a number of different strategies in your instruction. For example, you might first ask students to summarize a news article in one sentence. That sentence could become the topic sentence in a Single-Paragraph Outline (SPO), which could become the draft of a paragraph. Students could then practice their revising and editing skills to create a more polished version.

- When first introducing a strategy, it's best to *model an activity for the class and then have students practice it orally as a group*. This is certainly true for younger students, but older students also need to have some demonstrations and participate in whole-class activities. Once students understand the concept, you can have them try the activity on their own in writing. When demonstrating a strategy for the first time, you may want to ground the activity in a topic from outside the classroom that all students are familiar with. Otherwise, all TWR activities should be embedded in the content you're teaching.

- When you model an activity for the whole class, make sure that you're displaying your work in a way that *enables all students to see what you're doing and follow along.* You might use a chalkboard, whiteboard, flip chart, SMART Board, or document camera to do this.

- As you adapt TWR strategies and activities to the content of your curriculum, *always anticipate student responses* to the questions you pose or activities you create. It's surprisingly easy to create an activity that is clear to you but confusing to students. At the same time, make sure you have a clear idea of what you want your students to understand about the content the activity is focused on, and plan the activity backward from that goal.[9]

- When we provide examples of activities, we usually include one version for Level 1 students and another for Level 2. These categories apply to students with more basic and more advanced writing skills, and to some extent they correspond to grade levels in terms of the subject matter we have used in the examples. Level 1 examples tend to focus on elementary-level material, and Level 2 examples focus on secondary-level material. But we are well aware that even students in high school often lack basic writing skills, so we have avoided using grade-level designations. You will need to use your knowledge of your students' needs and abilities when adapting TWR activities to the content you're teaching.

- As you progress through the school year, you should be giving students *prompt feedback* on their writing and continuously *assessing their progress* to determine what TWR strategies to focus on, how quickly to move through TWR sequence, and which students need modifications suited to their individual needs.

- TWR method works best when it is implemented *across the curriculum* in as many subject areas as possible. In secondary schools and elementary schools where different subjects are taught by different teachers, this approach requires coordination between teachers and common planning time. To facilitate collaboration, we have provided key terms that all teachers can use as a common vocabulary and to share tips about the best ways to introduce and implement TWR strategies and activities. These terms are boldfaced in the text, and their definitions are found in the Glossary.

How This Book Is Organized and What It Covers

This book is divided into three sections. The first section focuses on sentences and a system of note-taking. The second section addresses longer forms of writing—paragraphs and compositions. The third section covers how to assess your students' writing and adapt TWR method to your students' specific needs.

Sentences and Note-Taking

The strategies in this section will help your students understand the purpose and structure of sentences and develop the ability to compose complex sentences that reflect extended thinking.

The sentence strategies will teach your students how to do the following:

- Understand the concept of a sentence by distinguishing between sentences and fragments.

- Use the four types of sentences (statements, questions, exclamations, and commands).

- Develop questions.

- Use conjunctions to extend responses (*because, but,* and *so*).

- Use subordinating conjunctions to reflect written language structures (*although, unless*).

- Insert appositives to describe a noun.

- Combine two or more short sentences into a longer one.

- Expand a basic "kernel" sentence with details.

In addition, this section will introduce a system of abbreviations and symbols your students can use to take notes on their reading. You'll find activities that give your students practice in converting text they have read into notes, using key words and phrases, which they'll later convert back into text they write themselves. This process ensures that your students will actually process and understand what they read, rather than merely copying it.

Paragraphs and Compositions

In this section, you'll learn why it's important for students to plan before they tackle longer forms of writing. You'll be introduced to an outlining process that will enable your students to shape coherent paragraphs through the use of topic sentences, supporting sentences that provide key details, and concluding sentences. Our revision activities will provide your students with the techniques they need to make their writing flow.

We'll also cover the powerful strategy of summarizing and then move on to the challenges of writing compositions: selecting a topic, developing a thesis statement, crafting introductions and conclusions as well as body paragraphs, and incorporating quotations.

TWR covers five types of paragraphs and, ultimately, compositions: expository, compare-and-contrast, narrative, descriptive, and opinion or argumentative. We have a separate chapter (Chapter 8) devoted to writing argumentative essays, given the complexity of that particular genre and the emphasis that has recently been placed on it in many state standards.

Assessing Student Writing and Adapting TWR to Your Students' Needs

The final section will guide you through the sometimes tricky process of assessment, which involves collecting independent writing samples early in the school year in order to set goals for individual students and for the class. (Bear in mind that you'll need to be familiar with the contents of this entire book before you'll be able to set those goals.) You'll want to administer similar assessments at the middle and end of the year to see how your students are progressing. In addition, you'll need to give your students periodic diagnostic assessments that test their mastery of the specific strategies you've been teaching.

The final chapter gives you tips on how to tailor TWR strategies and activities to the particular needs of your students, along with ideas on how to differentiate the same activity for students in your class with varying ability levels. We'll also detail the sequence in which the strategies should be taught, and you'll be able to access sample pacing guides online—with the caveat that you are the person who knows your students best, and you'll need to use your own judgment about pacing.

Soon after Monica got to New Dorp High School, she encountered the new method of teaching writing that faculty members had decided to adopt in every class except math. In her chemistry class, for example, Monica got a worksheet to fill out after learning about the properties of hydrogen and oxygen. She had to write three sentences, one beginning with *although*, one with *unless*, and one with *if*. She wrote:

> *Although hydrogen is explosive and oxygen supports combustion, a compound of them puts out fires.*
> *Unless hydrogen and oxygen form a compound, they are explosive and dangerous.*
> *If hydrogen and oxygen form a compound, they lose their original properties of being explosive and supporting combustion.*

Monica found that the writing activities her teachers gave her dramatically boosted her reading comprehension. "Before, I could read, sure," she said. "But it was like a sea of words. The more writing instruction I got, the more I understood which words were important."

By her sophomore year, Monica—along with the rest of her class—had moved on to outlining and revising paragraphs and compositions. One of the strategies that she found helpful was using transition words. "There are phrases—*specifically, for instance, for example*—that help you add detail to a paragraph," she said. After a pause, she added, "Who could have known that, unless someone taught them?"

By senior year, Monica said, she was able to "write paragraphs and paragraphs, and essays, and *pages.*" Despite having entered high school reading far below grade level, she was able to score a 77 on her New York State Regents exam, two points above the cut-off signaling a student is ready for college-level course work. On her American History and Government Regents exam, she got a 91.

The essay she wrote for her Global History Regents exam, which she hurried through, began:

> *Throughout history, societies have developed significant technological innovations. The technological innovations have had both positive and negative effect on the society of humankind. Two major technological advances were factory systems and chemical pesticides.*

Although that may not be knock-your-socks-off writing, the essay went on for six paragraphs, was logically ordered, cited examples, and used transitions to connect ideas.

As a special education student, Monica had assumed she would never go to college. But as she developed her writing abilities—along with her reading, speaking, and thinking abilities—that assumption changed.

"I always wanted to go to college," she said during her junior year, when she was starting the process of applying, "but I never had the confidence that I could say and write the things I know." She smiled and swept her brown bangs from her eyes. "Then someone showed me how."[10]

Notes

1. P. Tyre, "The Writing Revolution," *The Atlantic* (October 2012), www.theatlantic.com/magazine/archive/2012/10/the-writing-revolution/309090/.

2. National Center for Education Statistics, *The Nation's Report Card: Writing 2011* (Washington, DC: Institute of Education Sciences, US Department of Education, 2012), https://nces.ed.gov/nationsreportcard/pdf/main2011/2012470.pdf.

3. M. Will, "As Teachers Tackle New Student-Writing Expectations, Support Is Lacking," *Education Week* (July 20, 2016), www.edweek.org/tm/articles/2016/06/20/as-teachers-tackle-new-student-writing-expectations-support.html?cmp=eml-eb-popweek+07012016.

4. G. Gillon and B. Dodd, "The Effects of Training Phonological, Semantic, and Syntactic Processing Skills in Spoken Language on Reading Ability," *Language, Speech, and Hearing Services in Schools* 26 (1995): 58–68.

5. K. A. Ericsson and R. Pool, *Peak: Secrets from the New Science of Expertise* (New York: Houghton Mifflin Harcourt, 2016).

6. B. Saddler, *Teacher's Guide to Effective Sentence Writing* (New York: The Guilford Press, 2012), p. 6.

7. P. C. Brown, H. L. Roediger III, and M. A. McDaniel, *Make It Stick: The Science of Successful Learning* (Cambridge, MA: The Belknap Press of Harvard University, 2014); Ericsson and Pool (2016).

8. S. Graham and D. Perin, *Writing Next: Effective Strategies to Improve Writing of Adolescents in Middle and High Schools. A Report to Carnegie Corporation of New York* (Washington, DC: Alliance for Excellent Education, 2007).

9. For more on this kind of "backward planning" and how it relates to writing instruction, see Vermont Writing Collaborative, *Writing for Understanding* (South Strafford, VT: Author, 2008).

10. Most quotations from Monica are from Tyre (2012), with additional details from a video created by students at New Dorp and posted on YouTube (www.youtube.com/watch?v=l8Q5MaqO5Ig).

CHAPTER 1

Sentences
The Basic Building Blocks of Writing

If you were building a house, would you start with the roof? Probably not. But for far too long, I was attempting to do just that with my writing assignments.

A student I'll call Roger was in the eighth grade—well past the point where he should have learned to write a good, clear sentence. But somehow, he was still struggling to produce one. Some of his sentences continued on and on—maybe with a comma where there should have been a period, maybe with no punctuation whatsoever—trailing off only when he seemed to run out of energy. At other times, his sentences were short and dull, each repeating the same simple structure. Sometimes his "sentences" lacked a subject or a verb. Sometimes I had no idea what he was trying to say.

But Roger was in the eighth grade, and so I felt I had to assign him—and his classmates who were having similar problems—paragraphs and compositions to write. When I returned these written pieces to Roger, I would point out the run-on sentences, the fragments, the sentences that didn't say much of anything, and ask him to do better next time. But it didn't seem to make any difference. The next time I assigned Roger a paragraph or a composition, the same sentence-level problems would stubbornly appear.

Eventually I realized that if I wanted my students to write good paragraphs and compositions, I was going to need to start building a solid foundation first—just the way I would start building a house. And in writing, that foundation consists of **sentences**.

The importance of spending plenty of instructional time working with sentences can't be stressed enough. Sentence-level work is the engine that will propel your students from writing the way they speak to using the structures of written language. Once they begin to construct more sophisticated sentences, they'll enhance not only their writing skills but also their reading comprehension.[1] And sentence-level work will lay the groundwork for your students' ability to revise and edit when they tackle longer forms of writing.

Clearly, not all sentences are the same. Some are far more informative, complex, and interesting to read than others. Many students, when asked to compose a sentence, are likely to write something like this:

The Union Army won.

The goal of TWR sentence-level strategies and the activities that support them are to enable students to write something more like this:

In April 1865, the Union Army, a well-trained and well-equipped force, won a decisive battle against the Confederates at the Battle of Appomattox Court House.

The second expanded sentence has an appositive and is expanded to answer the questions *where, when* and *why.* If you teach all of these elements explicitly through TWR sentence-level strategies, it will enable your students to construct far more sophisticated and informative responses.

The second sentence also demonstrates far more content knowledge than the first one—content knowledge that students can express only if they're actually learning it. When giving students any writing assignment, including those at the sentence level, first ensure that your students have sufficient knowledge or resources at their disposal to write intelligently about the subject at hand. That means you'll need to figure out in advance what you want your students to understand as a result of the activity and plan backward from that goal.[2]

Make It Correct: Using Sentence Activities to Teach Grammar and Conventions

As we've mentioned, your best bet for teaching your students the grammar and conventions of English is to do it in the context of their writing. And the best way to do that is through sentence activities. If you wait until they're writing paragraphs and compositions, the number of mechanical errors can be overwhelming, for you and for your students. Of course we don't expect students to master all the conventions of written English at once, but there's no reason to hold off on gradually introducing the rudiments.

If you're working with Level 1 students, you may need to start by teaching them to begin each sentence with a capital letter and end it with a period. As your students progress, you can introduce the use of question marks and exclamation points. Once they have a grasp of those conventions, you can begin to focus on the capitalization of **proper nouns**.

When introducing students to the first **subordinating conjunctions** they'll encounter—*before, after, if*, and *when*—show them that the comma should go after the dependent clause at the beginning of the sentence. For example:

Before I go to bed, I always brush my teeth.

A subordinating conjunction introduces a **dependent (subordinate) clause** and signals the relationship between that clause and the main idea. Subordinating conjunctions are often used in written language, and they are more likely to appear at the beginning of a sentence in writing than in speech.

For example, in the sentence, "Although it is raining, I'm going to take a walk," the subordinating conjunction is *although*. Together with "it is raining," it forms a dependent clause. When speaking, we would be more likely to say, "I know it's raining, but I'm going to take a walk anyway."

For Level 1 students, it's best not to use technical grammatical terms such as *subordinating conjunction* or *dependent clause* when explaining the placement of the comma. Simply give them examples of sentences using these words and point out where the comma goes. Of course, as with other conventions, you'll also need to ensure that students are placing commas correctly in their own writing.

Some grammatical errors may be quite persistent—for example, using a **verb** form that doesn't agree with the subject of a sentence, as in "They was going to school." This is a particular problem with students who are still learning English or who speak non-standard English. As an initial approach, it's a good idea to highlight the most common mistakes and bring them to the attention of the class as a whole. But that's unlikely to solve the problem. You will also need to correct the mistakes as they appear in students' own writing—as they almost inevitably will continue to do.

TECHNICAL TIP

As you introduce the sentence activities in this chapter to your students, you should keep the following points in mind:

- When introducing a new activity, model it for students first.
- Have students practice sentence-level activities orally as well as in writing, even if you're teaching older students.
- Embed the sentence activities in the content you're teaching.
- Differentiate the activities for students at different ability levels while covering the same content.
- When planning activities, write out the responses you anticipate getting from students and make sure your directions and questions are clear.
- Plan your instruction so that your students will have the content knowledge they need to practice the activity successfully.
- As you progress through the sequence of activities, have students keep practicing TWR activities you've already covered to build on the skills they've acquired. You can use a number of different sentence activities at the same time.

What Makes a Sentence a Sentence: Fragments, Scrambled Sentences, and Run-Ons

Practicing sentence-defining and sentence-ordering activities:

- Helps students understand the concept of a complete sentence and discern sentence boundaries
- Helps students understand correct word order
- Provides practice with capitalization, punctuation, and using new spelling and vocabulary words
- Serves as a comprehension check
- Helps students understand the meanings of subjects, predicates, and prepositional phrases
- Encourages careful reading

A **fragment** is a group of words that is not a grammatically complete sentence. Usually a fragment lacks a subject, verb, or both, or it is a dependent clause that is not connected to an independent clause (for example, "Although I read the book"). A **phrase** is a group of words in a sentence that does not contain a verb and its subject. For example, in the sentence, "The teacher, a recent arrival to the school, was happy because I did my homework," "a recent arrival to the school" is a phrase.

A sentence consists of a group of words that includes a **subject** and a **predicate** and that expresses a complete thought. Students who haven't yet developed good writing skills often struggle with the concept of a complete sentence. We all use sentence fragments or incomplete sentences in spoken language, and students may continue to use them as they learn to write.

If you've tried to explain the concept of a sentence to students by giving them a definition to memorize—for example, "A set of words that is complete in itself, typically containing a subject and predicate, conveying a statement, question, exclamation, or command, and consisting of a main clause and sometimes one or more subordinate clauses"[3]—you've probably discovered that approach doesn't work very well. Simply learning to repeat the definition of a sentence won't help most students learn to craft one. It's far too abstract an exercise. They need to spend time hearing and reading complete sentences alongside sentence fragments and distinguishing between the two. And teachers need to ask their students questions about fragments that will guide them to turn the fragments into complete sentences.

When you introduce your students to the concept of a complete sentence as opposed to a fragment, it's helpful to explain that fragments may be fine in conversation but that written speech requires more precision. Then give students examples of sentence fragments and ask them to correct them by supplying whatever element is missing. Your students may need a lot of practice working with examples you provide before they can recognize fragments in their own writing.

Start With Speaking: Oral Activities With Fragments

Initially, when you give examples of fragments, it's best to present them orally rather than in writing. For example, you might say to the class:

ate a great meal

To guide them to supply a subject, you could follow that up with, "Does that tell us *who* ate a great meal? How can we make these words into a complete sentence?"

Another example could be:

Robert and Jack

You might say, "we need to know *what they did*. Let's make this fragment into a complete sentence." Students would then supply a verb (such as *ate*) and perhaps a predicate (*a great meal*) to create a sentence.

You can also give your students oral examples of fragments that are related to the content they're studying. These examples can be more or less challenging, depending on the complexity of the content and the knowledge demands of the fragment you choose to give them. When you make up fragments, you'll need to anticipate the correct responses and be sure that your students have the knowledge they need to correct them.

Level 1 Example

Let's say you've been teaching your students about early settlement in the American colonies, and you're not too sure of their grasp of the material. You might give them this fragment:

settled near rivers

Your students could then draw on the content they've learned to turn the fragment into a sentence, such as the following:

Early Americans settled near rivers.

Level 2 Example

If you're teaching a higher-level class on the history of the early American republic and you're fairly confident your students have some command of the interplay between the founders—particularly the role played by Alexander Hamilton—you might give them this fragment:

developed a set of principles

They might respond:

Alexander Hamilton developed a set of principles that explained how the new nation would be governed.

With Level 1 students, you'll want to avoid using technical grammatical terms such as *subject, verb,* and *predicate,* which may just confuse them.

If you're teaching Level 2 students, though, you might say, "The subject (or predicate) is missing in this fragment. Can you make it into a complete sentence?"

Put It in Writing: Written Activities With Fragments

Once your students are familiar with distinguishing fragments from sentences through oral practice, it's time to have them practice with written examples.

Fragments or Sentences?

Begin by giving your students a list that includes fragments and complete sentences, and have them mark the sentences with an *S* and the fragments with an *F.* They should also convert the fragments into complete sentences with appropriate capitalization and punctuation. When creating the examples, be careful not to capitalize or punctuate either the fragments or the sentences.

As always, when you embed this activity in content, you'll need to make sure your students already have the information they'll need to turn the fragments into sentences. This activity will also alert you to gaps in students' knowledge and comprehension.

Level 1 Example

If you've been teaching your students about the story of Columbus, you could give them a list such as the following:

___ queen isabella and king ferdinand

___ columbus never reached

___ the sailors were tired and frightened

___ in three small ships

___ columbus an italian sailor

After marking these examples *F* or *S,* students should convert the fragments into sentences at the bottom of the page and add the correct punctuation and capitalization to the sentences.

Level 2 Example

Let's say you're a math teacher with a pre-algebra class and you want to review rational numbers—while also helping your students develop an understanding of sentences. You might give them the following two fragments and ask them to correct them with proper punctuation and capitalization:

> can be expressed as a fraction or a ratio

> rational numbers

Their responses might be:

> *A rational number is a number that* can be expressed as a fraction or a ratio.

> Rational numbers *can be ordered on a number line*.

BE CAREFUL

Keep the following points in mind when you're creating sentence fragment activities for your students:

- When you give students isolated written examples, don't capitalize or punctuate either the fragments or the sentences. For example, give students the fragment "in the forest" rather than "In the forest." Similarly, give them the sentence "the bear lived in the forest" rather than "The bear lived in the forest." Capitalizing and punctuating only the sentences would be a dead giveaway as to which examples are which!
- Be sure not to use commands (e.g., "ride bikes") when you're giving students examples of fragments. Commands can be complete sentences.
- Similarly, avoid using **kernel sentences** (e.g., "they fought") as examples of fragments, because they are in fact complete sentences.

Find the Fragment: Embedding Fragments in Text

In addition to giving your students isolated written examples of fragments, have them find and correct fragments that are embedded in sample texts. Unlike the isolated examples, fragments that are embedded in text should be capitalized and punctuated, as in the following examples for different ability levels. Have students underline the fragments, as shown in the examples, and then turn them into complete sentences.

Level 1 Example

If your students have been studying colonial-era clothing, you could give them a passage like the following, which you've modified to include fragments. Your students will need enough knowledge to supply the missing information in the fragments.

> A colonist's outfit began with underwear. But underwear wasn't what you might expect. All colonial men wore long-sleeved white under-

shirts that reached their knees. <u>Women and children wore shifts instead of.</u> A shift was a long-sleeved dress that fell below the knees. No one bothered with boxers or briefs. <u>Underwear wasn't common in America until.</u>[4]

After your students have underlined the two fragments in the text, they might convert them to the following complete sentences:

Women and children wore shifts instead of <u>skirts</u>.

Underwear wasn't common in America until <u>the 1830s</u>.

Level 2 Example

After your students have been studying the Holy Roman Empire for a while, you could give them a passage like this:

A year before Charlemagne died in 814, he crowned his only surviving son, Louis the Pious, as emperor. Louis was a devoutly religious man but an ineffective ruler. He left three sons: Lothair, Charles the Bald, and Louis the German. <u>They fought one another for.</u> In 843, the brothers signed the Treaty of Verdun, dividing the empire into three kingdoms. <u>As a result, Carolingian kings.</u> The lack of strong rulers led to a new system of governing and landholding—feudalism.[5]

Your students could convert the fragments they've underlined to complete sentences such as the following:

They fought one another for <u>control of the empire</u>.

As a result, Carolingian kings <u>lost power and central authority broke down</u>.

Piece It Together: Unscrambling Scrambled Sentences

Students enjoy rearranging jumbled sequences of words into correctly punctuated and capitalized sentences. At the same time, they're developing and honing their grasp of the concept of a complete sentence, learning correct word order, and reinforcing their knowledge of the rules of punctuation and capitalization. When you embed the activity in the content you've been teaching, your students also will be deepening their understanding of that content and of new vocabulary words they've learned.

Scrambled sentences can include statements, questions, and exclamations. It's best to avoid using commands, especially with Level 1 or younger students. With commands—such as "Get the book"—the subject (*you*) is implied rather than stated explicitly, and that can be confusing.

For Level 1 students who need additional support, consider capitalizing the first word of the sentence or writing it in bold letters. Try to use between six and nine words per sentence for Level 1 students and up to 9 or 10 for Level 2 students.

Level 1 Examples

Here are some examples of scrambled sentences with anticipated student responses. In the first example, we've put the first word in bold as an example of how you can help students who need more support.

apples **Tim** oranges bought and bananas

Tim bought apples, oranges, and bananas.

divided twenty-one equals by seven three

Twenty-one divided by three equals seven.

away yellow the did bird why fly

Why did the yellow bird fly away?

Level 2 Examples

functions take in life cytoplasm most the place

Most life functions take place in the cytoplasm.

Dill summer Scout in 1933 the of and Jem met

In the summer of 1933, Scout and Jem met Dill.

advocate passive against the British why Gandhi did for resistance

Why did Gandhi advocate for passive resistance against the British?

Put the Brakes On: Correcting Run-On Sentences

Run-on sentences are an all-too-frequent problem in student writing. Although there's no quick solution, we have found a few effective ways to help students become aware of run-ons and learn how to correct them.

If your students have trouble with run-ons, try putting a run-on sentence on the board daily, preferably embedded in content or relating to a subject students already know something about. When you first start this routine, ask a student to read the sentence aloud, without pausing, and then ask the class what's wrong with it. After doing this a few times, you can just put run-ons on the board and have students correct them without hearing them read aloud. You'll want to continue to do this as a daily activity until you stop seeing run-ons in your students' writing.

If the word *and* is the biggest culprit in the run-ons your students write, tell them to go back and look at every *and* they've put into a sentence. Have them ask themselves whether they're joining two ideas that should be in separate sentences.

You can use a variety of techniques to give your students practice in correcting run-ons: do-now activities, exit slips (tickets), and in the earlier grades, **turn-and-talk**. As with sentence fragments, you can also embed run-ons in text and have the students identify, underline, and correct them.

Introduce Some Variety: The Four Basic Sentence Types

Practicing sentence-type activities does the following:

- Enables students to vary sentence structure
- Provides one way to improve topic and concluding sentences in a paragraph
- Introduces students to forming questions
- Helps students learn correct punctuation

All sentences, no matter how complex, can be boiled down to these four types:

- **Declarative sentence (statement):** the most common type of sentence; a statement of an idea or argument

  Example: Theodore Roosevelt created five national parks.

- **Imperative sentence (command):** gives advice or instructions or expresses a request or command

  Example: Describe the effects of the many visitors to national parks.

- **Interrogative sentence (question):** asks a question and always ends with a question mark

  Example: How can the national parks be protected?

- **Exclamatory sentence (exclamation):** expresses force or a strong emotion and ends with an exclamation point

  Example: We must save the national parks!

Introducing students to the four sentence types will pay off when it comes time for them to write paragraphs and essays and you ask them to vary their sentence structure. You can simply suggest that they write one of the sentence types as a topic or concluding sentence.

You can also use sentence-type activities to teach punctuation. For example, you can give students different types of unpunctuated sentences and ask them to add the appropriate punctuation. If one sentence says, "Are you coming," students will need to add a question mark. If another says, "Get over here," they need to add an exclamation point or perhaps a period.

Another way to use sentence-type activities is for vocabulary and spelling practice. If you are teaching the root word *retract,* for example, you can ask students to write a statement, a command, and a question using the word in any of its forms. Students might give the following answers:

The teacher retracted what she had said.

Retract that statement.

Will he retract that remark?

Getting to Know the Sentence Types

After explaining the four different sentence types, have your students practice distinguishing between them. You might give them the following activity:

Identify the sentence type:

____ I don't want to go.

____ Do you want to go?

____ I'm not going!

____ Go now.

One way of helping students understand the different types of sentences is to ask them to change questions into statements and vice-versa. For example:

Change this statement into a question: Sam is coming with us.

Change this question into a statement: Did she take the dog for a walk?

Using Sentence Types in Writing

Once your students have a grasp of the different sentence types, they can start formulating sentence types in their own writing.

Level 1 Example

If your students have been studying immigration, you can ask them to write a question using the word *immigrants*, a statement using *Ellis Island*, an exclamation using *freedom*, and a command using *citizen*. Students might write the following sentences in response:

> *Are your grandparents immigrants?*

> *Many immigrants were documented at Ellis Island.*

> *We are so fortunate to have freedom in this country!*

> *Become a citizen now, if you aren't one already.*

You may want to omit the command sentence from the activity, depending on the topic. Often, topics having to do with the past don't lend themselves to commands.

Level 2 Example

Let's say your students have been doing a unit on the International Space Station. You might ask them to write four sentences on the topic, using each of the four sentence types, without providing them with prompting words. They might write:

> *The International Space Station is the largest and most complex international scientific undertaking in history.*

> *How many crew members live and work at the International Space Station?*

> *Almost an acre of solar panels provides electrical power to state-of-the-art laboratories!*

> *Continue the space program.*

HOW TO DIFFERENTIATE SENTENCE-TYPE ACTIVITIES

If some of your students need extra support or additional challenge, here are some possible modifications:

- Ask more advanced students to create all four sentence types, while asking others to create only two.
- Give struggling students prompts with specific words to use in each sentence type, but ask others to create their sentences from scratch.

What Do You Know? Developing Questions

Practicing question activities does the following:

- Encourages students to think about the important features in text

- Encourages close reading

- Helps students to focus on the key elements of questions

- Gives students practice in understanding and using expository terms

- Helps students anticipate what questions they may be asked

It's as important for students to learn how to generate questions as it is for them to learn how to answer them. When students formulate questions, they're developing higher-level cognitive functions while at the same time focusing on the main idea of the content that provides the basis of their question.

Imagine, for example, that you needed to formulate a question about the paragraph you just read. You might need to read it several times, asking yourself what it's really all about. Perhaps you'd come up with the following:

Why is it important for students to learn how to generate questions?

Or:

What skills or abilities do students develop when they learn to formulate questions?

If you embed question activities in the content your students are learning, you'll spur them to read and reread text closely and think deeply about what they're learning while at the same time developing their writing skills.

Worth a Thousand Words: Developing Questions About Pictures

An excellent way of introducing your students to the skill of developing questions is to show them a picture and ask them to come up with two or three questions based on what they see. If the picture is related to the content of the curriculum—for example, a political cartoon or a depiction of a historical event in a history class—you'll be able to probe your students' understanding of it. This activity can also serve as a good introduction to a topic, piquing your students' curiosity and giving you insight into their background knowledge.

EXHIBIT 1.1

Write a question about the picture.

Who are the dogs waiting for?

EXHIBIT 1.2

Paleolithic Age

Directions: Write two questions about the picture.

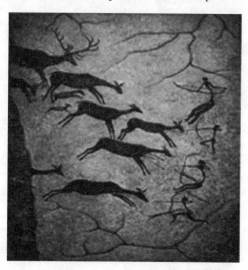

1. What civilization made this cave painting?

2. When was this cave painting made?

Level 1 Example

You could give your Level 1 students the picture shown in Exhibit 1.1 to practice developing questions. They might write the question, "Who are the dogs waiting for?"

Level 2 Example

If your Level 2 class has been studying the Paleolithic era, you could give them the activity as shown in Exhibit 1.2.

Test Yourself: Developing Questions About Content

If you're teaching Level 2 students, try asking them to write essay questions they think might appear on an upcoming test. You can tell students that if their question is selected for use on the test, they'll get bonus points.

You can also ask Level 1 or 2 students to develop comprehension questions after reading a text. This activity can be expanded to allow students to write commands as well as questions, using **expository terms** such as *discuss, explain, justify,* or *describe.* A list of terms used to describe different types of **expository writing** can be found in Appendix A ("Expository Writing Terms").

Students might write the following:

Describe the formation of igneous rock.

Trace the events leading up to the War of 1812.

Explain the continuing public interest in The Diary of Anne Frank.

Let's Play Jeopardy: Giving Students Answers and Asking for Questions

Another good exercise is to provide students with answers relating to a text they've read and having them write questions to go with them. For example, you might give them the word *abolitionists.* The student response might be as follows:

What term was used to describe people opposed to slavery?

Ask your students to make their questions as precise as possible. For example:

Q. _____

A. 1600 Pennsylvania Ave.

The question should be, "Where is the White House?" or "Where does the president of the United States live?" The question, "Where does the president live?" isn't specific enough.

Conjunctions, Complexity, and Clauses

Practicing conjunction activities does the following:

- Develops the ability to write extended responses
- Checks student comprehension
- Develops analytical and deeper thinking
- Fosters close reading
- Assesses the ability to use new vocabulary words correctly
- Develops the ability to craft linguistically complex sentences that use written rather than oral language conventions
- Enhances reading comprehension by familiarizing students with more complex syntax and sentence structure
- Provides a way to develop topic and concluding sentences

Conjunctions include words such as *and, because,* and *but.* Using conjunctions to connect words, phrases, and clauses helps make writing clear and linguistically rich. It also provides more information to the reader.

A **clause** is a group of words in a sentence that contains a subject and a verb. There are two types of clauses:

- An **independent (main) clause** represents a complete thought and can stand alone as a sentence. For example, in the sentence, "The teacher was happy because I did my homework," "The teacher was happy" is an independent clause.

- A dependent (subordinate) clause does not express a complete thought and could not stand alone as a complete sentence. In the previous example, "because I did my homework" is a dependent clause.

Much of what students hear, read, and write in their everyday lives is couched in simple language and structures. But much of what they're expected to read in school, especially at higher grade levels, is linguistically complex.

The large amber windows were open, and the fish swam in, just as the swallows fly into our houses when we open the windows, excepting that the fishes swam up to the princesses, ate out of their hands, and allowed themselves to be stroked.[6]

Somewhere in the dead of the southern night my life had switched onto the wrong track and, without my knowing it, the locomotive of my heart was rushing down a dangerously steep slope, heading for a collision, heedless of the warning red lights that blinked all about me, the sirens and the bells and the screams that filled the air.[7]

When in the course of human events, it becomes necessary for one people to dissolve the political bonds which have connected them with another, and to assume, among the powers of the earth, the separate and equal station to which the Laws of Nature and of Nature's God entitle them, a decent respect to the opinions of mankind requires that they should declare the causes which impel them to the separation.[8]

When confronted with complexity in literature, expository text, and original documents, students often have difficulty extracting the text's meaning. Conjunction activities enable students to craft more complex sentences themselves. As they do so, they also develop the ability to understand such sentences when they encounter them in their reading.[9]

The Power of Basic Conjunctions: *Because, But,* and *So*

A popular—and powerful—TWR sentence activity is what has become known as *because-but-so*. It's a great illustration of how an exercise that seems simple can actually require students to think analytically. It's also the first conjunction activity you should give to your students.

Here's how it works: You'll give students a **sentence stem**—the beginning of a sentence—and ask them to turn it into three separate sentences using each conjunction in turn. This approach requires them to engage in far more specific and focused thinking than just asking them to respond to an open-ended question. Think about the difference between asking students, "Why do seeds need light to grow?" and framing the assignment as follows:

Seeds need light to grow because _____.

Seeds need light to grow, but _____.

Seeds need light to grow, so _____.

Make sure your students understand the meanings of each conjunction. You could explain it to them this way:

- *Because* explains why something is true.

- *But* indicates a change of direction—similar to a U-turn.

- *So* tells us what happens as a result of something else—in other words, a cause and its effect.

As with other TWR activities, the content of *because-but-so* drives its rigor. When you adapt the activity to the content you're teaching, be sure to anticipate student responses and ensure that your students have enough content knowledge to complete the activity successfully.

In addition to guiding your students to create more informative sentences, this activity will prod them to think critically and deeply about the content they're studying—far more so than if you simply asked them to write a sentence in answer to an open-ended question. At the same time, *because-but-so* activities will provide you with a more precise check of your students' comprehension.

You can also use this activity to give students practice with new vocabulary or spelling words. Just embed those words in the stems you create, or have your students embed them in the sentences they write. For example, if your students have just learned the word *mediocre*, you can give them the following sentence stems:

The critic thought the book was mediocre because _____.

The critic thought the book was mediocre, but _____.

The critic thought the book was mediocre, so _____.

Level 1 Example

With Level 1 students, practice this activity orally before having students try it in writing. It's also best to begin with just one conjunction at a time—students generally find *because* the easiest to use.

To introduce the idea, start with a simple stem that is not based in the content you're teaching—for example, "The teacher was happy _____." Students might respond orally with answers such as these:

The teacher was happy because *we raised our hands*.

The teacher was happy, but *she still gave us homework*.

The teacher was happy, so *she gave us a longer recess*.

Once your students have gotten the hang of the concept, it's time to embed the activity in content. If your class is studying Abraham Lincoln, you could give students the stem, "Abraham Lincoln was a great president _____." The activity would look like this:

Abraham Lincoln was a great president because _____.

Abraham Lincoln was a great president, but _____.

Abraham Lincoln was a great president, so _____.

Student responses might be as follows:

Abraham Lincoln was a great president because *he kept the North united during the Civil War*.

Abraham Lincoln was a great president, but *many Americans didn't like him while he was alive*.

Abraham Lincoln was a great president, so *more books have been written about him than any other American leader*.

Level 2 Example

Let's say you're teaching students about American composers and they've recently been learning about George Gershwin. You could use the stem "George Gershwin is considered a musical genius _____." Their response might look like this:

George Gershwin is considered a musical genius because *he captured and expressed the spirit of American life in his rhythms, harmonies, and melodies*.

George Gershwin is considered a musical genius, but *some have criticized him for the structural weaknesses in some of his works*.

George Gershwin is a musical genius, so *many composers have tried to emulate his style*.

BE CAREFUL

Keep the following points in mind when creating and assigning *because-but-so* activities:

- It is extremely important to anticipate your students' responses when developing activities with these conjunctions. Always try completing the stems yourself before asking your students to do so.
- Explain to students that in this activity, the word *so* isn't being used in the sense of "I like Abraham Lincoln *so* much." Instead, it introduces a phrase that tells us what happened as a result of something else.

- Not every text will lend itself to activities using all three conjunctions. For example, if a text provides only positive information about Abraham Lincoln's presidency, students will have difficulty completing the *but* sentence shown in the example. In that case, you should only give students the conjunctions *because* and *so*.
- Don't let students use *because, but,* and *so* at the beginnings of sentences. If they do, they're likely to write a fragment rather than a complete sentence. As they become more competent writers, they can begin to use these conjunctions to start sentences.

HOW TO DIFFERENTIATE CONJUNCTION ACTIVITIES

You can easily modify the *because-but-so* activity to differentiate your instruction for students at different ability levels. You can give all students the same stem but ask more advanced students to provide complete sentences for all three conjunctions while asking others to write a sentence for only one or two. For example, you could have struggling students use only the conjunction *because* and more advanced students also tackle *but*. Using *but* requires students to juggle two contrasting ideas and can be a more difficult task, depending on the stem.

How to Say It in Writing: Subordinating Conjunctions

Practicing subordinating conjunction activities does the following:

- Promotes the use of complex sentences
- Improves reading comprehension
- Enables students to vary sentence types
- Boosts vocabulary development
- Encourages close reading and references to text
- Checks student comprehension
- Enables students to extend their responses
- Provides a good option for topic and concluding sentences

Here are the subordinating conjunctions used most frequently to begin written sentences, listed in the order in which they are taught to Level 1 students:

1. before
2. after
3. if
4. when
5. even though
6. although
7. since
8. while
9. unless
10. whenever

Most students don't use subordinating conjunctions such as *although* in their spoken language—especially at the beginning of a sentence, as the introduction to a dependent clause—so they may not know what some of these conjunctions mean or how to use them. If they encounter such constructions in their reading, that lack of familiarity can interfere with their comprehension. When students learn to use this kind of syntax in their own writing, they become better able to understand complex texts, and their oral language becomes more sophisticated as well.

Once your students learn to use subordinating conjunctions, they'll also be able to write extended responses that are rich in complexity and content. When they begin writing paragraphs and essays, they can use subordinating conjunctions to create topic or concluding sentences that are interesting and full of information. Several of these conjunctions—such as *while*, *although*, and *even though*—are particularly useful in composing argumentative or persuasive writing.

Although We've Never Met . . .: Introducing Your Students to Subordinating Conjunctions

To develop your students' skill in using subordinating conjunctions, give them introductory dependent clauses that you've created and ask them to complete the sentences. As with sentence stems using *because-but-so*, this approach demands more analytical thinking and precision than merely asking open-ended questions.

For example, there is a significant difference between asking a student this question:

Why was the Industrial Revolution important?

and asking them to complete the following sentences:

Although the Industrial Revolution was important, _____.

Before the Industrial Revolution, _____.

To finish a stem that begins with *although*, students need to find contrasting or contradictory information. When using a subordinating conjunction such as *before*, students need to demonstrate their understanding of the chronology of events.

Obviously, students will need to have knowledge of the content in order to successfully complete activities with subordinating conjunctions.

Level 1 Examples

Students in primary grades can practice completing stems based on books you've introduced in read-alouds. They can complete the stems either orally or in writing. With Level 1 students, it's best to start with conjunctions that depend on chronology (*before, after, when*) or the conjunction *if*.

If you've been reading them the book *How Rocket Learned to Read*,[10] for example, you could give them stems based on the story. The stems and the answers students provide might look like these:

Before Rocket heard the story about the dog, *he wasn't interested in learning to read*.

After Rocket listened to part of the story, *he wanted to know if the dog found the bone*.

When Rocket learned to read, *he was excited and proud*.

If you've read your students a book about penguins, the stems and answers might look like these:

After emperor penguins build nests, *they have babies on the sea ice*.

If sea ice melts, *penguins won't have enough food*.

Before the late 1980s, *there were a lot more Adelie penguins*.

Level 2 Examples

If you're teaching English and your students have been reading *Of Mice and Men*, you might give them the following stems to complete, and they might provide the answers shown:

Since Lennie has a mild mental disability, *George looks out for him*.

After Lennie meets Curley's wife, *George warns him to stay away from her*.

Although Lennie promised to keep the farm a secret, *he tells Crooks about it*.

In math class, the stems and answers might look as follows:

If a mid-segment touches a side, *then it bisects it*.

Since the side that the mid-segment does not touch is 22 units long, *the mid-segment must be 11 units long*.

Although a mid-segment is half as long as the side it does NOT touch, *it is not necessarily half as long as the side it does touch*.

Once students have become more familiar with this structure, you can make the exercise more difficult by giving them just a subordinating conjunction and a term and asking them to create a complex sentence. Be sure to tell students to *begin* the sentence with the subordinating conjunction. For example, in science class you might give them:

Unless hydrogen _____.

A student answer might be:

Unless hydrogen *and oxygen form a compound, they are explosive and dangerous*.

Another Name for a Noun: Appositives

Practicing appositive activities does the following:

- Provides an effective strategy for creating topic and concluding sentences
- Enables students to vary sentence structure
- Enables students to include more information in a sentence and add complexity
- Improves reading comprehension
- Enables teachers to check for comprehension
- Encourages careful reading
- Familiarizes students with a form that is often seen in text and rarely heard in spoken language

An **appositive** is a second **noun**, or a phrase or clause equivalent to a noun, that is placed beside another noun to explain it more fully. For example:

New York City, the largest city in the United States, is a major tourist attraction.

In that sentence, the appositive is "the largest city in the United States." Although appositives can include verbs in some circumstances, this activity should be limited to appositives that don't include verbs. Tell your students to use "the largest city in the United States," not "*which is* the largest city in the United States. The latter is actually a relative clause, not an appositive. An appositive usually follows the noun it describes, as in the example, but it can also precede it ("The largest city in the United States, New York City, is a major tourist attraction.")

In addition to sentence types and subordinating conjunctions, appositives are a third strategy that will help students compose complex and interesting topic sentences when they write paragraphs and compositions. Level 1 and younger students (below third or fourth grade) may have trouble grasping the concept of appositives. They may confuse them with relative clauses, which begin with *who* or *which* and include a verb. You'll need to use your judgment about whether your students are ready to be introduced to appositives.

Identifying, Matching, and Creating Appositives

To introduce appositives, give students examples of sentences containing them and have them underline the appositives. When creating examples, remember that for these activities, an appositive should not include a verb.

To help students identify the appositive in a sentence, tell them that it's a phrase that can be removed or covered up without making the entire sentence incomplete. If we omitted the phrase, "the largest city in the United States," in the previous example, we would still have a complete sentence:

New York City is a major tourist attraction.

You could also tell students that an appositive defines or describes a person, place, or thing.

Once students have begun to grasp the concept of an appositive, you'll want to start embedding activities in content. For example, you can create a matching activity based on a text your class has been studying: List nouns from the text on one-half of a sheet of paper and appositives on the other, and have students match each noun with the appositive that best describes it.

For example, if your class has been reading *A Raisin in the Sun*, you could list the major characters on the left side of the sheet and noun phrases that describe each of them on the other—not in the same order, of course. For example, you could have the name *Beneatha Younger ("Bennie")* on the left side and *an independent young woman* on the right side (see Exhibit 1.3).

Next, you can have your students fill in blanks with their own appositives in sentences that you create. Again, it's best to embed this activity in content students have been studying in order to boost learning at the same time that you're developing writing skills.

EXHIBIT 1.3

Match Appositives

Name:_____   Date:_____

Match each noun with the appositive that best describes it.

_____1. Walter Lee Younger   a. an independent young woman

_____2. Lena Younger ("Mama")   b. an ambitious person

_____3. Ruth Younger   c. an emotionally strong woman

a. _____4. Beneatha Younger ("Bennie")   d. the matriarch of the family

_____5. Joseph Asagai   e. a Nigerian student

Source: Copyright © 2017 The Writing Revolution.

Level 1 Example

If your class is studying explorers of the New World, you might give them the following:

Henry Hudson, _____ , explored what is now known as the Hudson River.

A student might answer:

Henry Hudson, *an employee of the Dutch East India Company*, explored what is now known as the Hudson River.

Level 2 Example

A more demanding activity is to give students a topic and have them write a sentence about it that includes an appositive. This activity develops students' abilities to paraphrase and summarize material they have read. For example, if you're teaching biology, you could give your students the topic "natural selection." A student response might be:

Natural selection, a process of evolution, results in species with favorable traits.

You can also provide an appositive—such as *a renewable resource*—and ask students to write a sentence that includes it.

Wind energy, a renewable resource, can produce electricity to power a city.

HOW TO DIFFERENTIATE APPOSITIVE ACTIVITIES

There are several ways to differentiate appositive activities for struggling students. One way to make the activity less challenging is to underline the appositives in the sentences you provide for students. For example:

Primary sources, <u>*firsthand accounts of events*</u>, are used to study history.

An even easier alternative would be to give struggling students the same activity you've designed for others but include a list of appositives at the top of the page. Students can then choose appositives from the list and insert them in the appropriate sentences. For example:

a. a Virginia slave
b. a leader in the movement to end slavery
c. a conductor on the Underground Railroad

1. Harriet Tubman, _____, was born in 1821 on a plantation in Maryland.
2. John Brown, _____, met Harriet in 1858.
3. Nat Turner, _____, led a famous rebellion in 1831.

Put Them Together: Sentence Combining

Practicing sentence-combining activities does the following:

- Effectively teaches grammar and usage

- Encourages students to produce more complex sentences

- Enables students to see various options for crafting sentences

- Exposes students to varied writing structures and enhances syntactic flexibility

- Helps students focus on what is important to include in a sentence

- Improves fluency in writing

Sentence combining involves giving students a series of short declarative sentences and having them find various ways of combining those sentences into one longer, complex sentence. It is one of the most powerful strategies in writing instruction. Extensive research has found it to be the most effective way of teaching grammar. It also gives students greater control over **syntax**, which is the way words and sentences are put together and ordered.[11]

If you've already taught your students how to use conjunctions, appositives, and subordinating conjunctions, they'll be able to draw on those techniques in finding ways to combine sentences. They'll also be able to practice using **pronouns**.

To introduce students to sentence combining, give them a series of short, declarative sentences that can be combined into one longer, complex sentence. Begin with just two or three sentences, adding more as students' skills develop.

For example, you could give your students the following short sentences:

> Nate took the subway every day.
>
> Nate did not like the subway.
>
> Nate needed to get to work.

There are a variety of ways these sentences could be combined into one longer sentence. You could, for example, put the second sentence first and introduce it with a subordinating conjunction. You could also use a conjunction to connect the third sentence to the other two:

> Although Nate did not like the subway, he took it every day because he needed to get to work.

There are usually various correct ways to combine sentences. The previous example could also be combined like this:

> Nate didn't like the subway, but he took it every day because he needed to get to work.

While students are learning this strategy, it may be helpful to provide them with a cue that will guide their combining, such as "use an appositive" or "use a conjunction." Once they've started to feel comfortable with the concept of sentence combining, it's time to start embedding the activity in the content you're teaching.

Level 1 Example

If you've been teaching your students about two of the ancient civilizations of India, you could give them the following sentences to combine:

> Mohenjo-Daro and Harappa were twin cities.
>
> Mohenjo-Daro and Harappa had urban planning.
>
> The cities had a system of plumbing.

One possible response would be as follows:

Mohenjo-Daro and Harappa were twin cities that had urban planning and a system of plumbing.

Level 2 Example

My colleague Betsy Duffy, director of language arts at The Windward School, and I created the following example for a science class studying the periodic table:

The periodic table is a chart of chemical elements.

The chart displays the elements in horizontal rows.

They are displayed horizontally in order of increasing atomic number.

They are displayed vertically in order of the structural similarity of their atoms.

A student might combine these sentences to create this sentence:

The periodic table, a chart of chemical elements, displays elements horizontally in order of increasing atomic number and vertically in order of the structural similarity of their atoms.

A Daily Dose of the Revolution: Using Sentence Activities in the Classroom

Given that the ability to craft a good sentence is the necessary foundation for all good writing, it's important to offer as many opportunities as possible for students to practice writing sentences. Once you and your students have become acquainted with various TWR sentence activities, you'll find there are many ways to use them in your classroom—no matter the grade level or the subject you're teaching.

Here are a few possibilities:

At the beginning of class, you can give students a do-now to review material you've taught previously.

Although Egyptians built the pyramids, _____.

Mid-lesson, you may want to pause and have students do a **stop and jot** by asking them to develop a question about what they've learned so far.

You could also have students turn-and-talk to try to put new vocabulary words in sentences using subordinating conjunctions.

Since / persevere

Even though / mediocre

After / captivate

Be sure to tell them that they can use alternative forms of the given term, for example, *perseverance, mediocrity, captivated.*

At the end of class, consider having students fill in exit slips responding to highlights in the lesson.

Egyptians built pyramids because _____.

Egyptians built pyramids, but _____.

Egyptians built pyramids, so _____.

On tests and in homework assignments ask students to use the expository terms found in Appendix A ("Expository Writing Terms") to develop and answer questions about what they are studying. In addition to prompting students to think carefully about content, this activity will help them understand the different meanings of these expository terms when they encounter them on tests or elsewhere. If they've used the terms *trace* and *justify* in formulating their own questions, for example, they're less likely to become confused when they see directions using those terms. Perhaps, for example, you've had the experience of asking students to *justify* a series of events on a test, but many students only *traced* them.

You can ask your students to formulate their own test or assignment instructions, using the expository terms, and then respond to them. Depending on the content the class is studying, students might come up with some of the following instructions:

Describe the relationship between Charlotte and Fern.

Trace the events leading up to the Civil War.

Justify the arguments for year-round school.

Enumerate the reasons for following a vegan diet.

If you weave these kinds of sentence-level activities into your instruction on a daily basis, you'll be giving your students the tools they need to create effective paragraphs and compositions, while at the same time boosting their understanding of the content you're teaching.

TO SUM UP

- Use sentence activities to teach grammar and conventions.

- When introducing a new activity, begin by modeling it and having students practice it orally.

- Have students practice activities with sentence fragments, scrambled sentences, and run-on sentences to grasp the concept of a complete sentence.

- Familiarize students with the four sentence types—statement, command, question, and exclamation—to equip them to vary their sentence structure and create effective topic and concluding sentences.

- Have students develop questions about texts or pictures to spur them to read closely and deepen their content knowledge.

- Give students sentence-stem activities with *but*, *because*, and *so* to enable them to think critically and to use and understand more complex sentences in their writing and reading.

- Have students practice beginning sentences with subordinating conjunctions (*although, since,* etc.) to familiarize them with the syntax used in written language, help them extend their responses, enhance their reading comprehension, and provide a way to create interesting topic sentences.

- Introduce students to appositives to help them create effective topic sentences and give a reader more information.

- Have students practice sentence combining to teach grammar and help them create longer sentences using varied structures.

- Embed sentence activities in the content you're teaching as much as possible to check students' comprehension and deepen their understanding.

Notes

1. S. Graham and M. A. Hebert, *Writing to Read: Evidence for How Writing Can Improve Reading* [A Carnegie Corporation Time to Act Report] (Washington, DC: Alliance for Excellent Education, 2010).

2. For more on backward planning, see The Vermont Writing Collaborative, *Writing for Understanding* (South Strafford, VT: Author, 2008).

3. *Webster's Dictionary for Students.*

4. E. Raum, *The Scoop on Clothes, Homes, and Daily Life in Colonial America* (Mankato, MN: Capstone Press, 2012).

5. R. Beck, L. Black, L. Krieger, P. Naylor, and D. Shabaka, *World History* (Evanston, IL: McDougal Little, 2005).

6. Hans Christian Anderson, "The Little Mermaid" (1836), http://hca.gilead.org.il/li_merma.html.

7. Richard Wright, *Black Boy* (New York: Harper and Brothers, 1945).

8. The Declaration of Independence (1776).

9. C. M. Scott, "A Case for the Sentence in Reading Comprehension," *Language Speech and Hearing Services in Schools* 40 (2009): 184–91.

10. T. Hills, *How Rocket Learned to Read* (New York: Schwartz & Wade, 2010).

11. S. Graham and D. Perin, *Writing Next: Effective Strategies to Improve Writing of Adolescents in Middle and High Schools. A Report to Carnegie Corporation of New York* (Washington, DC: Alliance for Excellent Education, 2007); B. Saddler, *Teacher's Guide to Effective Sentence Writing* (New York: The Guilford Press, 2012).

CHAPTER 2

Sentence Expansion and Note-Taking

Getting Students to Process What They've Read

Ms. Anderson wanted her eighth-grade English students to write about the book they were reading, *Animal Farm*. She knew some were struggling writers, and she didn't want to overwhelm them. So, after the class had read the first couple of chapters, she asked students to write just a few sentences in response to the following question: "What event first gave the animals on the farm the idea of rebelling against human control?"

Ms. Anderson was pleased with the question. It was specific enough, she thought, that even struggling students would be able to write something, but also open-ended enough that more advanced ones could expound at some length on the speech given by Old Major, the elderly prize boar, and his dream of a more equal and just society.

When she got back the assignment, though, most of the results were disappointing. A couple of students had simply written, "He called a meeting," without explaining who had called the meeting, why it was called, or what happened. Ms. Anderson asked one of them, a girl named Alia, why she hadn't written more. Was the problem that she didn't remember any more about the story?

Alia shrugged. "I just didn't think I needed to. I mean, *you* already know that stuff, right? So I figured you'd understand what I meant."

When they're writing, students often assume that a reader has extensive prior knowledge of the subject matter they're covering. Although that may be true for you—the teacher—students need to learn to anticipate what an unknown reader may need or want to know to better understand what they are trying to convey. This is a crucial step in developing students' abilities to write clearly, coherently, and convincingly. Often it's also one of the most difficult.

Sentence expansion is one of the best techniques available to help students gauge what information they need to include to make their writing intelligible. At the same time, practicing this activity will ensure students grasp the meaning of content. Alia may or may not have actually understood or remembered more about what happened in *Animal Farm*. Getting her to expand her sentence would be one way for her teacher to determine whether or not she did.

Here's how sentence expansion works: Give your students a bare-bones, brief—but complete—sentence called a *kernel sentence*. At the same time, give them a list of question words to respond to: *who, what, when, where, why,* and *how.* Your students will provide answers in the form of notes and then convert those notes into a complete sentence.

Before you introduce your students to sentence expansion, you'll need to show them how to take notes using key words and phrases, abbreviations, and symbols. We discuss note-taking techniques in the second part of this chapter.

Bigger and Better: Expanding Sentences to Expand Students' Knowledge and Responses

Practicing sentence expansion activities does the following:

- Enables students to anticipate what a reader needs to know and to provide that information
- Checks comprehension
- Teaches note-taking strategies (key words and phrases, abbreviations, and symbols)
- Enables students to craft written language structures
- Develops the ability to summarize

To familiarize your students with the concept of sentence expansion, use a simple, declarative sentence as your sample kernel sentence. It should have only one verb and no modifiers. You might use something like "Jane ran" or "The candidates will debate." When you introduce this strategy, it's not necessary to embed the example in content you're teaching. It is important, though, to use a kernel that's grounded in a topic your students already know about.

How to Create a Kernel Sentence

When creating kernel sentences, you'll want to make sure that you're not using a sentence fragment or omitting an object. To get the most out of this exercise—especially later on, when you embed it in content—be sure the kernel is a complete sentence. "They seem" or "She enjoys," for example, are not sentences and can't be used as kernels—they don't express a complete thought. Avoid using commands, such as "Run fast," because students may have trouble determining who should be doing the running.

Choosing Your Question Words

Before sharing your kernel with the students, make sure you've posted a chart in the classroom listing the following question words, in this order:

Who?

What?

When?

Where?

Why?

How?

You don't need to use all of the question words with each kernel. When introducing the sentence expansion strategy, it's a good idea to present just two or three. The question words *when, where,* and *why* are the best to begin with.

Generally, the question words you choose will depend on the kernel you're using and the information you want your students to add. For example, if you use the kernel "Jane ran," you won't use the question word *who,* because the reader already knows the answer. However, if the kernel is "She ran," it would make sense to use the question word *who.* It may help to keep in mind that the question words *who* and *what* will always correspond to pronouns in the kernel. If you were going to use the kernel about Jane and give your students the question word *what,* you'd want to change the kernel to "Jane ran it." They might respond with "the 5K race."

Demonstrating How to Expand a Sentence

Once the students have answered the question words, you can demonstrate how to use the answers to make the sentence longer and more informative. For example, let's say you've used the kernel "Jane ran," and your students have given the following answers to the *when*, *where*, and *why* question words:

> When: *7 a.m.*
>
> Where: *park*
>
> Why: *to get into shape*

Note that when you're writing these answers on a board or on chart paper, they should appear on dotted lines because they are not complete sentences (see the "Technical Tip" box). Let your students know that when expanding a sentence, they should always begin with the answer to *when*. Not only does that help students get started, it also gives them practice with a construction that is common in writing but not in speech.

Show your students that the expanded sentence would read as follows:

> *At seven in the morning, Jane ran in the park because she wanted to get in shape.*

When you demonstrate this sentence in writing, be sure to put it on a solid line.

Next, you might want to give your students another kernel, with appropriate question words, and have them try expanding the kernel on their own. With sentence expansion activities, the *teacher* should always be the one to supply the question words—not the students. Students can practice expanding sentences independently when doing their own writing.

Make sure you provide your students with a worksheet that has dotted lines for the notes following the question words and solid lines for their expanded sentence. They'll need to incorporate *all* the information they provide in response to the question words into their sentences—and, of course, their expanded sentences will need to be grammatically correct.

Once your students have the idea of sentence expansion, it's time to give them a sentence expansion activity that's embedded in content. As always, you'll first need to decide what you want your students to get out of the activity, anticipate their responses, and assess whether they have enough knowledge to produce the responses you're looking for.

TECHNICAL TIP

When your students provide written answers to the question words you give them, they will be writing notes rather than complete sentences. (We'll explain how to have them write notes in the second part of this chapter.) That means you'll want to provide them with worksheets that have *dotted* lines after the question words, like this:

Who: ....

What: ....

When: ....

Where: ....

Why: ....

Below that, provide *solid* lines where they'll write their expanded sentence, like this:
Expanded sentence:

_____

_____

_____

In TWR, dotted lines are *always* used for notes (key words and phrases, abbreviations, and symbols), and solid lines are *always* used for complete sentences. You'll want to make sure your students understand the difference between what is expected on the dotted lines and the solid ones.

It's important to remember to provide the appropriate kind of lines so that students understand what they are being asked to provide. If you've worked hard to get your students to understand the difference between a fragment and a sentence, you won't want to blur that distinction for them now!

Level 1 Example

If you've been teaching your students about the pyramids in ancient Egypt, you could give them this kernel sentence:

Pyramids were built.

If you've taught your students *when, where,* and *why* the pyramids were built, you could give them those question words to check comprehension and reinforce their learning.

You'll want to be sure to remind them to write their answers to the question words in the form of notes rather than complete sentences, using the abbreviations and symbols that we'll cover later in this chapter. That will help ensure that they're actually processing information rather than just copying it. Also remind your students to begin their expanded sentences with *when.*

The completed version of the student worksheet might look like what is shown in Exhibit 2.1.

EXHIBIT 2.1

Sentence Expansion

Directions: Expand the following sentence using the question words.

Pyramids were built.

When: ...ancient times................................

Where: Egypt................................

Why: ...protect body of deceased pharaoh

Expanded Sentence:

In ancient times, pyramids were built in Egypt to protect the body of the deceased pharaoh.

Source: Copyright © 2017 The Writing Revolution.

Level 2 Example

If you're teaching math and covering the distributive property, you might give your students the following problem:

$$2(x + 6) = 14$$

Then you might show them two possible solutions, step by step: one for a student called Jasmine who gets the wrong answer—because she doesn't apply the distributive property—and the other for a student called Maya, who gets the right answer.

You could give students the kernel:

She made a mistake.

Students would then have to answer the question words _who, when,_ and _why._ The resulting student answer might look like what is shown in Exhibit 2.2.

EXHIBIT 2.2

Example 1:

Problem: 2(x+6)=14

	Jasmine	Maya
Step 1	2x + 6 = 14	2x + 12 = 14
Step 2	2x = 8	2x = 2
Answer	x = 4	x = 1

She made a mistake.

Who: .....Jasmine..

When: .....Step 1..

Why: .....Didn't distribute 2 to both terms inside ()

Expanded Sentence:

In step 1, Jasmine made a mistake because she
didn't distribute the 2 to both of the terms
inside the parentheses.

Source: Copyright © 2017 The Writing Revolution.

HOW TO DIFFERENTIATE SENTENCE EXPANSION ACTIVITIES

When you're working with Level 1 students or those who need more support with sentence expansion, it's a good idea to provide them with only one, two, or three question words, usually starting with *where, when,* or *why.* You can give additional question words to students who are more advanced in their writing skills. Remember, though, that you—not your students—will always be the one to select the question words when you give your students a kernel to expand.

Another way to provide support is to put a star next to the word *when* on the worksheet to remind students to start their expanded sentences with their answer to that word. To provide even more support, you can number all the question words in the order you want students to use the answers in their expanded sentences.

Later on, when your students are writing drafts, you may find that they're writing sentences that need to be expanded. With Level 1 students, your feedback should be very explicit. For example, you might insert *when?* or *why?* at specific points in their writing. With Level 2 students, you'll be able to just write *expand* on their work. That should encourage them to consult the question word chart you've posted on the wall, and they should be able to determine which of the question words are relevant to their sentences.

What Do You See? Using Sentence Expansion to Write Captions for Images

One variation on expanding sentences is writing one-sentence captions for paintings or other images. As with converting notes to text, this activity will require that your students have a fair amount of background knowledge about the subject of the image.

For example, if your students have been studying the American Revolution, try asking them to write a caption for the famous painting of George Washington crossing the Delaware River. Be sure to identify the subject that you want students to write about. Although it may seem obvious to you that the subject here is George Washington, we've seen students identify the subject as "The American Revolution," "Crossing the Delaware," and "The Battle Against the British."[1]

Exhibit 2.3 provides a template that shows the caption a student might write about this painting.

EXHIBIT 2.3

Name _____ **Date** _____

Write a sentence about the picture.
Answer the following questions first.

Who / What? . *Gen. George Washington* ....

(did) What? . *crossed Delaware River w/troops* ....

When? . *during American Revolution* ....

Why? . *hoped to surprise Hessian forces celebrating Christmas* ....

Sentence: <u>During the American Revolution, General George</u>
<u>Washington crossed the Delaware River with his troops</u>
<u>because he hoped to surprise the Hessian forces who were</u>
<u>celebrating Christmas.</u>

Source: Copyright © 2017 The Writing Revolution.

BE CAREFUL

It's important to be especially careful when giving students sentence expansion activities—there are many possible ways to create unintended confusion. Here are some guidelines to keep in mind:

- The question word *when* should refer only to a specific time or time period, not in the sense of *whenever* (as in, "When I eat too much, my stomach hurts").
- When creating kernels, it's important not to omit objects: "Upton Sinclair wrote" is not a good kernel. Instead, say, "Upton Sinclair wrote it," because it is likely that you'll be asking what he wrote.
- If you will be using *who* or *what* as question words, include a corresponding pronoun in the kernel. If one of the question words is *who,* and the answer is "Lincoln," the kernel should read, "He issued an order." If one of the question words is *what,* and the answer is "the handkerchief," the kernel should read, "It was stolen."
- Commands don't make good kernels. "Ride cars" or "Go fast" can be confusing because the subject is implied. If you ask *who,* it's not clear what response you're expecting.
- Fragments can't be kernels. "In the school yard" and "Irrigation of deserts" are not kernels.
- Tell your students they must use the same words in their expanded sentence that they've used in their notes on the dotted lines.
- You'll also want to tell them to use *all* the information in their notes—and not to add any other information.
- Even though you want students to begin with the answer to *when*—if that's one of your question words—always list the question words on the worksheet in the same order as they appear on the wall chart: *who, what, when, where, why,* and *how.* This particular sequence of the terms is commonly used, and it's helpful for students to get used to it.
- You'll want to be the one who chooses the question words—it's best not to leave that decision to students. If students choose their own question words, they're likely to leave out important information. Once they become more experienced writers, they can come up with question words to expand sentences when they're revising their own writing.

The Power of Note-Taking: Key Words and Phrases, Abbreviations, and Symbols

Having students reduce sentences to key words and phrases, abbreviations, and symbols does the following:

- Helps students distinguish essential from nonessential material
- Boosts comprehension
- Enables the absorption and retention of information
- Promotes analytical thinking
- Teaches efficient note-taking
- Enables students to outline paragraphs and compositions before drafting them

As we mentioned in the first part of this chapter, to practice sentence expansion, your students will need to know how to write brief notes rather than complete sentences. Learning to identify key words and phrases in a text and reduce them to notes and abbreviations is a crucial step in TWR's method. In addition to using this technique to respond to the question words you give them during sentence expansion activities, your students will use it later on to produce outlines for paragraphs and compositions—and to take notes on their reading or what they're learning in class.

Converting text or speech to notes is one of the most valuable skills you can teach your students. It's far more than just a quick way to get information down on paper—although it does serve that purpose. It's a way of forcing students to process and understand what they've read, heard, and learned. Converting sentences to notes requires students to extract the most important words and phrases and render them in a different mode of expression. That exercise prevents rote copying, ensures comprehension, and promotes absorption and retention of information.

ASK THE EXPERTS

Studies have shown that people who take notes by hand retain more information than those who take notes on a laptop or tablet—apparently because those who take notes by hand are extracting the information that is important, just as students do when they reduce sentences to key words and phrases, abbreviations, and symbols. People who take notes on a laptop tend to just write everything down without prioritizing the main points.

One study involved 65 college students who watched a TED Talk in small groups. Researchers asked the students to take notes on the talk either by hand or on a laptop. Although both types of note-takers did equally well on questions about the talk that just asked them to recall facts, the laptop note-takers did significantly worse on questions that required them to apply concepts from the lecture. Similar results were found one week later, when participants were tested again after being given a chance to review their notes.

The problem for the laptop note-takers wasn't distraction because they were checking Facebook or buying stuff from Amazon—researchers gave them laptops that were disconnected from the Internet. Rather, those taking notes on a laptop were likely to simply transcribe whatever the speaker was saying, without analyzing the material to determine what was essential.

"It may be that longhand note-takers engage in more processing than laptop note takers, thus selecting more important information to include in their notes, which enables them to study this content more efficiently," the researchers concluded.[2]

Make a Note of It: Introducing Students to Note-Taking

As with all TWR activities, when you're introducing students to note-taking, model the activity first. Although it's not essential to embed the sentences in the content of the curriculum at this point, it will provide an opportunity to boost students' learning if you do. Initially, you'll want to be the one to decide which words and phrases are key and should be underlined. Later on, you can have your students identify key words and phrases, either by coming up to the board and underlining them or simply telling you which words they think should be underlined.

TECHNICAL TIP

It's much better for students to use a pen or pencil to underline key words and phrases than to use a highlighter. Once they have a highlighter, students have a tendency to highlight too much. It's also harder to annotate a text when using a highlighter, because students need to put down the highlighter and pick up a pen or pencil to do so. Sometimes they lose their thoughts in the process.

Next you'll need to show your students how to extract these key words and phrases and write them down as notes, without reproducing the entire sentence. When you're modeling this strategy, introduce your students to the abbreviations and symbols for common words and concepts (see Appendix B, "Abbreviations and Symbols"). You and your students may already be familiar with some TWR abbreviations and symbols, although others will be new.

Introduce your students to abbreviations such as *b/c* for *because*, *w/* for *with*, and *w/o* for *without*. Remind them that when they're writing notes, they should omit words such as *the, and,* and *a*.

Here are some of the most frequently used symbols:

- An equal sign (=) indicates a definition or explanation.

- A plus sign (+) stands for *and.*

- A horizontal arrow ($\rightarrow$) indicates that one thing has resulted in another, or cause and effect.

- An upward arrow ($\uparrow$) means more, an increase.

- A downward arrow ($\downarrow$) means less, a decrease.

- A slash (/) indicates a comma or a period—or signals the beginning of a new idea.

It's a good idea to post a chart of the most frequently used abbreviations and symbols from Appendix B and keep it in the classroom where students can refer to it. Once they get used to the technique of converting text or speech into notes, they'll be able to use the symbols and abbreviations to take notes in class.

After you've introduced your students to the concept of note-taking through this whole-class guided activity, it's time to have them practice converting sentences to notes on their own. Start by giving them sentences embedded in the content they're learning and ask them to convert the sentences to notes: key words and phrases, abbreviations, and symbols. Once they've had some practice with that activity, try giving them some notes and have them convert the notes to a complete sentence.

Level 1 Example

If you've been teaching your students about the history of the early American republic, you might give them this sentence and ask them to convert it to note format:

George Washington was the first president of the United States.

Your students might respond with the following:

G.W. = 1st pres. / U.S.

When you think they've gotten the hang of converting text to notes, give them a collection of key words and phrases, abbreviations, and symbols and have them reverse the process: convert the notes to text. For example, you might give them these notes:

Continental Congress = meeting of states → plan for entire nation

Your students might turn that into the following sentence:

The Continental Congress was a meeting of states that wrote a plan for the entire nation.

Obviously, converting notes into text requires students to have enough knowledge of the subject matter to interpret the meaning of the notes.

BE CAREFUL

When using abbreviations and symbols, make sure you don't use slashes to break up a thought cluster. For example, you would not want to write the example about the Continental Congress like this:

Continental Congress = meeting / of / states

Level 2 Example

Perhaps your class is studying ancient China, and you want to assess and consolidate what they've learned about the terra-cotta army buried with a Chinese emperor in the 3rd century bce. First you might give them the following sentence to convert into note format:

> Qin Shi Huang Di, China's first emperor, will be remembered forever for his elaborate tomb.

Your students might write:

> *Qin Shi Huang Di = China's 1st emperor / remembered forever → elaborate tomb*

Once they've practiced converting text to notes, and you think they also have sufficient background knowledge to reverse the process, you could ask them to convert these notes to a complete sentence:

1974 / discovered by farmers / Xian China

A possible response is as follows:

> *In 1974, the terra-cotta army was discovered by farmers near the city of Xian in China.*

If Ms. Anderson, the teacher we met at the beginning of this chapter, had taught her students how to expand sentences, she would have had an easy way of helping her student Alia anticipate what information a reader needs to know. She could have used Alia's simple sentence about *Animal Farm*—"He called a meeting"—as a kernel sentence for an expansion activity.

Underneath the four-word sentence, she could have listed question words that would elicit the information Alia needed to include: *who, where, when,* and *why.*

Alia's response might have looked like this:

> Who: *Old Major*
> Where: *Manor Farm*
> When: *3 days before he died*
> Why: *to encourage animals → revolt*

Beneath that, Alia could have produced a complex, information-packed sentence that she and her teacher would have been proud of:

> *Three days before he died, Old Major called a meeting at Manor Farm to encourage the animals to revolt.*

TO SUM UP

- List question words on a wall chart in this order: *who, what, when, where, why,* and *how.*

- Provide kernel sentences that express complete thoughts but are not commands or questions.

- Have students start expanding sentences using the question words *when, where,* and *why.*

- Teach students how to reduce text to key words and phrases, abbreviations, and symbols to help them process what they have read and take notes more efficiently.

- Have students write answers to question words in the form of notes on dotted lines only, and write their expanded sentences on solid lines only.

- Have students begin their expanded sentences with the answer to *when* if it is one of the question words provided.

- Make sure that students' expanded sentences contain all the information in the responses they've noted on the dotted lines.

- Use sentence expansion activities to help students anticipate what readers need to know.

- Use sentence expansion activities to check students' comprehension of content.

Notes

1. Emanuel Leutze, "Washington Crossing the Delaware" (1851), Metropolitan Museum of Art, New York, Gift of John Stewart Kennedy (1897), www.metmuseum.org/art/collection/search/11417.

2. Association for Psychological Science, "Take Notes by Hand for Better Long-Term Comprehension" (April 14, 2014), www.psychologicalscience.org/news/releases/take-notes-by-hand-for-better-long-term-comprehension.html; P. A. Mueller and D. M. Oppenheimer, "The Pen Is Mightier Than the Keyboard: Advantages of Longhand Over Laptop Note Taking," *Psychological Science* 25, no. 6 (2014): 1159–68, http://pss.sagepub.com/content/25/6/1159.

CHAPTER 3

One Step at a Time
Why Students Need to Plan
Before They Write

My student Ben's composition at the end of our unit on monarch butterflies began promisingly enough: "Monarch butterflies have learned to adapt to their environment in many ways." But soon Ben had veered off topic to discuss his trip to Butterfly World and the many varieties of butterflies to be found there. He went on to describe his excitement when one butterfly landed on his shoulder.

Eventually he returned to the theme of adaptation in his third paragraph, but it largely repeated what he had said in his first paragraph. Then, in the fourth paragraph, he launched into a discussion of spiders that appeared to have no relationship to monarch butterflies at all or to adaptations to the environment. Ben just liked spiders.

"Ben," I told him gently, "this is a great start. You've got a lot of ideas here. But can you go back now and make sure that everything you're saying here is actually about monarch butterflies and how they adapt to their environment? Can you take out the stuff about Butterfly World and spiders and save that for another composition? And you need to make sure you're not repeating yourself so much."

Ben's face fell. He'd worked hard on the composition, using his best handwriting and embellishing his account of Butterfly World with lots of details. I could see that the last thing he wanted to do now was to start all over again. He slunk back to his seat, crumpled up the composition he'd invested so much effort in, and put his head down on the table. It looked like I wasn't going to get much more writing out of him that day, or maybe ever.

I only wish I'd realized then what I've learned since: When you help students plan carefully before they write, they'll learn to avoid the all-too-frequent pitfalls of going off topic and repeating themselves.

If you're about to embark on a road trip, try a new recipe, put together an Ikea table, develop a football play, build a Lego model—or engage in just about any complex, multistep task—you need to have a plan. Without one, it is far more likely that your efforts will be disappointing at best and end in failure at worst. Athletes, architects, artists, playwrights, chefs, physicians, lawyers, and members of countless other professions rely on plans to accomplish their objectives. Yet when we teach our students to write in lengthier forms such as paragraphs and compositions, we rarely help them come up with the kind of plan they need to produce an effective piece of writing.

I've heard people say that planning, or outlining, will constrain students' creativity. I disagree. We've found that teaching students to plan can actually *enhance* their creativity. If students are working from a plan, they're liberated from the need to figure out the overall structure of what they're writing as they go along. As a result, they have the mental space they need to conjure up vivid imagery or telling details.

True, some authors prefer to simply freewrite as a first step in their writing process, allowing their thoughts to take them where they will. But that approach doesn't work for most students, for at least two reasons. First, virtually all the students we work with are not experienced writers. They may be still struggling with figuring out everything from punctuation or word choice to larger questions such as the overall organization of their thoughts. If they're asked to plunge into a longer piece of writing with no outline to follow, they'll need to juggle all these tasks at once. As we'll explain in more detail in the following sections, they're likely to be overwhelmed.

Second, the freewriting approach to drafting is best suited to relatively free-form genres such as memoirs, poems, plays, short stories, or (perhaps) novels. Students are unlikely to be asked to engage in that kind of writing in college or the workplace. What they will be asked to do, in countless situations, is to explain, inform, justify, enumerate, summarize, and describe. (A comprehensive list of these expository writing terms can be found in Appendix A.) As compared to more creative writing forms, this kind of writing demands that authors figure out in advance where they're going to end up and chart a clear and logical course that will lead a reader there. Even many experienced writers find planning to be essential if they're going to communicate clearly and effectively when producing explanatory or analytical pieces.

As a classic writing handbook points out, "planning must be a deliberate prelude to writing. The first principle of composition, therefore, is to foresee or determine the shape of what is to come and pursue that shape."[1] In short, if you want your students to be able to move from writing effective sentences to writing coherent paragraphs—and, ultimately, compositions—you'll need to teach them how to plan before they write. As with revising—which we'll turn to in Chapter 5—planning is a stage of writing that rarely gets enough instructional time and attention.

Planning Matters: The Cognitive Demands of Writing at Length

Why is it so important for students to plan before they write? Largely because of the demands that writing places on what are called *executive functions.* These are cognitive processes, housed primarily in the prefrontal cortex of the brain, that enable us to perform a series of actions and that are essential to good writing. The abilities associated with executive functions begin to develop in early childhood, but they don't reach their peak until people are in their mid-20s. That means that virtually all students in kindergarten through 12th grade are working with executive function abilities that are still a work in progress.

When assigning writing tasks, teachers need to be keenly aware of the demands they place on a student's executive functions. These functions enable a writer to do the following tasks:

- *Strategize.* Selecting a topic demands the ability to foresee consequences. A topic shouldn't be so narrow that students have too little material to write about. If the topic is too broad, students will need a great deal of skill to sort essential from unessential information. For beginning writers, the teacher rather than the student selects the topic.

- *Initiate a series of actions.* This ability comes into play, for example, during the process of finding textual evidence to support a topic sentence or thesis. Students must identify the point they want to support, locate the corresponding evidence in a text, and figure out how and where to insert it into their writing.

- *Plan.* Students must be able to develop an outline that provides a road map for presenting a body of information, an explanation, or an argument.

- *Organize.* Students need to sequence information in the order that suits a particular piece of writing, whether it's a narrative, an argument, or a comparison of two or more different things.

- *Resist distractions.* The typical classroom and home are full of potential distractions, and the modern era—with its cell phones and ubiquitous Internet connections—seems to have made students' attention spans shorter than ever.

- *Sustain effort.* Students must maintain the stamina necessary to focus on the writing task at hand.

- *Self-monitor.* When working on a draft, for example, students need to continually assess it against their outline to ensure they're not going off track.

- *Institute needed changes.* These changes can range from reorganizing an entire sequence of ideas to executing smaller modifications such as choosing more accurate words, varying sentence structure, and inserting transitions.

Closely related to executive functions is what cognitive scientists call **working memory.** Essentially, working memory enables us to manipulate multiple inputs and process them simultaneously, drawing on the surrounding environment and on information stored in long-term memory. While writing, people need to juggle a host of factors at the same time: word choices, spelling, syntax, background information or content knowledge, the nature of the audience they're addressing, and their purpose in writing, among other things. In addition, many Level 1 students have not yet achieved automaticity in letter formation, punctuation, capitalization, and other foundational skills.

An individual's working memory can hold only a limited number of items simultaneously, which means that the complex task of writing places heavy demands on this aspect of cognition. Yet many writing assignments ask students who are still struggling with learning English or with lower-level aspects of writing, like punctuation, to focus on challenging tasks, such as writing paragraphs, comparing and contrasting, or summarizing text.

Teachers need to be aware that executive functions are compromised by stress. Stress can be caused by many factors, and nearly all children experience it to some extent. Those who are most likely to experience the levels of stress that interfere with executive functions include students who have language and learning disabilities, those who are still learning English, and those who live in chronically stressful conditions, such as those associated with poverty. Students who are under a great deal of pressure to succeed or who have suffered loss also can feel stressed.

When students experience high levels of stress, they can have difficulty concentrating and organizing their thoughts. Learning to juggle the multiple demands imposed by writing paragraphs and compositions can be daunting for any student, but for those who are stressed it can be overwhelming. That's why it's particularly important for them to have a clear, written plan before they begin writing at length.

ASK THE EXPERTS

Although some levels of stress are normal and healthy, in recent years researchers have used the term *toxic stress* to describe the effects of frequent or prolonged exposure to fear and anxiety, especially in children living in poverty. Stress activates the release of certain hormones, particularly cortisol, that trigger a "fight-or-flight" response to perceived threats. When excessive amounts of cortisol are released, it can affect the development of children's brain structures and impair their executive functions and working memory, as well as their ability to control their impulses.

Although we're not aware of any research that specifically addresses the relationship between toxic stress and writing ability, it's clear that any student dealing with the effects of toxic stress will be challenged by an activity that imposes so many demands on executive functions. Students who are still learning English, for example, are likely to be overwhelmed by an assignment that doesn't take into account their difficulties with syntax and vocabulary. One way to help such students cope with these demands is to break the writing process into manageable parts so that students don't need to focus on so many things at the same time. That's what TWR strategies and activities are designed to do.[2]

Defining Our Terms

A **paragraph** is a group of sentences that includes details supporting a specific point. To be effective, a paragraph should have the following characteristics:

- *Structure.* The sentences in the paragraph are sequenced in a way that ensures clarity for the reader.

- *Coherence.* The sentences are logically connected with transition words that signal that connection or indicate a change of direction or emphasis.

- *Unity.* Every sentence supports the main idea of the paragraph.

- *Sentence skills.* The sentences are grammatically correct and clear, and their types and structures should vary (some simple, others compound or complex).

A **composition (essay)** is a series of paragraphs united by a common theme. The characteristics of effective compositions mirror those of effective paragraphs:

- *Structure.* The paragraphs are sequenced in a way that ensures clarity for the reader.
- *Coherence.* The paragraphs are logically connected with appropriate transition words.
- *Unity.* Every paragraph supports the main idea or thesis of the composition.

Step by Step: How to Make Writing a Manageable Task

To make writing manageable for your students, you'll need to break the process down into four basic steps before students produce a final copy—planning and outlining, drafting, revising, and **editing**—as shown in Exhibit 3.1.

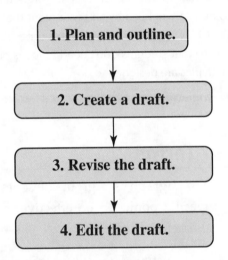

You'll need to spend the majority of instructional time on the first and third steps: planning and outlining, then revising. A lesson can end after Steps 1 or 4—but not after Steps 2 or 3. Always have your students revise and edit a draft, whether or not they go on to turn it into a final copy.

The planning-outlining and revising-editing stages need to be broken down into a number of smaller steps—first in the context of paragraphs and later in the context of compositions. We'll go into those steps in detail in Chapters 4 and 5 on outlining and revising.

Briefly, however, planning and outlining include these steps:

1. Gathering information

2. Distinguishing between essential and irrelevant material

3. Putting ideas and supporting details into categories

4. Arranging the ideas and details in an appropriate order

5. Developing a topic sentence for a paragraph or an introductory paragraph for a composition

Later, when students have converted their outlines into drafts—whether of paragraphs or compositions—they'll need to focus on turning those drafts into flowing and coherent pieces of writing through the process of revision. That process includes the following steps:

1. Varying sentence structure

2. Making sentences more informative and interesting

3. Using vivid, varied, and precise words

4. Using transition words and phrases to connect their ideas

Introduce each of these steps by guiding the discussion and then model the strategies and activities—in a way that all students can observe—and provide feedback. As students become more proficient in the activities, they can begin to do them independently.

In keeping with this step-by-step approach, you'll want to be sure that your students are comfortable with writing paragraphs before you ask them to start learning to craft compositions. Given the heavy demands that writing even a single coherent paragraph can place on students' cognitive abilities, it's important to spend ample time guiding them through that process before moving on to longer pieces of writing—just as you spent time having them practice sentence activities before moving on to paragraphs.

Once students understand how to write a good paragraph, they will have acquired the skills they need to write clearly and coherently at greater length. It may be tempting to have students write at length before they've mastered the essentials of a paragraph, but ultimately it will be counterproductive.

First Steps: Identifying Topic, Audience, and Purpose

To plan a paragraph or a composition, your students first need to understand three things: what they're writing about, whom they're trying to communicate with, and why they're writing. Initially, most students will find it difficult to answer these questions on their own. Until they're ready to engage in the process independently, it's important for you to lead them in class discussions that establish the topic, audience, and purpose.

The What: Choosing a Topic

As with all TWR strategies and activities, it's best to embed your students' paragraphs and compositions—and the activities that lead up to them—in the content they're studying. If students have recently read about a topic, writing at length about it—or even just planning to write about it—will boost their comprehension and help ensure they'll absorb and retain the information.

In any event, it's crucial to determine how much background knowledge students have about a topic before beginning the planning process. If they need more information, class discussions should help them identify the best sources to provide it.

The Who: Determining the Audience

One of the most difficult aspects of writing for many students is to imagine themselves in the mind of an intended reader and to anticipate what the reader would need or want to know. For example, a paragraph describing New York City that's directed at an audience of first-time tourists may be very different from one aimed at people who already live or work there. Students need to be reminded to tailor the structure, facts, and arguments in their writing to the kinds of readers they're planning to reach.

The Why: Understanding the Purpose

Are students trying to persuade the reader to adopt a certain position, or are they simply narrating a series of events? The purpose of a piece of writing influences many of the choices students will make in planning it. A paragraph that is intended to persuade a reader usually has a different kind of topic sentence than one that is merely describing a situation, place, or person. Similarly, the concluding sentence of a persuasive piece of writing might be a call to action rather than a summary of what's been said.

Writers will also organize details differently depending on their purpose. If they're writing about a series of events or a process, it will make sense to relate them in chronological order. But if they're trying to persuade a reader to adopt a particular point of view, they will probably want to begin with their "soft" arguments and end with their strongest. Transition words will also vary: Words such as *first, then,* and *ultimately* will connect the sentences in a narrative, whereas pro-con and argumentative writing will call for words such as *although, specifically,* and *moreover.*

A Guide to Purpose: Four Types of Writing

The last of these steps—identifying the purpose of a piece of writing—can be particularly tricky for students. It's also particularly important, because it will determine much of the tone and organization of the paragraph or composition.

To help students identify purpose in writing, TWR emphasizes four types of paragraphs and compositions: expository (including **compare-and-contrast**), **narrative, descriptive,** and **opinion** or **argumentative.** In the real world, of course, a single piece of writing often contains more than one of these types at a time. In this book, for example, the anecdotes about our experiences with students are usually examples of narrative writing, while other parts are expository or argumentative. But when students are first learning to write at length, they need practice with one type of writing at a time. Later on, when they've become comfortable with the demands of each type, they can begin to blend them in the way experienced writers often do.

The language you use when creating a writing prompt or posing a question for students can signal the particular purpose of the writing you're looking for, so you'll want to acquaint your students with the various expository terms and their meanings (see Appendix A). For example, if you ask them to *justify* something, this means the purpose of their writing is argumentative. If you're teaching high school English, you might use some of the following expository terms to help students identify the purpose of a writing assignment:

Contrast the motives of Finny and Gene in *A Separate Peace.*

Summarize the plot of *The Scarlet Letter.*

Describe the symbolism in the setting of *Wuthering Heights.*

Justify the killing of Lennie in *Of Mice and Men.*

Even younger Level 1 students can practice responding to some of the expository terms. For example:

Explain why Rocket became interested in the story.

Discuss why the disappearance of sea ice is affecting penguins.

Describe the garden where Mary meets Ben.

Summarize Chapter 2.

Expository Writing

Expository writing is writing that explains or informs. Classes in English, social studies, and science tend to generate assignments that require expository writing, at least from third or fourth grade on, so it's important to devote the greatest amount of instructional time to this kind of writing. Expository assignments might use terms such as *define* or *discuss.*

Compare-and-Contrast Assignments

Some expository assignments ask students to compare and contrast certain things and to draw a conclusion based on the facts presented. The assignment might be to compare and contrast meiosis and mitosis, for example, or the styles of two authors. When introducing this type of writing assignment, be aware that organizing compare-and-contrast essays—and especially paragraphs—can try the skills of many writers. It can be difficult to write a single paragraph interweaving the two points of view.

Narrative Writing

Narrative writing relates a process or event in chronological or sequential order and is usually organized with transition words that signal time or sequence, such as *first, next, then, later,* and *finally* (see Table 5.1, "Transition Words and Phrases," in Chapter 5, near "Connect the Dots: Using Transitions to Create Flow"). In general, narratives are written in either the first person (as a participant) or third person (as an observer). In English classes, a narrative assignment might be to write a plot summary. A math teacher might ask students to explain the sequence of steps in solving a problem, and a science teacher might ask the same with regard to a scientific process. In social studies, the assignment might be to trace the steps leading to a historic event.

Students tend to write at greater length when writing narratives, but their sentences are typically less complex than when they're writing, for example, expository, opinion, or argumentative passages.

Descriptive Writing

While narrative writing draws on organizational skills, descriptive writing taps the five senses to effectively conjure images of people, places, and things. Varied and vivid vocabulary is important for developing a descriptive passage. Appropriate activities for descriptive writing lessons include brainstorming for **adjectives** and listing varied nouns and verbs. An assignment might be to describe a person students have learned about or the setting or characters in a story or novel they have read.

Some aspects of giving directions or orienting readers to the layout of a particular place also require descriptive writing. Students may want to organize that kind of information using words such as *below, beyond, next to, left,* and *right.*

Opinion Writing and Argumentative Writing

We discuss opinion writing and argumentative writing in detail in Chapter 8, but we'll provide a brief overview of these types of writing here. Opinion writing, usually assigned to elementary students, seeks to change how the reader thinks or feels without providing evidence or opposing views. By contrast, argumentative writing presents both sides of an issue, appeals to logic, and marshals evidence and reasons for supporting one side or the other. The conclusion usually proposes the action or point of view that the writer would like the reader to take.

Education experts consider argumentative writing the most complex and cognitively demanding form of composition.[3] Only about 25% of students' argumentative essays were considered competent according to the results of a nationwide writing test in 2012.[4] In argumentative writing, students may be required to support their claims with evidence, especially as they become more proficient writers. They must weigh the pros and cons of both sides, then take a position and justify it to the reader. To write an effective argumentative essay, students must be able to assume the perspective of their intended audience. Perhaps most challenging, they must be able to accurately represent a position with which they may not agree.

Most argumentative assignments are given in middle and high schools. Students might be asked to criticize an author's technique or to evaluate the importance of a historical event. But most state writing standards call for students to begin writing "opinion pieces" in the early elementary grades, and it's certainly a good idea to begin instruction in this kind of writing earlier than middle school. It may, however, be more difficult to find opinion or argumentative assignments for young children that are embedded in the content of the curriculum. If necessary, you might assign young children opinion pieces on non-curricular topics such as "Homework on Weekends" or "Preventing Global Warming."

Before your students begin to write an outline for an opinion or argumentative paragraph or composition, have them engage in class discussions about their topic. That kind of dialogue can help them formulate arguments that their intended audience would find persuasive.

Building the Framework: Outlining

Having students outline before they write does the following:

- Enables students to visualize the beginning, middle, and end of a paragraph or composition
- Helps students distinguish between essential and nonessential material
- Guides them to place their ideas in a logical order
- Prevents repetition
- Improves students' ability to stick with a topic

Writing an outline may not be as overwhelming a task as trying to write a draft without first making a plan, but it's still a challenging undertaking. Students will need to practice a number of skills before they're ready to embark on constructing an outline for even a single paragraph on their own. We will detail these skills, and how they should be introduced, in Chapter 4.

For now, bear in mind that it doesn't work to simply hand students the template for an outline and ask them to fill it out. You need to lay the groundwork first. And even after that groundwork has been laid, you'll need to model the process of creating an outline with the class as a whole before asking students to complete an outline independently.

Also bear in mind that you should continue to have students practice sentence-level skills even after they move on to planning and drafting. They will be drawing on many of those skills in crafting and revising longer-form writing.

Last, creating an outline can be a valuable end in itself, regardless of whether or not students turn it into a finished piece of writing. In creating an outline that is embedded in the content they're learning, they'll be delving into material they have read, mining it for the information they need, and making decisions about how to categorize and order that information. All of these tasks will be honing their thinking and writing skills while at the same time developing and reinforcing their content knowledge. Be sure to provide your students with ample opportunities to develop outlines without asking them to move on to drafts and final copies.

TO SUM UP

- Writing places heavy demands on the aspects of cognition known as executive functions and working memory.

- Break the writing process down into a series of four steps—planning and outlining, drafting, revising, and editing.

- Spend the most instructional time on planning and outlining and revising.

- Students don't need to take every piece of writing through all four steps, but they shouldn't stop after the drafting step—they should always revise and edit.

- Before students can plan a piece of writing, they need to identify the topic, the audience, and the purpose.

- Introduce students to the meaning of expository terms such as *enumerate* and *justify* to help them understand the purpose of an assignment or a prompt.

Notes

1. W. Strunk and E. B. White, *The Elements of Style* (New York: Longman, 1999), p. 15.

2. E. Yu and P. Cantor, "Poverty, Stress, Schools: Implications for Research, Practice, and Assessment" (New York: Turnaround for Children, 2016), www .turnaroundusa.org/wp-content/uploads/2016/05/Turnaround-for -Children-Poverty-Stress-Schools.pdf; National Scientific Council on the Developing Child, "Persistent Fear and Anxiety Can Affect Young Children's Learning and Development: Working Paper No. 9" (2010), http://

developingchild.harvard.edu/wp-content/uploads/2010/05/Persistent
-Fear-and-Anxiety-Can-Affect-Young-Childrens-Learning-and-Development
.pdf; P. Tough, *Helping Children Succeed* (2016), www.paultough.com/helping/
pdf/Helping-Children-Succeed-Paul-Tough.pdf?pdf=hcs-pdf-landing.

3. R. P. Ferretti and W. E. Lewis, "Best Practices in Teaching Argumentative
   Writing," *Best Practices in Writing Instruction.* 2nd ed. (New York: The
   Guilford Press, 2013), pp. 113–40.

4. National Center for Educational Statistics, *The Nation's Report Card: Writing
   2011 for Education Sciences* (Washington, DC: US Department of Education,
   2012).

CHAPTER 4

First Steps in Planning
The Single-Paragraph Outline

Recently, while visiting a third-grade class that consisted mainly of English language learners, I observed a dedicated teacher, whom I'll call Ms. Jones, struggling to help her students with a writing assignment based on an abridged version of *Peter Pan*. (As in most abridged versions of the classics, the fluency and beauty of the language were lost and the flow of the narrative was fragmented. Most abridgements actually impede comprehension, but that's another story.)

Ms. Jones gave the children 10 minutes to write an exit ticket about whether Wendy or Tinker Bell was more important to the story. The students had to include evidence to support their choice and they were given this hint: "There is no right answer to this question. But be sure to think carefully about each character's actions and how she moved the story forward." Ms. Jones provided her students with copies of interconnected webs that had little boxes radiating from each character's name. The students were expected to write their observations about Wendy and Tinker Bell in the appropriate boxes and then use those observations to construct a paragraph.

"What happened?" Ms. Jones said later, reading over the students' efforts—all of them incoherent. "They seemed to be getting the story. I don't know why they couldn't do this!"

One basic problem with Ms. Jones's assignment was that it was extremely complex—especially for students still learning English. But even if the assignment had been more manageable, students would still have had trouble converting their sprawling webs of information into linear, logically sequenced paragraphs. That's a challenging task for many students.

Call them what you will—*thought webs, brainstorming webs, bubble maps*—these frequently used devices may be helpful for vocabulary instruction or helping students grasp certain concepts, but they don't provide an effective template for transferring those ideas into a coherent piece of writing. A crucial step is missing: taking the material in the bubbles or boxes and figuring out what is most important, what is least important or irrelevant, and how to put the ideas and points in a logical order.

What Ms. Jones didn't yet know was that before asking her students to write, she needed to help them through the process of constructing a simple outline. If she had, she might have found that her students' paragraphs were far clearer and more coherent.

Outlining That Works

Some teachers may have tried the so-called Harvard Outline, with its main ideas, sub-ideas, sub-sub-ideas, Roman numerals, and capital and lower-case letters. Although it has the advantage of a linear structure, and it can serve as a great study guide, we've found that the Harvard Outline doesn't translate well into paragraphs. It goes to the other extreme from the free-form bubble map, requiring such high-level categorization and classification skills that students can get bogged down and confused in the planning process. Even if they do manage to complete such a detailed outline, they may find it difficult to convert the complex structure to written text.

The **Single-Paragraph Outline (SPO),** however, has a format that is linear and simple. It provides students with a road map they can follow to plan the beginning, middle, and end of a unified, coherent paragraph. It's a template they can easily duplicate themselves, and it encourages a way of thinking that will enable them to construct almost any type of text structure, including the following standard ones:

- Cause-and-effect
- Problem-solution
- Narrative
- Descriptive
- Compare-contrast
- Opinion

Exhibit 4.1 shows a blank SPO template, also available full-size in Appendix I. Exhibit 4.2 shows one that has been completed. Exhibit 4.3

EXHIBIT 4.1

<table>
<tr><td colspan="2" align="center">Single-Paragraph Outline</td></tr>
<tr><td>Name: _____</td><td>Date: _____</td></tr>
<tr><td colspan="2">T.S. _____</td></tr>
<tr><td colspan="2">_____</td></tr>
<tr><td colspan="2">_____</td></tr>
<tr><td colspan="2">1. ....</td></tr>
<tr><td colspan="2">2. ....</td></tr>
<tr><td colspan="2">3. ....</td></tr>
<tr><td colspan="2">4. ....</td></tr>
<tr><td colspan="2">C.S. _____</td></tr>
<tr><td colspan="2">_____</td></tr>
</table>

Source: Copyright © 2017 The Writing Revolution.

EXHIBIT 4.2

<table>
<tr><td colspan="2" align="center">Single-Paragraph Outline</td></tr>
<tr><td>Name: _____</td><td>Date: _____</td></tr>
<tr><td colspan="2">T.S. <u>The Brooklyn Bridge, an iconic structure, is a key feature</u></td></tr>
<tr><td colspan="2"><u>of the New York City skyline.</u></td></tr>
<tr><td colspan="2">1. East R. connects Manhattan + Bklyn</td></tr>
<tr><td colspan="2">2. opened 1883 / millions of commuters + tourists</td></tr>
<tr><td colspan="2">3. free passage → ↑ traffic</td></tr>
<tr><td colspan="2">4. footpath → walk + bike / avoid traffic</td></tr>
<tr><td colspan="2">C.S. If you want to see one of the most spectacular views</td></tr>
<tr><td colspan="2">of the city, make the trip across the Brooklyn Bridge!</td></tr>
</table>

Source: Copyright © 2017 The Writing Revolution.

EXHIBIT 4.3

> The Brooklyn Bridge, an iconic structure, is a key feature of the New York City skyline. The span soars over the East River, connecting the boroughs of Manhattan and Brooklyn. Since its opening in 1883, the bridge has been traveled by millions of commuters and tourists. Passage across the bridge is free, so traffic can be high. However, travelers can avoid the traffic by walking or biking between the two boroughs by using the bridge's famous footpath. If you want to see one of the most spectacular views of the city, make the trip across the Brooklyn Bridge!

Source: Copyright © 2017 The Writing Revolution.

shows a paragraph that a student might write based on the outline. As you can see, the SPO requires a student to create a complete topic sentence (T.S.) and concluding sentence (C.S.) for the paragraph—on solid lines. On the dotted lines, students write notes for the sentences that provide supporting details. *Remember that dotted lines tell students to write notes and solid lines tell them to write complete sentences!*

This chapter provides you with an array of strategies and activities that you can use to guide your students toward creating outlines and paragraphs such as these on their own. They'll be using the note-taking skills they learned when doing sentence expansion, described in Chapter 2, to write the notes for their detail sentences. They'll also be drawing on the three sentence-level skills you've had them practice to craft engaging and informative topic and concluding sentences: the four sentence types, appositives, and subordinating conjunctions.

We'll show you how to teach your students to put these skills together while also developing the new skills they'll need to construct paragraphs: extracting the main idea from a mass of information, figuring out which details relate to that main idea and how, and deciding how to sequence those details. We've broken the planning process down into a series of logically sequenced steps.

These stepping stones to the SPO are challenging for many students. You'll need to model each step along the way for the class as a whole and provide individualized feedback for each activity. The ultimate objective is to enable students to produce an outline independently, but handing them a blank SPO without first teaching them the necessary underlying skills won't produce that outcome.

Keep in mind that the steps leading toward the SPO have value in themselves: They will help students think more analytically, find important points more efficiently, and take notes more effectively. And once students have learned these steps, they will not only be ready to construct an SPO but also will have the skills they'll need when they move on to planning compositions. In addition, they'll acquire an understanding of the structure of a paragraph that will enhance their reading comprehension.

Here's an overview of the steps you'll need to take with your students to get them ready to create their own SPOs and paragraph drafts:

1. Be sure your students are familiar with the concept of a topic sentence.

2. Introduce students to the three TWR techniques for creating effective topic and concluding sentences. (Level 1 students should begin with just the sentence-type technique.)

3. Practice brainstorming or relating details about a specific topic and organizing them.

4. Have students generate a complete topic sentence for that topic, using the solid line at the top of the outline.

5. Have students select, categorize, and sequence the details they will use on the outline.

6. Write notes for the detail sentences on the dotted lines.

7. Generate a complete concluding sentence on the solid line at the bottom.

Although we'll present this process as a linear sequence, in practice you and your students will probably be combining some of these steps. Let's say you're at the stage where students are selecting details to use on their outline, and you notice they're having trouble distinguishing relevant from irrelevant details. At that point, you might decide to return to a previous exercise that's designed to give them practice with that skill—for example, giving them a list of sentences, including a topic sentence, and having them eliminate the one that is least relevant.

Home in on the Main Idea: Topic and Concluding Sentences

Practicing the development of topic and concluding sentences does the following:

- Enables students to make generalizations

- Promotes analytical and abstract thinking

- Provides focus

Developing topic and concluding sentences can be difficult tasks. Both require students to consider a collection of facts and information and decide what fundamental characteristics unite them—in other words, to develop the ability to make abstractions. Many of the activities that follow will help students in identifying and creating both kinds of sentences. But we'll focus on topic sentences here, because that's what students will confront first when making their outlines. And once students have created a solid topic sentence, constructing the concluding sentence is often an easier job.

Rather than simply going through each of the activities described in the next sections, you'll need to decide which of them are necessary for your particular students—or some subgroup of your students—and how long to spend on each of them. Inevitably, some students will pick up a skill more quickly than others.

Familiarizing Your Students With the Concept of a Topic Sentence

Before asking your students to try drafting topic sentences, you'll want to make sure they understand the concept—that is, that a **topic sentence** expresses a paragraph's main idea. You'll also want them to see that the sentences that follow in the body of the paragraph should all provide details that relate to the general idea contained in the topic sentence. The following activities will help them grasp these fundamental points.

The Forest and the Trees: Distinguishing a Topic Sentence From Supporting Details

Practicing distinguishing a topic sentence from supporting details does the following:

- Enables students to connect supporting details to a main idea
- Helps students organize facts and ideas
- Aids in sequencing

One effective way to help students understand the concept of a topic sentence is to present them with a series of sentences and ask them to identify the one that is the topic sentence and the ones that provide supporting details. You could start with just two sentences, and ask students to mark one with *T.S.*, for *topic sentence*, and the other with *S.D.*, for *supporting detail.*

Level 1 Example

This example doesn't require specific background knowledge:

___ Thanksgiving is a popular American holiday.

___ Our meal is very traditional.

Students should put T.S. next to the first sentence and *S.D.* next to the second.

Level 2 Example

If you're a biology teacher, you can give your students something like this:

___ In the cell nucleus, chromosomes are separated into two identical sets.

___ Mitosis is a process of cell division.

In this example, students should put T.S. next to the second sentence and *S.D.* next to the first.

You can increase the level of difficulty by giving students groups of three to five sentences and asking them to identify the topic sentence. They should then number the remaining sentences in the order that would be most logical. This activity will help them understand how to sequence ideas or a narrative within a paragraph.

For example, students who have been studying the years leading up to the Civil War might do the following activity:

Identify topic sentence (T.S.), then sequence details:

___ Harriet Tubman helped slaves to freedom.

___ John Brown led a small rebellion against slavery.

___ The anti-slavery movement began to grow in the 1850s.

___ Abraham Lincoln won the presidential election.

Students would put T.S. next to the third sentence and number the remaining sentences in the appropriate order (1, 2, and 3).

Tell Me More: Brainstorming Details for a Given Topic Sentence

In this activity, you provide students with a topic sentence you've created and have them generate details to go with it. This exercise will help your students grasp the relationship between a general topic and supporting details.

Level 1 Example

For a Level 1 group, you might start with the following sentence—which, like the previous Level 1 example, requires only general knowledge:

Dogs are popular pets.

Students could brainstorm key words relating to the topic of dogs being popular pets, such as *protective, loyal,* and *playful.* If you write the words down on a lined piece of paper or template, make sure they appear on dotted rather than solid lines.

Level 2 Example

If you've been teaching Level 2 students about public health and nutrition, you could give them this sentence:

The rise in obesity rates has created a serious health problem in the United States.

Students might respond with words and phrases such as *larger portion sizes, heart disease,* and *diabetes.*

The Match Game: Which Details Go With Which Topic Sentence?

To further help students understand the relationship between a topic sentence—or main idea—and supporting details, you might give them a collection of details and two different topic sentences. Students need to write each detail under the topic sentence it belongs with.

Level 1 Example

In the following example, one topic sentence relates to George Washington and the other to Abraham Lincoln. Students need to look at each of the words and phrases in the list at the bottom and decide which topic sentence it goes with. For example, they would write a detail such as "Revolutionary War" under the sentence about George Washington, and a detail such as "log cabin/self-educated" under the sentence about Abraham Lincoln.

T.S. George Washington, the first president of the United States, had a remarkable life.

1. ....

2. ....

3. ....

4. ....

T.S. Although Abraham Lincoln came from humble beginnings, he became one of the greatest American presidents.

1. ....

2. ....

3. ....

4. ....

log cabin / self-educated

Revolutionary War

Gettysburg Address

father of his country

Emancipation Proclamation

leader/Continental Congress

crossed Delaware/1776/Christmas

Civil War/preservation of the Union

Level 2 Example

The following example is somewhat more complex because both topic sentences relate to the same person, Andrew Jackson. The difference is that one presents him in a positive light and the other in a negative one. This activity requires students to distinguish between facts that support different points of view about the same historical figure.

T.S. Andrew Jackson, the seventh US president, was a hero of the common man.

1. ....

2. ....

3. ....

4. ....

T.S. President Jackson should be remembered as an unjust leader.

1. ....

2. ....

3. ....

4. ....

spoils system = rewarded unqualified supporters

nullification crisis / preserved union

relocation of Native Americans → Trail of Tears

many vetoes = power-hungry/dictatorial

Tariff of Abominations

born in log cabin

voting ↑ → spirit of equality

When embedded in content, an activity like this not only helps students distinguish between main ideas and details but also provides an effective comprehension check and a boost to learning. It's excellent preparation for the challenging task of planning and writing an argumentative essay, when students will present claims and acknowledge counterclaims (see Chapter 8).

Which One Doesn't Belong? Eliminating the Least Relevant Sentence

If students are having difficulty distinguishing relevant from irrelevant details when given a particular topic sentence or are going off topic when they write, try this: give them a group of sentences and have them underline the topic sentence. Then have them cross out the sentence that has the weakest connection to the topic sentence and the other detail sentences.

For example, you could give Level 1 students the following sentences:

1. Harriet Tubman escaped from slavery.

2. Harriet Tubman risked her life many times by helping other enslaved people.

3. Harriet Tubman was an extraordinary woman.

4. At seven years old, Harriet Tubman was sent to work in the fields.

5. During the Civil War, Harriet Tubman became an armed scout and spy for the Union Army.

In this example, students would underline the third sentence—which is the topic sentence—and cross out the fourth sentence. Although it relates to Harriet Tubman, it doesn't strongly support the idea that she was extraordinary.

A similar activity is to give students a paragraph that has one irrelevant sentence and have them cross it out (see Exhibit 4.4).

Ready to Write: Drafting Topic and Concluding Sentences

Once your students have a general understanding of the nature of a topic (or concluding) sentence, you can give them activities that lead them through the process of drafting a topic sentence. As with all TWR activities, you'll want to model each of these with the class as a whole before asking students to try them independently.

Three Strategies for Constructing Topic and Concluding Sentences

If you are guiding students through the formulation of topic sentences and concluding sentences, tell them there are three excellent strategies for coming up with interesting topic sentences that convey a lot of information. They should remember these strategies from their sentence-level work:

1. *Using one of the sentence types.* Students may use a statement, a question, an exclamation, or (possibly) a command. For example, the topic

EXHIBIT 4.4

> **Eliminate the irrelevant detail.**
>
> Why is the New York City subway system unique? There are approximately 468 stations, which is more than any other city in the world. Over a billion people use the city's transportation system each year! In addition, it was designed to make traveling around the city easier for its passengers. For example, mezzanines allow passengers to use any entrance without having to cross the street. ~~Beijing, Moscow, and Tokyo have a very fast rapid transit rail system.~~ If you need to get around New York City, the subway is a great alternative to driving.

Source: Copyright © 2017 The Writing Revolution.

sentence for a paragraph about New York might be, "Have you ever been to New York City?" A paragraph about the Taj Mahal might start with, "The design of the Taj Mahal is spectacular!"

2. *Including an appositive.* A paragraph about New York City could start with, "New York, the nation's largest city, is a fascinating place." A paragraph about Genghis Khan might begin, "Genghis Khan, a powerful Mongol leader, created a large empire."

3. *Starting with a subordinating conjunction.* A Level 1 student might use a subordinating conjunction such as *before* to form a topic sentence. For example: "Before you get a dog, you need to make some preparations!" A Level 2 student might use a more sophisticated conjunction such as *although*—as in "Although the New Deal did not solve all of the nation's problems, it saved the United States from complete economic collapse." Beginning with a subordinating conjunction such as *although* works well for compare-and-contrast topic sentences and, later on, argumentative thesis statements.

These three strategies are also very useful in formulating concluding sentences—a challenge we'll address further on in this chapter.

If you're teaching Level 1 students in the early elementary grades, just introduce them to the first of these strategies: the four sentence types. Otherwise, you'll want to have your students practice using all three of these strategies to transform boring topic sentences into engaging, informative ones. You can start by getting them to recognize the difference between a boring and an interesting sentence. For example, you can show them two topic sentences and ask them which is better:

Dogs are fantastic pets!

Here are the reasons dogs are good pets.

Hint: They should choose the first one! Then you can provide them with some additional boring topic sentences and guide them through the process of using one of the three strategies to liven them up.

Level 1 Example
You might give students a boring topic sentence such as this one:

Thanksgiving is fun.

Then ask them to make it more interesting by using a different sentence type, an appositive, and a subordinating conjunction. They might come up with these sentences:

Thanksgiving is a great family holiday!

Thanksgiving, a popular holiday in the United States, is always celebrated on the fourth Thursday in November.

Although all Americans celebrate Thanksgiving, not everyone knows why.

Level 2 Example

The students in a 10th-grade social studies class at New Dorp High School on Staten Island had been studying the Indian independence movement and were analyzing primary sources. Their teacher, Toni-Ann Vroom, decided to guide the class of English language learners through a topic sentence activity.

Toni-Ann started by putting a simple sentence on the whiteboard— "Gandhi had an impact"—and asked students to improve it. One student suggested using a subordinating conjunction, and another proposed changing the sentence to a different sentence type, perhaps a question.

Toni-Ann agreed these were good ideas, but she settled on the suggestion of a third student: "You could use an appositive."

She then asked students to brainstorm four appositives with a partner and got responses from various pairs. "A nonviolent leader?" one girl offered.

"Excellent!" Toni-Ann said, turning to the whiteboard to write the phrase down. She repeated the process with several more student-generated appositives: "a civil rights activist," "a pacifist," "a nationalist leader," "an intelligent leader."

She then asked the students to pick one of the appositives and work individually to "improve that boring topic sentence." After getting several suggestions, she chose one sentence to write on the board: "Gandhi, a nationalist leader, had a significant impact on India."

Make It Sparkle: Choosing Vivid Words

One way of enlivening a topic sentence—or any sentence, for that matter—is to use strong and varied nouns and verbs, as well as modifiers and descriptive phrases. You may need to show Level 1 students where to place adjectives and descriptive phrases in sentences at first, but eventually students will be able to find the correct placement on their own.

If students favor overused, easy-to-spell adjectives such as *fun* or *good*, encourage them to find descriptive words that are more specific and unusual. You can provide students with a list of suggested alternative words. Instead of *fun*, for example, a student might substitute *memorable* or *sensational*. Instead of *good,* you might suggest *enjoyable* or *delightful.* It's often a pleasant surprise to see the better choices students make when they brainstorm for more precise and varied alternatives.

Some teachers have gone so far as to ban certain words from their classrooms, including the verb *said.* In some instances, however, a simple, direct word can be the best choice. Rather than prohibiting the use of simple words, we suggest encouraging students to use more unusual and vivid ones when appropriate.

As students move to more sophisticated expository and argumentative writing, try posting lists of words that are geared to those types of writing. For example, topic sentences using words such as *although* work particularly well for argumentative writing. See Table 8.1 in Chapter 8, near "Consider the Alternatives: Planning and Writing Four-Paragraph Pro-Con Compositions," for a list of suggested nouns and verbs for argumentative writing.

More Than One Way to Say It: Creating Multiple Topic Sentences for a Single Topic

After students have had some practice making boring topic sentences more interesting, try giving them a topic and asking them to create two or three topic sentences for it.

Level 1 Example

If your Level 1 students have been studying weather, you might give them the topic of "climate change" and ask them to write three interesting topic sentences using each of the three strategies: sentence types, appositives, and subordinating conjunctions. They might come up with these sentences:

Do you think the earth is getting warmer?

Climate change, a problem all over the world, is getting more attention.

If we don't do something about climate change, the world will keep getting warmer.

Level 2 Example

If you're teaching biology and your class has been studying the digestive system, you can give students the topic "digestion." They might produce topic sentences such as the following:

Digestion, a system consisting of a group of organs that breaks food down in order to enable the absorption of nutrients, also rids the body of waste.

Although some bacteria cause disease, others have positive effects, such as helping to digest food.

What Do These Things Have in Common? Using Notes to Create a Topic Sentence

A slightly more difficult exercise is to give students an SPO with the details in the form of notes—key words and phrases, abbreviations, and symbols—and have them generate a topic sentence. (See Chapter 2 for a discussion of TWR note-taking techniques.) When embedded in the content you're teaching, this activity will require students to draw on what they've learned, so you'll want to be sure they have acquired enough knowledge to complete the exercise successfully. This activity will also require students to synthesize a number of details to come up with a sentence that brings them all together.

Level 1 Example

If Level 1 students have been learning about weather, you could give them an SPO such as the one shown in Exhibit 4.5 and have them provide a topic sentence.

Students might write this as their topic sentence:

A thunderstorm can be scary!

EXHIBIT 4.5

Single-Paragraph Outline

Name:_____   Date:_____

T.S. _____

_____

_____

1. cumulonimbus clouds ....

2. wind + rain + hail ....

3. lightning → thunder ....

4. dog under bed ....

C.S. _____

_____

Source: Copyright © 2017 The Writing Revolution.

EXHIBIT 4.6

Single-Paragraph Outline

Name:_____ Date:_____

T.S. _____

_____

_____

art   1. Michaelangelo / DaVinci ....

education 2. Gutenberg / printing press ....

inventions 3. watches / microscope ....

science 4. Copernicus / Galileo → astronomy ....

C.S. _____

_____

_____

Source: Copyright © 2017 The Writing Revolution.

Level 2 Example

Students might use the details shown in Exhibit 4.6—and the knowledge that enables them to identify the era being discussed—to generate a sentence such as the following:

> *The Renaissance was a time of tremendous advancements in many areas.*

In Conclusion: The Challenge of Creating Non-Repetitive Concluding Sentences

The same basic techniques that have enabled students to craft effective topic sentences will work for concluding sentences—with one twist. A concluding sentence should echo the idea of the topic sentence but not repeat it verbatim.

In some types of writing, the concluding sentence should introduce something new—perhaps, especially in an opinion piece, a call to action or a personal opinion. Often, however, a paraphrase or summary of the topic sentence can serve as the concluding one. For example:

> T.S. In *Charlotte's Web,* a resourceful spider saves the life of Wilbur, a little pig.

C.S. In conclusion, *Charlotte's Web* is a wonderful story about an unlikely friendship.

T.S. In *To Kill a Mockingbird,* the verdict against Tom Robinson reveals the racism that was prevalent during the 1930s.

C.S. Although Tom was clearly innocent, the jurors are swayed by their racial prejudices.

As we'll discuss in Chapter 5, one way to make a sentence sound more like a concluding one is to introduce it with an appropriate transition, such as *finally* or *in conclusion.* It's also best if the topic and concluding sentences don't repeat the same structure. For example, if the topic sentence includes an appositive, then encourage students to use a different structure for the concluding sentence—perhaps using a subordinating conjunction or an exclamation.

Concluding sentences may seem formulaic and unnecessary. Certainly most published writers don't end each paragraph with a formal concluding sentence. And as students become more adept and fluid writers, you can relax the requirement that they include one as well. But when students are first beginning to construct a paragraph, a concluding sentence will help them see the group of sentences that form it as a cohesive whole. The process of creating a concluding sentence will also prepare them for the work of creating a concluding paragraph when they start writing multiple-paragraph compositions.

Reverse the Process: Turning a Paragraph Into an SPO

A great way to help your students grasp the underlying structure of an effective paragraph is to give them a paragraph or brief article and have them deconstruct it into an SPO. You can use a variety of text structures for this activity. Whatever structure you choose, your students will get practice identifying topic and concluding sentences, recognizing detail sentences, and analyzing the order in which ideas or steps in a sequence are presented.

Level 1 Example

Ms. Schlesinger's second-grade class had spent plenty of time observing her model the process of crafting a narrative SPO and then creating that kind of SPO as a whole class. When Ms. Schlesinger decided her students were ready to try the activity independently, she had them write their own

EXHIBIT 4.7

I have a routine when I do my
①
homework. First, I start my first
②
page of homework. Next, I get a
③
drink of iced tea. Then, I get rid of
my brother, Nicky, because he
④
comes into my room. Finally, I try
to do my homework in peace. Over
the years, this routine has worked
very well for me.

Source: Copyright © 2017 The Writing Revolution.

EXHIBIT 4.8

Single-Paragraph Outline

Name:_____   Date:_____

T.S. __I have a routine when I do homework._____

_____

_____

1st ⟍ 1. 1 pg. of hw. ....

Next ⟍ 2. iced tea ....

Then ⟍ 3. rid of Nicky ....

Finally ⟍ 4. do h.w. ....

C.S. __Over the years, this routine has worked very__
    __well for me._____

_____

Source: Copyright © 2017 The Writing Revolution.

SPOs about their routines for doing homework. Afterward, they turned their SPOs into finished paragraphs.

Then Ms. Schlesinger gave one of the student-written paragraphs to Mr. Harris's second-grade class, where his students turned it back into SPOs. Mr. Harris instructed his students to do the following:

1. Underline the topic and concluding sentences.

2. Number the detail sentences.

3. Underline the key words and phrases in each sentence.

4. Convert the paragraph into an SPO.

Exhibit 4.7 shows the completed paragraph that the student in Ms. Schlesinger's class wrote, with annotations by a student in Mr. Harris's class:

The next step was for Mr. Harris's students to convert the paragraph into an SPO, copying the topic and concluding sentences and converting the detail sentences into key words and phrases (see Exhibit 4.8).

Level 2 Example

When having your students deconstruct paragraphs, you can either write a paragraph based on the material they've been studying or use an appropriate paragraph from a published text on the topic.

If your students have been studying the role of the Catholic Church in the Middle Ages, you might give them the following paragraph:

> The Catholic Church was the most dominant force during the Middle Ages. The church was the center of town life. The pope was the religious leader of the Catholic Church. He had the power to crown kings and excommunicate people from the church. The church collected a tithe, a church tax, which led to the construction of convents, monasteries, and great cathedrals. Overall, the Catholic Church was an extremely powerful institution.

As Mr. Harris did with his second-grade class, you'll want to tell students to underline the topic and concluding sentences and number the four detail sentences. Then they'll copy the topic and concluding sentences onto the solid lines of an SPO and convert the detail sentences into note form on the dotted lines. Because this is a Level 2 class, they'll be able to use not just key words and phrases in their notes but also abbreviations and symbols. You can provide some examples of abbreviations and symbols students can use, if they're still developing their note-taking skills.

The student's notes for detail sentences might look like this:

1. church = center / town life

2. pope = rel. leader / Catholic Church

3.   pope → crown kings / excomm. people

4.   tithe → convents, monasteries, cathedrals

A Writing Road Map: Building an SPO

Having students create an outline before writing a paragraph does the following:

- Provides structure (beginning, middle, and end)
- Eliminates repetition
- Improves adherence to topic
- Enables students to distinguish essential from nonessential material
- Aids in sequencing
- Promotes analytical thinking

As we've mentioned, an outline provides students with a kind of road map for their writing journey. It's also easier to revise than a draft: If students see they've omitted some important information or have gone off track, they can make changes without rewriting an entire sentence or paragraph. Often, students can produce an outline more quickly and efficiently than a draft. And—especially if it requires students to convert text they've read to notes—using an outline ensures that students will actually think about the meaning of a text and determine its main points. It's a step in writing that you won't want your students to skip.

The topic and concluding sentence activities we've just described will help prepare students for much of the work of creating the SPO. But even if students have spent a fair amount of time practicing those skills, you'll still need to provide a great deal of modeling and ample opportunities for whole-class work before they'll be ready to construct an SPO on their own.

Before beginning, you'll need to let students know the topic of the outline you'll be modeling with them and the intended audience. They may also need to know what type of writing will be involved—expository, narrative, descriptive, or opinion. It's important to make those factors clear.

Generally, you'll want to follow these steps for developing an SPO with your class:

1. Identify the topic, purpose, and audience.

2. Brainstorm or relate details.

3. Generate a complete topic sentence (this can be done before the brainstorming if preferred).

4. Select, categorize, and sequence details.

5. Write notes for the detail sentences on the dotted lines.

6. Generate a complete concluding sentence.

Generating a Topic Sentence: Develop an Eye for Details

The first step in the process of generating a topic sentence is to establish the topic. It's good to have a minimum of 10 to 15 details before trying to formulate a topic sentence, so the topic should be one that students already have some knowledge of. As always, a topic embedded in the curriculum will work best, because it will enhance learning while simultaneously teaching writing skills.

If your students are creating a topic sentence for a narrative paragraph, have them relate the steps or events in a logical or chronological order. The topic might be the steps in a math problem or scientific process, the plot of a novel or story, or the sequence of occurrences leading up to a current or historical event.

Other kinds of topics lend themselves to brainstorming: After you've stated the topic, students can brainstorm details about it and use those details to create a topic sentence. Alternatively, you might provide the topic sentence first and then have students brainstorm details.

As students provide details, you'll want to write them on the board or a flip chart. Be careful to write them as notes rather than sentences, using only key words and phrases, abbreviations, and symbols. If students state the details as sentences, model the process of paring them down to notes.

If students need help brainstorming about a topic, you can provide a prompt—perhaps asking "What about the weather?" if the topic is Halloween. Their answers can be grouped into a "weather" category when you reach the next stage of creating the outline.

Time to Choose: Selecting and Categorizing Details

Once students have brainstormed or otherwise generated ideas, the next step is to guide them to select the three to five most important details. If possible, group the details into categories. For example, if the topic is New York City, the details might fall into categories such as culture, shopping, poverty, and transportation. Within the "culture" category, the details might be museums, opera, Broadway, and ballet.

If the students are outlining a narrative paragraph, the process will be different: The details should be grouped chronologically or in the sequence determined by the narrative.

Putting It All Together: Filling in the Single-Paragraph Outline as a Class

Next, display a blank SPO template, using whatever method of modeling you choose, and distribute a photocopy to each student. If you have provided a topic sentence, or the class has collectively come up with one through relating or brainstorming details, have them write it at the top, on the solid line following the abbreviation T.S.

Now you're ready to guide students through the process of filling in the dotted lines—numbered one through four—with the appropriate details rendered in key words and phrases, abbreviations, and symbols. Tell students that it's not necessary to include every detail they generated. What *is* important is to write down the details as notes rather than complete sentences. This will make it easier to change or rearrange the details, if need be, and will also get students in the habit of using notes for their detail lines. When they're relying on texts as the sources for details, converting the text into notes will ensure that they are actually processing what they've read rather than simply copying it.

Depending on the type of writing involved, there may or may not be a logical sequence for these details. If the paragraph is a narrative that involves a series of events, you will want to put the details in chronological order. If the paragraph is an opinion piece, tell students it's a good idea to put the strongest argument last, because readers will be more likely to remember it.

Last, generate a concluding sentence as a class. Students may be able to do this independently by creating a variation on the topic sentence. For example, if the topic sentence has an appositive, the concluding sentence can express a similar idea but take the form of a sentence type or begin with a subordinating conjunction.

You'll probably want to model this process for one or two class sessions before having your students try to create an SPO on their own.

HOW TO DIFFERENTIATE AN SPO ACTIVITY

For students who need more support in completing an SPO, you can provide the topic or the concluding sentence—or both—and just have them write in notes for the details. Students who need less support can come up with their topic and concluding sentences independently.

Another way to differentiate this activity is to have some students use only key words and phrases for their notes on the dotted lines, while requiring others to use abbreviations and symbols as well.

Level 1 Example

Mr. Clark, a teacher at a New York elementary school, decided to lead his Level 1 class through the process of creating an SPO on the topic of autumn. He introduced the topic and explained the purpose of the paragraph: to describe the fall season. Then he specified the audience: people in other parts of the country, such as Florida or Hawaii, who might not be familiar with autumn the way it's experienced in the Northeast.

Next, Mr. Clark asked his students to brainstorm ideas about autumn. He wrote down each response in the form of notes on the board:

colder weather

frost

scarves

jackets

shorter days + longer nights

leaves turn colors + fall

pumpkins

turn back clocks

After coming up with these ideas, the students seemed stuck. They needed at least a few more.

"How about animals?" Mr. Clark suggested. "Do they do anything different in the autumn?"

"They hibernate!" a student remembered. "And some of them build shelters."

Mr. Clark added that detail to the list. Once the class had about 15 details, he led them through the process of creating a topic sentence.

"Is there something that most of these details have in common?" he asked.

One student pointed out that a lot of them had to do with things changing. Mr. Clark agreed and asked, "So if we wanted to create a topic sentence for a paragraph about autumn, using these details, what could it be?"

"Something like . . . 'Autumn is a time when a lot of things change'?" one student offered.

"Good!" Mr. Clark said. "Let's make that, 'The autumn season brings many changes.'"

Next he guided the class through the process of putting the details into four categories—one for each detail line of the SPO. The students eliminated the details that didn't fit with the idea of change or didn't fit into one of the four categories. Once the class had two or three details in each category, Mr. Clark asked them to take out their templates and follow along as he transferred the detail notes onto the dotted lines of the template.

Finally, it was time to come up with a concluding sentence. Mr. Clark suggested using a different sentence type than the one they'd used for their topic sentence, and the students decided on a sentence in the form of a question.

The class's completed SPO looked like that shown in Exhibit 4.9.

EXHIBIT 4.9

Single-Paragraph Outline

Name: _____ Date: _____

T.S. __The autumn season brings__
___many changes.___

_____

time 1. .turn back clocks / shorter days & longer nights....

temperature 2. .colder weather → frost / sweaters & jackets......

nature 3. .leaves turn colors & fall...................................

animals 4. .animals make shelters / give ex............................

C.S. __Isn't autumn an exciting__
___time of year?___

_____

Level 2 Example

In one Level 2 class that had been studying ancient native American civilizations for a couple of weeks, students began the SPO process by brainstorming a list of key words and phrases about the Aztecs. Some of them consulted the texts they had been reading for ideas. As the students suggested ideas, their teacher, Ms. Klein, wrote them on the board in the form of notes, as shown in Exhibit 4.10.

Ms. Klein had the students work in pairs to come up with topic sentences for at least some of these details. For some students who needed a little more help, she suggested that they use an appositive. For others, she suggested using a subordinating conjunction. After a few minutes, she called on several pairs to report what they had come up with. Some

EXHIBIT 4.10

Aztecs Facts

polytheistic = worship many gods

herbal treatments → cure for diseases

practiced human sacrifice

women's clothes = beads + flowers + metals

prisoners + children = most sacrificed

1519 / Cortez = conquistador / conquered empire

adv. math system → used area for construction

1st civ. / developed educational system → all children attended

smallpox → Aztec ↓

constructed pyramids + temples / used for ceremonies

created advanced calendar → improved farming

practiced polygamy = > 1 wife

Aztecs = fierce warriors

built chinampas = floating gardens → crops ↑

Source: Copyright © 2017 The Writing Revolution.

suggestions were too specific, while others—such as "The Aztec civilization did many different things"—were too general.

After some discussion, Ms. Klein and the class agreed on the following sentence, which one of the pairs had come up with:

The Aztecs, a Mesoamerican civilization, had many outstanding achievements.

Ms. Klein wrote the sentence on the SPO template, which she had projected onto the board, and the students followed suit.

"Now, are there some details here that don't belong with this topic sentence?" Ms. Klein asked.

Students suggested several that should clearly be eliminated: human sacrifice, smallpox, polygamy. And there were far too many details to fit into one paragraph. Students had a lively debate over which four details to include on their SPOs. Some argued for "herbal treatments" over "floating gardens," but "floating gardens" won.

By the end of class, Ms. Klein had the outline shown in Exhibit 4.11 on the board, and students had the same information on their individual copies.

EXHIBIT 4.11

Single-Paragraph Outline

Name: _____   Date: _____

T.S. **The Aztecs, a Mesoamerican**
      civilization, had many outstanding
      achievements.

1. advanced math. system → used area for construction…

2. 1st civ. / developed edu. system → all children attended.

3. constructed pyramids + temples / used for ceremonies…

4. built chinampas = floating gardens → crops ↑……………

C.S. _____

_____

_____

An Intermediate Step: Turning an Outline into a Draft

Once your students have done the hard work required to put together a coherent SPO, converting the outline into a draft will be a relatively simple matter. All they'll need to do is to translate their detail notes into complete sentences—something they'll have had practice doing during sentence expansion and SPO scaffold activities—and combine those sentences with the topic and concluding sentences they've already written.

As we've mentioned, the two stages of writing that require the most instructional time are planning and revising. Drafting is the stage that comes in between. When students translate their SPOs into a draft, the resulting paragraph will be logically organized, on topic, and non-repetitive. At the same time, though, it may sound wooden and flat. When you introduce them to revision techniques in the next chapter, they'll learn to add transition words that connect their sentences and to vary their sentence structure to make their writing flow.

But bear in mind that leading your students through the process of developing an SPO, and later having them complete one independently, is a valuable exercise in itself, regardless of whether it results in a written paragraph. Remember that making an outline enables students to do the following:

- Visualize a beginning, a middle, and an end in their writing.
- Distinguish essential from nonessential information.
- Make connections between a main idea and a detail that relates to it.
- Order ideas or events in a logical sequence.

You'll want to give your students plenty of opportunities to develop outlines without turning them into drafts and final copies.

TO SUM UP

- An outlining format should be linear and simple, enabling students to rank material in order of importance, eliminate irrelevant information, and put points in a logical order.

- To help students understand the concept of a topic sentence, have them distinguish topic sentences from supporting details, generate detail sentences, match details with the appropriate topic sentence, and eliminate the least relevant detail sentences.

- Build on students' knowledge of sentences to **introduce the three strategies** for constructing topic and concluding **sentences: sentence types,** appositives, and subordinating conjunctions.

- Have students practice writing topic sentences from **notes you provide.**

- Guide students through the process of creating **non-repetitive** concluding sentences.

- Have students convert a paragraph you provide into an SPO to help them grasp the structure of a paragraph.

- Model the process of creating an SPO as a whole-**class activity:** brainstorming or relating details and crafting a topic sentence, **putting details** in categories or a logical sequence, writing them as notes on **the dotted** lines of the SPO, and generating a concluding sentence.

- Have students create their own SPOs and convert **them into draft** paragraphs.

CHAPTER 5

Putting Flesh on the Bones
Revising a Draft

When I was a young teacher, I remember looking with dismay at the paragraph my fourth-grade student Brittany had just handed in, which was similar to so many others I'd gotten back.

"I really really like summer," the first sentence read. There were two more sentences that essentially repeated the same idea, without much elaboration.

"Brittany," I said encouragingly, "you can do better! Try making the topic sentence more interesting. And how about adding more details?"

Brittany went back to work, biting her lip. She was trying hard, but the end result was little better. She had changed the first sentence to "Here are some reasons why I like summer." She had added one sentence about how she liked to go to the beach and another about how she liked to stay up late when there was no school the next day, but the paragraph was still disjointed and wooden—and, frankly, boring.

I mustered a smile, not wanting to discourage her. "That's getting better," I lied, my heart sinking. How could I get my students to write clear, coherent paragraphs, with one well-structured and informative sentence leading seamlessly to the next? Why didn't they respond to my suggestions the way I wanted them to?

The reason, as I eventually learned, is that students need much more than vague comments like "make it better." They need explicit instruction, including clear directions, teacher-led demonstrations, group participation, and a careful sequence of activities. They need to learn how to edit their writing. But first, and more important, they need to learn how to revise it.

Two Different Processes: Revising Versus Editing

Many people see the concepts of revising and editing as one and the same. After all, both processes are necessary to make a piece of writing better. But in fact, revising and editing differ in important ways. Helping your students understand the distinction between the two is a crucial first step in transforming a boring and disjointed piece of writing into one that engages the reader and flows smoothly.

Put Yourself in the Reader's Shoes: Revising

Revising means clarifying or altering the content or structure of a draft. It's what all good writers do, sometimes repeatedly, to make their writing clear, accurate, and fluid. It can be as simple as substituting a powerful adjective for one that falls flat or as complex as reorganizing the sequence of ideas in an essay to make an argument stronger. For beginning writers, it often involves turning simple rudimentary sentences into rich, complex ones or fleshing out vague ideas with details and examples. For other writers, it may mean eliminating unnecessary verbiage or streamlining convoluted sentence structure.

At its core, revising requires writers to put themselves into the shoes of a reader, anticipating what information that reader will need or want to know and how to communicate it as effectively as possible.

To revise, students will need to draw on the skills they learned when practicing the sentence-level activities. They will also build on the planning they engaged in when creating their Single-Paragraph Outlines (SPOs). And they'll need to learn how to harness the power of transitions to make their writing flow.

Correct Mechanical Errors: Editing

Editing, although important, is a much more cut-and-dried affair. It involves identifying and then correcting errors in grammar, punctuation, capitalization, syntax, and spelling.

When teaching writing, most teachers focus on editing, probably because they are most comfortable with the mechanics of writing. Similarly, if you ask students to improve on a piece of writing, they're likely to make mechanical changes, because it's easier: Adding a comma or capitalizing a proper noun isn't nearly as complex as imagining what a reader needs to know. But it's revising that deserves the lion's share of instructional time. And it rarely gets it.

Revising needs to come *before* editing. Only after students grow familiar with the process of revising should they be expected to edit, proofread, and otherwise refine their work. Revising may change the wording and structure of a piece of writing, so there's no point in fine-tuning words and passages that may disappear in the next draft. Editing an assignment before it has been revised is like icing a cake before it's fully baked.

However, that doesn't mean that you should wait until students have reached the editing stage to start correcting their mechanical errors. As we pointed out in Chapter 1, it's best to begin that work when students are practicing sentence-level activities.

At the end of this chapter, we'll go into further detail on how and when editing should be done.

Polish a Draft: The Process of Revision

Practicing revision activities does the following:

- Helps develop clarity and **coherence**
- Enables students to use sentence strategies when writing at length
- Provides a way of incorporating substantive changes into a piece of writing in addition to mechanical ones
- Leads to smoothly flowing, logically connected prose

Students may find it challenging to revise their writing. Providing them with an array of activities—which we'll outline in the following sections—will help. But even after you've introduced your students to these activities, they'll have to practice applying them to a bare-bones paragraph that you provide before they'll be equipped to revise their own writing.

We've observed that students find it easier to revise a paragraph when they don't feel a sense of ownership. Giving them what we call an *unelaborated paragraph*—which we'll describe in detail in the next section—is a great way to have them practice inserting transitions and varying their sentence structure. Eventually, they'll be able to apply those strategies independently to their own writing.

Generally, revision assignments should be kept brief. It's best for Level 1 writers to limit their writing to one paragraph of five or six sentences. That's also true for more able writers who are still learning how to make substantive revisions. If students write at greater length, they may find it difficult to revise and edit and become discouraged. *Clarity and accuracy, not length, are the goals.* Stress to students that they should leave room on their papers for revising and editing their work.

For drafting and revising written work and printing final copies, computers are invaluable—as long as students learn keyboarding skills and become proficient typists. If they have to hunt and peck at a keyboard, students will be distracted during the complex process of composing.

Practice on Someone Else's Text: The Unelaborated Paragraph

Having students revise unelaborated paragraphs does the following:

- Helps them learn to use TWR strategies with careful scaffolding and then apply them to their own writing independently.

- Enables them to practice revision techniques on text for which they don't feel a sense of ownership

- Deepens their understanding of content

We often notice that students can apply TWR techniques they've been taught when a teacher provides them with structure but then have difficulty when writing independently. You may see this issue emerge when students revise their outlines and drafts. A student might, for example, improve a sentence by adding an appositive when you specifically suggest that strategy but won't come up with the idea on his own.

One of the most effective ways to solve this problem and see improvement in students' independent writing is by using the unelaborated paragraph. The idea is to give students a bare-bones paragraph consisting of brief, simple sentences and then guide them through the process of improving it. These paragraphs should have no spelling, capitalization, punctuation, or grammatical errors so that students can focus on revision, not editing. Students will be drawing on a variety of sentence-level strategies to expand and enrich the sentences and using their knowledge of transitions to knit ideas together and make the paragraph flow.

In addition to helping students learn to use various TWR strategies independently, practicing with unelaborated paragraphs is also a great first step in acquainting them with the revision process. Because students have no sense of ownership over these simple paragraphs, they're likely to be more objective and more willing to revise them.

As with all TWR activities, the unelaborated paragraph ideally should be embedded in content students have studied. If that's not possible, choose a subject students are very familiar with. If they don't have a command of the subject, students won't be able to provide the details they'll need to improve and expand the paragraph.

The first step is to display an unelaborated paragraph, using whatever method of modeling you choose, and have the students follow along on hard copies as you improve the example one sentence at a time.

TECHNICAL TIP

Be sure to provide students with unelaborated paragraphs that have no grammar, spelling, punctuation, or capitalization errors. Your objective is to remove editing issues so that students can focus on the task of revising.

Level 1 Examples

Ms. Green used the following unelaborated paragraph with her Level 1 students about the class's Halloween activity:

> We carved a pumpkin. We drew the face. We cut the top. We took out the seeds. We carved the face. The pumpkin looked good.

"This is a pretty boring paragraph, isn't it?" Ms. Green asked after putting the paragraph on her classroom's SMART Board, and the students agreed. "Let's see if we can make it more interesting. When did we carve the pumpkin?"

"Today!" the students called out. Ms. Green added the word *Today* to the beginning of the first sentence.

"Okay, great!" Ms. Green said. "But what about this next sentence? What could we add to that?"

"We could say *first,*" a student said.

"That's a good idea. But how about if we also add something about *why* we drew the face first? Why didn't we just go ahead and start carving?"

As she made her way through the paragraph, Ms. Green continued the process of asking questions and adding students' responses on the SMART Board. Other questions she asked included the following:

> How did we cut the top off?

> What did we use to take the seeds out?

What did we do when we were almost finished?

Can we think of a better word than *good* in the last sentence?

At the end of the lively discussion, the paragraph on Ms. Green's SMART Board read as follows:

Today we carved a pumpkin. First we drew the face so it would be easier to carve. Next Ms. Green cut the top off with a knife. Then the best part was when we scooped out the seeds with a big spoon. Finally, we were so close to being finished that we only had to cut out the face. The pumpkin looked excellent!

After lots of practice with revision as a whole class, Ms. Green gave her students another unelaborated paragraph to tackle independently. However, she knew they would still need some guidance, so she provided them with specific directions about how to improve the paragraph. And she embedded the paragraph in the content the class had been studying—the sinking of the Titanic. The following brief paragraph is the one Ms. Green used, along with her directions. She asked the students to do the exercise in small groups.

The Titanic was a big ship. It sank. Many passengers died. There are new regulations.

- Expand the T.S. (telling *when* and *where*).

- Use an appositive in the T.S.

- Combine the first two sentences.

- Answer *why* the ship sank in your second sentence.

- Use examples after the fourth sentence in the paragraph, starting with an illustration transition.

- Write a C.S. beginning with a conclusion transition.

After revising the paragraph according to these directions and consulting the text, one group's final product looked like this:

On April 14, 1912, the Titanic, a huge ocean liner, sank in the North Atlantic. Fifteen hundred passengers died when the ship hit an iceberg. After the tragedy, many new safety regulations had to be followed by passenger ships. For example, more life boats, safety drills, and intensive training of the crew were required. In the end, the sinking of the Titanic led to new improvements in safety for future travelers.

HOW TO DIFFERENTIATE UNELABORATED PARAGRAPH ACTIVITIES

To adapt the unelaborated paragraph activities to your students' individual needs, you might give all students the same bare-bones paragraph but give some students fewer instructions on how to revise it. For example, give some students a list of six things to do and limit others to only one or two, such as "improve T.S. and C.S."

Level 2 Example

More experienced writers will be able to improve unelaborated paragraphs with less scaffolding. But don't stop giving more experienced or older students unelaborated paragraphs because you think they're too easy! They continue to be an extremely effective activity even for high school students as a check of comprehension and as an opportunity to practice revision.

Here is an example of a Level 2 activity that was completed by an eighth-grader, whom we'll call Andrea. Andrea had participated in several whole-class demonstrations and worked with other students on improving simple unelaborated paragraphs. As she became more proficient, Andrea was able to expand the following unelaborated paragraph, provided by her teacher, independently.

Eleanor Roosevelt was important. She was married to Franklin Roosevelt. She was the First Lady from 1933 to 1945. She made many contributions. Many people admired her.

Because she was working with a more experienced group of writers, Andrea's teacher needed to provide students only with a list of strategies for revision:

- Improve T.S. & C.S.
- Vary vocabulary.
- Expand sentences.
- Use an appositive.
- Use transitions.
- Give examples.
- Combine sentences.
- Use a subordinating conjunction.

Although Andrea had a list of strategies to work with, it was up to her to decide on the details. Here's the paragraph she ultimately produced:

Eleanor Roosevelt, one of the most admired women of the 20th century, was the wife of President Franklin Delano Roosevelt and First Lady from 1933 to 1945. Although she was born into great wealth and privilege, she

*was extremely aware of the injustices suffered by those less fortunate. She
became a passionate advocate for human rights and is remembered as **an**
author and activist. After FDR's death, President Truman appointed **her as**
a delegate to the United Nations where she gained worldwide respect and
received many honors and awards for her achievements. Truman called
Eleanor Roosevelt the "First Lady of the World."*

In composing this informative and smoothly flowing paragraph,
Andrea was demonstrating her ability to create sophisticated sentences
and her sense of organization. At the same time, she was drawing on and
deepening her knowledge of the topic.

How to Move From Unelaborated Paragraphs to Independent Revision

The ultimate goal of giving students unelaborated paragraphs, of course,
is to enable them to make similar revisions in their own writing—without
a teacher's prompting. This sequence of steps will lead your students to
that goal:

1. Revise an unelaborated paragraph as a class.

2. Display an unelaborated paragraph and have students suggest
   improvements.

3. Give students explicit directions and have them work together or independently to improve an unelaborated paragraph.

4. Have students improve an unelaborated paragraph without directions,
   either independently or with a small group.

5. Have students improve their own work after getting specific teacher
   feedback.

6. Have students improve their own work independently, incorporating
   the techniques they have practiced.

As your students become accustomed to revising their writing, encourage them to rework their drafts more than once. In fact, point out that in
most cases, the better the writer, the more times he or she will revise a
draft.

It's important to note that many lessons can end after revisions and
edits. Often, a polished final copy of an unelaborated or independently
written paragraph or composition is not necessary to achieve the lesson's
objectives.

TECHNICAL TIP

One extremely effective way of helping your students use revision techniques is to have them read brief paragraphs to their classmates and get feedback. Before you have students engage in this activity, be sure to provide them with the "Listening Evaluation Checklist" in Appendix C. The checklist will help listeners focus on the elements that enhance their classmates' writing and identify aspects that could be improved.

Although the checklist covers a range of factors, have your students concentrate on just a few during each reading. For example, you might ask students to focus on the following:

Does the topic sentence engage the audience?
Are there enough supporting details?
Is the vocabulary vivid enough?
Does the conclusion refer back to the main idea?

Next Steps: Writing Drafts From SPOs

The first step in turning an SPO into a paragraph is to have students copy the topic sentences they've written at the top of their outlines onto a separate piece of paper. Next comes the more challenging work of translating the notes they've written on the dotted lines into complete detail sentences. You can remind them that they practiced this kind of conversion when working on the activities that led up to creating SPOs in Chapter 4.

At this stage, students are drafting a paragraph rather than revising one. Their focus may be on accurately translating their key words and phrases, abbreviations, and symbols into complete sentences rather than on fashioning a fluid paragraph with appropriate transitions and a variety of sentence structures. As a result, the draft they produce may be stiff and stilted—and in dire need of the polishing that takes place during the revision process.

But as your students become more experienced writers, the drafting and revision stages may overlap. Students may eventually use many of the revision strategies outlined in the following section as they write their drafts rather than as part of a separate process.

Go Deeper: Enriching Simple Sentences Through Sentence Expansion

Your students may produce only brief, simple sentences when they convert their notes into sentences on their drafts, especially if they're beginning writers. Although short declarative sentences can provide emphasis and make facts plain, such sentences form the entire arsenal of many students. No one wants to read an entire paragraph or composition that relies on brief sentences and nothing else.

How can you guide students to expand these sentences into ones that are longer and richer? Remind them that when they were doing sentence expansion exercises, they used question words such as *who, what, when, where, why,* and *how* to transform kernels into complex, information-packed sentences (see Chapter 2). They can use the same kinds of questions to expand the brief sentences in their drafts—or, if they need some help, you can provide the appropriate question words as prompts.

For example, after his class had spent some time studying colonization in the United States, Michael's SPO had this notation on a dotted detail line:

settled near rivers

When Michael started to use the outline to draft his paragraph, he turned that phrase into this simple sentence:

The colonists settled near rivers.

"Do you remember *why* they settled near rivers?" his teacher asked him.

"Because they needed transportation," Michael answered. "And they needed water for their crops."

"Great!" the teacher said. "How about expanding the sentence to include that information?"

Michael then changed his simple sentence into this:

The colonists settled near rivers because they needed a way to travel other than over land and a way to water their crops.

As students learn to use the abbreviations and symbols, the notations on their SPOs will convey more information, making it easier for them to translate their notes directly into complex sentences. Eventually, the notation on Michael's SPO might look like this:

settled near rivers → transportation & crops

The Spice of Life: Introducing Sentence Variety

Another way your students can liven up a stilted draft is to make their sentences vary in length and type. Remind students of the four different sentence types they can use (statement, question, exclamation, and command) and the possibility of beginning a sentence with a subordinating conjunction (see Chapter 2).

If, for example, Michael's sentence about colonists settling near rivers followed another sentence or two using a similar structure, his teacher might suggest he change it to begin with the conjunction *since.* He might then write the following:

> *Since the colonists needed a way to travel and a way to water their crops, they settled near rivers.*

If you've been regularly assigning your students activities that give them practice with the various sentence-level strategies—embedded in the content they're studying—these techniques will be fresh in their minds.

Double-Check: Revisiting Topic and Concluding Sentences

If your students have completed an SPO, they've already engaged in the process of creating interesting and informative topic and concluding sentences and written them on the outline. As we detailed in Chapter 4, there are three basic ways to turn a flat, boring topic or concluding sentence into an engaging one:

- Choosing a different sentence type
- Adding an appositive
- Beginning the sentence with a subordinating conjunction

Le Mot Juste: Choosing Vivid, Varied, and Precise Words

As we discussed in Chapter 4, it's important that students employ words that are accurate and engaging in their topic and concluding sentences. The same is true of the detail sentences they're now creating. If you've provided them with a list of alternatives to overused, bland words such as *fun* and *good,* you'll want to remind them to consult the list when revising their detail sentences.

As students move to more sophisticated expository and argumentative writing, try posting lists of alternative words that are geared to those types of writing. For example, students may find themselves repeating, "Some people say…" and "Other people say…" You can add words to your list that provide students with alternatives—for example, "Advocates claim…" and "Opponents believe…" You'll find more ideas in Table 8.1, "Argumentative Nouns and Verbs," in Chapter 8.

Connect the Dots: Using Transitions to Create Flow

Practicing transition activities does the following:

- Helps students show the relationship between ideas
- Provides logical connections between sentences, paragraphs, and sections
- Enables students to signal how a reader should react to or process the information presented
- Makes student writing more readable and engaging

If you teach your students to insert appropriate transition words and phrases during the revision process, you'll see their writing become significantly more fluid and coherent. To demonstrate to your students how powerful these brief insertions can be, try showing them examples of writing with and without transitions. For example, you could show students the following transition-less paragraph:

> Being a student is not an easy job. You always have to pay attention even if something else is bothering you. You're not supposed to talk back to your teacher. This is difficult after your teacher has annoyed you. The hardest part of being a student is always doing your homework, after a day of classes and after-school activities. You acquire knowledge and skills and get the preparation you need to succeed in life. It is worth the hard work of being a student because you learn so much.

Then you might show them the same paragraph with transitions added:

> Being a student is not an easy job. You always have to pay attention even if something else is bothering you. *In addition*, you're not supposed to talk back to your teacher. This is difficult after your teacher has annoyed you. *However*, the hardest part of being a student is always doing your homework, *particularly* after a day of classes and after-school activities. *On the other hand*, you acquire knowledge and skills and get the preparation you need to succeed in life. *In conclusion*, it is worth the hard work of being a student because you learn so much.

Transitions are often called *signal words* because they signal, or indicate, a relationship between ideas. They can make text smoother and help minimize the confusion that fragmented statements can cause. You'll want to explain to students that some, but not all, transitions are set off by commas, and help them understand which ones require commas and which don't. For example, the transition *finally* requires a comma—as does *for example*—but the transition *then* does not.

A transition may begin a sentence, creating a link between that sentence and the one that has preceded it, or link thoughts within a sentence. When used at the beginning or end of a paragraph, transitions can underscore a theme or idea that knits the paragraph's various sentences together.

Because they help writers avoid short, choppy sentences, transitions—when used correctly—are vital to the creation of coherent paragraphs and compositions.

TECHNICAL TIP

It's a good idea to display posters of frequently used transitions as an easy reference and a reminder for students to use them. Transitional words and phrases can be found in Table 5.1. Note that the table presents transitions often encountered in the texts and literature students are likely to read but is not an exhaustive list. You might also want to give students Exhibit 5.1, which describes the purposes of the different kinds of transitions that we've provided in Table 5.1. (This chart and others can be ordered through our website, http://twr-resources.thewritingrevolution.org/.)

Table 5.1 Transition Words and Phrases

1A: Time and Sequence	1B: Time and Sequence	2: Conclusion
first	initially	in conclusion
second	previously	in closing
in addition	soon	in summary
after	later on	as a result*
last	at last	consequently*
then	additionally	finally
next	currently	therefore*
also	earlier	so*
before	meanwhile	thus*
finally	ultimately	in the end
later	during	

3: Illustration	4: Change of Direction	5: Emphasis
for example	however	especially
for instance	even though	in particular
specifically	in contrast	obviously
particularly	otherwise	above all
as an illustration	on the other hand	most important
namely	although	primarily
such as	but	certainly
expressly	yet	particularly
like	instead	moreover
including	on the contrary	notably
in particular		keep in mind

*Examples of cause-and-effect transitions; see the section "Conclusion Transitions" for more information.

Source: Copyright © 2017 The Writing Revolution.

(continued)

EXHIBIT 5.1.

Transitions

<u>Time</u>—sequence of events or steps in a process

<u>Conclusion</u>—summary, cause and effect, point of view, solution

<u>Illustration</u>—give examples, support details, explain or elaborate on a statement

<u>Change of direction</u>—contrasting thoughts

<u>Emphasis</u>—prove a point or statement; reaffirm something previously stated

---

Source: Copyright © 2017 The Writing Revolution.

Lay the Groundwork: Introducing Three Kinds of Transitions

In most cases, you'll want to introduce your students to transitions using sentence-level activity, before they use them to revise their drafts into more polished paragraphs. The only exceptions are the time-and-sequence transitions, which students can begin to use when they're actually converting their SPOs into paragraphs. We'll provide some examples of sentence-level transition activities later in this chapter.

The following three categories of transitions are the ones that students should be introduced to initially.

Time-and-Sequence Transitions

These are transition words and phrases such as *first, second,* and *finally.* Students will find them helpful when writing narratives that relate a chronological series of events or steps in a process. They are especially helpful when explaining a solution to a math problem or describing a process in science. As we mentioned previously, once you've introduced your students to the concept of time-and-sequence transitions and the specific words and phrases that fall into this category, you can have them try using them on their own draft paragraphs without having them practice at the sentence level first.

You may want Level 1 students to stick to simple time-and-sequence transitions such as *first, second,* and *finally,* along with *then* and *next* (category 1A in Table 5.1). More advanced students can use words such as *initially* and *previously* (category 1B in Table 5.1).

The time-and-sequence transitions are useful when writing a summary of a plot, explaining a process, or tracing the time line of an event. They can also be used to emphasize a particular point, such as the following:

> Assigning homework on weekends is a terrible practice. In addition, studying for two or three tests on the same day is a bad idea.

Conclusion Transitions

Students should use conclusion transitions to introduce the last sentence in a paragraph (or, possibly, a composition). Writers can use a conclusion that focuses on a solution or on their point of view. Some examples of conclusion transitions are *in closing, consequently,* and *in the end.*

There is a difference between stating a conclusion and summing up an idea, although sometimes the two overlap. More advanced students can practice deciding when it would be better to use a summation rather than a conclusion.

Some conclusion transitions, like *as a result* and *therefore,* should be used to introduce the endings of **cause-and-effect** paragraphs and compositions. For example:

> Often plastic waste is not recycled properly. Therefore, significant amounts of trash build up in rivers and oceans.

These cause-and-effect transitions are marked in Table 5.1 with an asterisk.

Illustration Transitions

Illustration transitions are used to give examples, to support a detail, or to explain or elaborate on a statement with evidence. For example, one illustration transition is—in fact—*for example*. Other examples are *such as* and *particularly*. Illustration transitions can be introduced to students who are at the higher end of Level 1.

Level 1 Examples

For less experienced writers, provide two sentences that are linked in some way but lack the illustration or conclusion transitions that make that link clear. As always, it's best if you can embed these activities in the content your students are studying, and it's a good idea to introduce them orally as a whole-class activity.

If your students are studying Greek mythology, you might give them the following two sentences:

> Each of the gods had his or her area of responsibility. _____, Apollo was the god of music and the sun.

Here, they might supply the transitions *for example* or *in particular*.

If the class has been learning about climate change and you'd like them to practice using conclusion transitions, you could give them the following:

> The earth is getting hotter. _____, there is less ice for walruses to rest on.

They might suggest the transitions *as a result* or *therefore*.

If your students need more support in doing this activity, you can give them a word bank of transitions to choose from.

Another way to have students practice using transitions is to give them a sentence followed by a transition word or phrase that introduces the next sentence. Students can complete the second sentence in a way that fits the transition word you've provided. For example, if your class is planning a trip to the nation's capital and has been reading about the sights there, you could give them this sentence:

> Washington, D.C., has many tourist attractions. In particular, _____
> _____.

They may need to reread their text to find a good answer. One possibility could be the following:

> Washington, D.C., has many tourist attractions. In particular, *the Lincoln Memorial and the Washington Monument are favorites of most visitors*.

HOW TO DIFFERENTIATE TRANSITION ACTIVITIES

If some of your students need more support in using transitions than others, you can give them a word bank of possible transitions—or tell them what category of transition they need to supply and have them consult Table 5.1, "Transition Words and Phrases."

Level 2 Examples

If your students are studying the connections between Europe and the Americas in the age of exploration, you could give them these two sentences and ask them to supply an appropriate transition from the chart.

> The European diet was enhanced by many foods from the New World. Europeans began to eat nutritious foods like tomatoes and potatoes.

They might choose *for example* or *as an illustration*.

If you're teaching math, you could have students use time-and-sequence transitions to write out the steps of a process. For example, you could give them:

Explain the steps to expand $(x-5)(x+5)$ into quadratic form.

Below that, you could provide them with a series of transitions, which they would need to turn into complete sentences:

First, _____.

Second, _____.

Next, _____.

Then, _____.

Finally, _____.

You can also give them a sentence followed by a transition word that will serve as the beginning of a sentence that they complete. If the class is studying the beginning of farming in ancient times, you could give them the following:

The Agricultural Revolution changed people's lives. Specifically, _____
_____.

They might respond:

The Agricultural Revolution changed people's lives. Specifically, *humans began to farm and plant on their own fields*.

This kind of activity is a great way to prompt students to engage with a text and extract relevant information, while at the same time helping them understand how to use transitions.

Hone the Skill: Two Kinds of Transitions for More Advanced Writers

If you're teaching Level 2 students who have no trouble using the three categories of transitions just described, introduce them to two other kinds of transitions: change-of-direction and emphasis.

Change-of-Direction Transitions

Change-of-direction transitions introduce contrasting thoughts. They are important signals to use in compare-and-contrast as well as in argumentative writing.

There is one change-of-direction transition that Level 2 students will already be familiar with: *but*. They will probably not be familiar, however, with many others—such as *however*. Other examples of these transitions are *in contrast* and *on the other hand*.

Remind students that some change-of-direction transitions such as *although* and *even though* need to be used as subordinating conjunctions that introduce a phrase. So, for example, it would be incorrect to write, "Although, Andrew Jackson was a popular president." If students want to begin a sentence with *although*, they will need to attach it to a group of words, like this:

> *Although* Andrew Jackson was a popular president, *some* observers criticized his use of the spoils system.

Emphasis Transitions

Emphasis transitions, such as *especially* or *in particular*, can be introduced at the same time as change-of-direction signals. They prove a point or statement or reaffirm something the writer has already stated. They are often used in argumentative and opinion writing, letters of complaint, and formal requests. These transitions can also be used as conclusion transitions.

Level 2 Examples

You can have your Level 2 students practice with these more complex transitions in much the same way that Level 1 students practice with simpler ones. To practice change-of-direction transitions, you can give students these two sentences and ask them to supply a transition at the beginning of the second one:

> Red blood cells carry nutrients throughout the body. _____ white blood cells fight infections.

They might use *on the other hand* or *in contrast* to link the two sentences.

This exercise will require students to recognize that the sentences present two contrasting ideas. To make an activity such as this less challenging, you can tell students in advance which category of transitions to use; to make it more challenging, you can leave that decision to them.

As with the transitions you've previously introduced, you can also ask your students to complete a sentence that starts with a transition word you supply. For example, if the class has been studying American history of the 1930s, you might give them the following sentence and transition word:

The Great Depression devastated some groups more than others. Notably, _____

_____.

They could complete the sentence with "African Americans faced discrimination and higher rates of unemployment."

Once your students have become comfortable with transitions through sentence-level activities, they can begin introducing them into their own drafts during the revision process. If they have trouble deciding what kind of transition to use, you can suggest a specific category from Table 5.1 for them to look at. With enough practice, they'll be able to find the right kind of transition independently.

Smoothly Flowing Compositions: Using Transitions to Link Paragraphs

Transitions are just as important to coherence and flow in longer pieces of writing as in shorter assignments. When your students are converting Multiple-Paragraph Outlines (MPOs) into drafts of compositions and revising them, you'll need to remind them to use transitions to link one paragraph to the next. Virtually any of the transitions they've learned that make connections between sentences can also be used to connect paragraphs.

For example, let's say a student is writing a compare-and-contrast composition about red and white blood cells—rather than just a sentence about each of them, as in the Level 2 examples. If she has written one paragraph about red blood cells and the next about white blood cells, she can use a change-of-direction transition to create a link between the two paragraphs:

Red blood cells carry respiratory gases throughout the body. These cells lack a nucleus, which means that there is room inside each cell for more of a pigment called hemoglobin. Hemoglobin gives red blood cells their color and is responsible for carrying oxygen around the body. Red blood cells also transport carbon dioxide.

On the other hand, *white blood cells fight infection . . .*

In argumentative essays, students can use a change-of-direction transition to introduce a paragraph that presents a counterclaim. They can use a time-and-sequence transition such as *in addition* or an emphasis transition such as *moreover* to introduce a paragraph that builds on their own argument. And they can use a conclusion transition to introduce their concluding paragraph.

Too Much of a Good Thing: Using Transitions Judiciously

One thing to be aware of: We've found that when students are learning how to incorporate transitions into their writing, they may overuse them or deploy them inappropriately. To help students use transitions judiciously, let them know that not *every* sentence in a paragraph should begin with a transition.

You can also create paragraphs that have blank spaces where specific transitions should go. Give them a list of possible transitions, and have students write the transitions on the appropriate blanks.

If your class is studying Asian history, you could give them a paragraph like the one shown in Exhibit 5.2.

EXHIBIT 5.2

Directions: Complete the paragraph by filling in the blanks with these transition words and phrases:

For example	In the end	However

China had an impact on the development of Japan. Prince Shotoku, a Japanese leader, sent spies to China to learn about their culture. _____, the Japanese learned about the Chinese government, economy, arts, and dress. _____, the Japanese adopted only the elements of Chinese culture they liked, which was known as selective borrowing. _____, Japan became a stronger country because of China's influence.

Source: Copyright © 2017 The Writing Revolution.

Bring in the Authorities: How to Incorporate Quotations

Quotations from text can strengthen almost any piece of writing, and they're particularly useful in argumentative essays and book reports Teachers often encourage students not only to cite evidence from text to support their claims but also to actually quote the text they're relying on.

But too often, students will plunk down a multi-sentence quotation in the middle of a paragraph or essay without providing any context, introduction, or attribution. And in many cases, it's not clear why students have chosen the particular quotation they've inserted. Sometimes students simply assume that the quotation's meaning and relationship to their point is obvious to the reader. In other cases students may not have really thought about or fully understood the words they're quoting. At times it seems that students are inserting a quotation simply to prove they've read the text rather than to support the point they're making.

If you want your students to use quotations effectively, you'll need to show them how to be judicious about selecting the text they'll quote and how to incorporate that text smoothly into their own writing. As the authors of the book *They Say/I Say* have suggested, it may help to tell your students that quotations are like orphans—they're "words that have been taken from their original contexts and that need to be integrated into their new textual surroundings."[1] To adopt those orphans, students will first need to make sure that the quotation they want to use actually supports the point they're making. They They'll need to frame it by answering these questions:

Whose words are they?

What does the quotation mean?

How does the quotation relate to their own text?

Understanding the Quote

First, you'll need to ensure that your students have actually understood the words they're quoting. A good way to do that is to have them convert the text they want to quote into note form, using key words and phrases and abbreviations, as they've learned to do on their outlines. Once they've done that, they can convert the key words and phrases into their own words and ask themselves if the quotation really supports the point they want to make.

Determining What's Noteworthy

You'll also need to explain that a longer quote isn't necessarily a better quote. A pithy phrase often has more impact than a discussion that goes on for several lines. Paraphrasing text can work just as well as a direct quotation in supporting a claim, and requiring your students to paraphrase will help ensure that they've understood what they've read—or at least alert you to the fact that they haven't understood it.

Quotations should be reserved for instances when the author of the text has said something particularly noteworthy or has worded an observation in a striking way. Be sure to guide your students in identifying those distinctive quotations before they attempt to select them independently.

It's also important to make sure they're selecting a quotation that matches the point they're making in their own writing and that they're placing the quotation where it will fit.

Weaving It In

Once they've settled on a quotation that directly supports their argument, students will need to learn how to weave it into their own writing. The authors of *They Say/I Say* advise having students think in terms of a "quotation sandwich . . . with the statement introducing it serving as the top slice of the bread and the explanation following it serving as the bottom slice."[2] The top slice will explain who is speaking and set up what the quotation will say. The bottom slice follows up with an explanation of why the quotation is important and what the writer thinks it means.

In argumentative essays, there are particular methods of providing these top and bottom slices. We'll address those in Chapter 8.

Laying the Groundwork: Introducing Quotations

There are a variety of ways that students can introduce a quotation. Here are a few examples adapted from *They Say/I Say*:

Jones states, "_____."

As the author of the article puts it, "_____."

According to Smith, "_____."

Following Up: Explaining Quotations

It's always a good idea to have students include a sentence after the quotation that paraphrases it. If they've already reduced it to key words and phrases and then put it in their own words, this should be easy for them.

They'll need to introduce the paraphrase with something similar to the following:

In other words, Jones is saying _____ .

Therefore, according to the author, _____ .

Smith's point is that _____ .

Level 1 Example

In the following example, the introductory and explanatory phrases—the top and bottom slices of the quotation sandwich—are in italics.

> In Aesop's fable, "The Fox and the Grapes," a hungry fox sees some grapes hanging on a trellis high above his head and wants to reach them. Over and over again, he runs, jumps, and tries to snatch the grapes, but he misses every time. At last, too tired to try anymore, he walks away. *The fox says,* "Well, I never really wanted those grapes anyway. I am sure they are sour, and perhaps wormy as well." *The point of the fable is that when people can't get something they want, they may decide it wasn't worth having in the first place.*

Level 2 Example

When students are quoting from primary sources or historical documents, setting up and paraphrasing quotations is particularly important. It won't always be clear to a reader where the quotation is from and—especially if the language is complex or archaic—what it means.

> *As the framers provided in Article III of the United States Constitution,* federal judges "shall hold their Offices during good Behaviour" and their salaries "shall not be diminished" while in office. *In other words, the Founding Fathers wanted to insulate members of the judiciary from political influence by giving them life tenure and preventing Congress from cutting their pay if they made unpopular decisions.*

Last but Not Least: Editing

Once students have a final draft, it's time to check for errors in spelling, capitalization, punctuation, and grammar. Many students, especially those at Level 1, will need help spotting those errors and correcting them.

As we discussed in the Introduction, researchers have unanimously concluded that teaching grammar rules in isolation doesn't work. **But** that doesn't mean that we shouldn't teach grammar. What *does* **work is** to teach grammar—along with writing conventions such as spelling **and** punctuation—in the context of a student's own writing.

In Chapter 1, we pointed out that it's easiest to teach grammar **and** conventions in the context of sentence-level work, where the number of errors is likely to be more manageable than in lengthier student writing. But even if you've done that, most students will continue to make at least some mechanical errors when they move on to paragraphs and compositions—although perhaps not as many as they would have otherwise! To give your students the skills that will enable them to avoid distracting readers with technical mistakes, you'll need to continue **to** identify and correct these errors in your students' drafts.

ASK THE EXPERTS

One significant problem you may encounter as students draft and revise their paragraphs and compositions **is** the poor quality of their handwriting. Many schools no longer focus on handwriting instruction. That has **led** to random acts of capitalization as well as to the failure on the part of many students to leave enough space between words. There are other negative consequences as well.

A couple of generations ago, children were introduced to cursive writing as soon as they entered school. Now, they usually don't encounter it until third grade, if at all. The Common Core standards don't require handwriting instruction, and there are reports that schools across the country have been dropping it entirely from the curriculum.[3]

That's a shame. Cursive is a much more efficient method of letter formation than printing, because **the** writer doesn't have to repeatedly pick up the pen or pencil and reset it in order to finish a letter or start a new one. Even when schools teach cursive, they generally don't reinforce that instruction or require students to use cursive as they move through the grades. As a result, students usually revert to printing, which is often sloppy and certainly slower than a well-practiced cursive.

When students have poor handwriting, the quality of their written work may suffer, especially when they're taking timed tests or are engaging in cognitively demanding tasks. Teachers are more likely to rate students' writing negatively when their handwriting is poor.[4] It's also a lot easier to take notes by hand when using cursive, because it's faster than printing—and, as we noted in Chapter 2, researchers have found that students who take notes by hand rather than on a laptop or tablet are more likely to retain information.

Beyond those considerations, there's evidence that the best predictor of academic ability for young children is how well they can copy a complex figure freehand on paper—which is, essentially, what handwriting requires.[5] The theory is that this kind of copying involves planning and execution, two skills that serve students well.[6] In addition, a child's inevitably imperfect first attempts to copy letters help reinforce the abstract concept of what letters stand for. Students learn that a messy *a* is still an *a*.[7]

Although those findings don't necessarily argue for cursive instruction—printing might serve the same purpose—other studies do. One study conducted in 2015 suggested that cursive gives children advantages in spelling and composing, perhaps because the connecting strokes between letters help children see groups of letters as words.

If schools want to boost their students' writing abilities, cognition, and retention, they would be well advised to teach cursive early and require frequent practice.

Saving Time With Proofreading Symbols

If you familiarize your students with standard proofreading symbols, such as a carat to indicate an insertion, you'll be able to use them to give quick and specific feedback on their writing. (You'll find a list of proofreading symbols in Appendix D.) If you simply circle a grammatical error such as a lack of subject-verb agreement, there's a good chance the student won't understand what the problem is. Take the time to make sure students know what mistakes they've made and that they know how to correct them. There's no other way to ensure that they'll learn the rules. And using symbols to communicate precisely what the error is will make the process much more efficient.

Busy teachers often have difficulty finding the time to provide detailed feedback on students' writing. But if you've laid the groundwork, you can provide shorthand feedback fairly quickly. And students will not only understand your abbreviations but also know how to follow through on the suggestions you've given them. You can use our Single Paragraph and Multiple-Paragraph Checklists, available online at http://twr-resources .thewritingrevolution.org/, to help you evaluate student writing.

When students become more adept at revision, you may only need to provide them with the "Revise and Edit Checklist" in Appendix E, adapting it as necessary to your students' needs and level of ability. Students can then go through the checklist on their own and ensure that their paragraphs and compositions are the best they can be.

When students submit drafts, they need explicit comments and feedback. If Brittany were my student today, I would have many more tools at my disposal. If she handed me a boring, wooden paragraph, I wouldn't just say "make it better" or "add more details" and hope for the best. After teaching her various sentence strategies, showing her how to craft an SPO, and familiarizing her with transitions, I could provide her with detailed suggestions for revision, knowing that she would understand my notes and abbreviations. It might look like this:

when? why? (expand this point)
ext w/ so → (extend with so)

ex. (provide an example)

app. in T.S. (use an appositive in topic sentence)

insert transition

sub. conj. in C.S. (begin concluding sentence with a subordinating conjunction)

combine sent. 2 & 3 (combine these sentences)

I might also point out, more generally, places where she got off track:

repetitive

irrelevant

Eventually, Brittany would have been able to consult the "Revise and Edit Checklist" in Appendix E and decide for herself what changes to make. And ultimately, she would have been able to simply look over her own writing—even without a checklist—and intuitively grasp ways to make it better.

TO SUM UP

- Revising, or making structural improvements to a draft, should be done before editing, which consists of correcting mechanical errors.

- Before you have students try to revise their own writing, have them practice on bare-bones unelaborated paragraphs that you provide.

- To create a draft of a paragraph, have students transfer their topic and concluding sentences from their SPOs onto a sheet of paper and convert the notes for their detail sentences into complete sentences.

- To help students revise their drafts, remind them to use sentence expansion, sentence types, and subordinating conjunctions to vary their sentence structure.

- Encourage students to use vivid and precise words in the revision process.

- Have students practice using the various types of transition words to signal the connections between their ideas and create smoothly flowing prose.

- Help students incorporate quotations by having them select the text to be quoted carefully, reduce it to note form to ensure they understand it, and frame it with an appropriate introduction and explanation.

- Make sure your students are familiar with proofreading symbols so that you can give them feedback briefly and efficiently.

Notes

1. G. Graff, C. Birkenstein, and R. Durst, *They Say/I Say: The Moves That Matter in Academic Writing* (New York: W. W. Norton, 2012), p. 43.

2. Ibid., p. 46.

3. T. Rees Shapiro, "Cursive Handwriting Is Disappearing From Public Schools," *Washington Post* (April 4, 2013), www.washingtonpost.com/local/education/ cursive-handwriting-disappearing-from-public-schools/2013/04/04/215862 e0–7d23–11e2-a044–676856536b40_story.html.

4. S. Graham, K. Harris, and M. Hebert, *Informing Writing: The Benefits of Formative Assessment. A Carnegie Corporation Time to Act Report* (Washington, DC: Alliance for Excellent Education, 2011), p. 21.

5. C. E. Cameron, L. L. Brock, W. M. Murrah, L. H. Bell, S. L. Worzalla, D. Grissmer, and F. J. Morriso, "Fine Motor Skills and Executive Function Both Contribute to Kindergarten Achievement," *Child Development* 83, no. 4 (2012): 1229–44, www.ncbi.nlm.nih.gov/pmc/articles/PMC3399936/; D. Grissmer, K. J. Grimm, S. M. Aiyer, W. M. Murrah, and J. S. Steele, "Fine Motor Skills and Early Comprehension of the World: Two New School Readiness Indicators," *Developmental Psychology* 46, no. 5 (2010): 1008–17, www.ncbi.nlm.nih.gov/ pubmed/20822219; L. Dinehart, "Handwriting in Early Childhood Education: Current Research and Future Implications," *Journal of Early Childhood Literacy* 15, no. 1 (2014), http://ecl.sagepub.com/content/15/1/97.

6. Maria Konnikova, "What's Lost as Handwriting Fades," *New York Times* (June 2, 2014), www.nytimes.com/2014/06/03/science/whats-lost-as -handwriting-fades.html?_r=0.

7. Perri Klass, "Why Handwriting Is Still Essential in the Keyboard Age," *New York Times* (June 20, 2016), https://well.blogs.nytimes.com/2016/06/20/ why-handwriting-is-still-essential-in-the-keyboard-age/.

CHAPTER 6

Summarizing
Mining Texts for the Essentials

After the first-grade class at one of our partner schools returned from a highly anticipated field trip to an amusement park, a teacher asked one of the students, Ana, to tell her about the trip.

"Oh, the park was really, really big," Ana began, her eyes widening at the recollection and her words tumbling out. "And it was *so* crowded. I was afraid I was going to get lost! And I saw this one girl there who looked like my cousin? I really thought it was her! I started to say hello to her, but then I realized it wasn't her—it was so funny. And there were all these cool rides. Like this one called "The Twister"? That one was kind of scary—I almost got sick. But this other one…"

Ana went on for several more minutes, describing every ride she went on, what she had for lunch, and whom she sat next to on the bus.

The teacher then moved on to Mario and asked him to tell her how the trip was.

"Good," Mario said.

First-graders aren't the only students who have trouble figuring out how much to say and what to focus on when they're asked to summarize. How much is too much? How much is too little? What's important and what's not? Teachers' guides often require students as young as second grade to summarize a chapter or an entire book. Yet even many high school students find it challenging to come up with a good summary, struggling to find the right level of succinctness or detail.

Not So Simple: The Power of Writing Summaries

Having students practice summarizing does the following:

- Boosts reading comprehension
- Helps generate concise and accurate responses to questions
- Maintains focus on the main idea and supporting details
- Teaches paraphrasing techniques
- Provides practice synthesizing information from multiple sources
- Enhances the ability to analyze information
- Develops the ability to make generalizations
- Aids in retaining information

A **summary** is a brief statement, sometimes called a *synopsis,* that presents the main points of a text in a concise form, whether oral or written. A graphic, such as a graph or chart, can also serve as raw material for a summary.

Summarizing information is something we all need to do, often many times a day—and not only inside a classroom. Just to name a few examples, summarizing comes into play when we're asked to do any of the following:

- Relate an experience or process.
- Describe someone or something.
- Sum up a plot.
- Give directions.
- Present a critical review.

Teachers sometimes underestimate the importance and the difficulty of having their students learn to craft effective summaries. In Bloom's taxonomy—the ranking of cognitive abilities that is widely known among educators—summarizing is often associated with *comprehension,* which is only level two out of Bloom's six levels.[1] That low ranking may lead teachers to feel that summarizing is a simple skill as compared to analyzing, contrasting, critiquing, or justifying—all verbs associated with higher cognitive levels in Bloom's taxonomy.

But as with any skill, the difficulty of summarizing varies with the material you're summarizing, the complexity of the language and syntax, and the depth of knowledge you have about the topic. To see what we mean, try summarizing the following paragraph, which appears on the first page of Immanuel Kant's *Critique of Judgment*:

> We proceed quite correctly if, as usual, we divide Philosophy, as containing the principles of the rational cognition of things by means of concepts (not merely, as logic does, principles of the form of thought in general without distinction of Objects), into *theoretical* and *practical*. But then the concepts, which furnish their Object to the principles of this rational cognition, must be specifically distinct; otherwise they would not justify a division, which always presupposes a contrast between the principles of the rational cognition belonging to the different parts of a science.[2]

Not so simple, especially if you don't have a graduate-level degree in philosophy!

Teachers are often told they should have students summarize material, but they're not necessarily told why or how. Now that we've explained why summarizing is important, we'll tell you how to teach this critical skill.

ASK THE EXPERTS

Summarizing can be difficult, but studies have shown it has powerful benefits. When you summarize—even mentally or orally—you have to figure out how to get to the essence of whatever you're trying to summarize. If you transfer that mental or oral summary to paper, you have to think even more intensively about it. Once you have the summary in writing, of course, it's easier to critique and rework it.

All of this makes summarizing a significant aid to reading comprehension: In studies of students in grades 3 to 12, researchers found that writing summaries about a text had a consistently positive effect on comprehension, especially for students in the elementary grades. Writing summaries worked better than simply having students read a text multiple times, read and study it, or receive instruction in reading skills.[3]

And as we mentioned in the Introduction, an experiment with more than 800 students showed that when students wrote summaries of key concepts in their own words—as opposed to simply copying information that a teacher provided—they scored significantly better on exams.[4]

Find the Right Moment: When to Teach Summarizing

Students at any grade or ability level can learn to summarize, although your approach may vary depending on your students' skill level, the complexity and knowledge demands of the text, and other factors. There are, however, some skills your students should be familiar with before you introduce them to summarizing activities.

Asking the Right Questions: Sentence Expansion and Summarizing

Students are ready to begin learning to summarize once they've had some practice with sentence expansion. As we explained in Chapter 2, sentence expansion involves giving students a kernel sentence—that is, a bare-bones declarative sentence such as "Pyramids were built." Students then expand the sentence by answering question words like *who, what, when, where, why,* and *how.* Using some of those question words, students can expand that sentence to this: "In ancient times, pyramids were built in Egypt to protect the body of the deceased pharaoh."

Summarizing and sentence expansion demand similar skills: figuring out what's most important in a given body of information, what details support that main idea, and how the details relate to one another.

If your students are in kindergarten through second grade or if they're older but their basic writing skills are still developing, use the question words to help them practice their summarizing skills orally rather than in writing. Older or more advanced students can also benefit from practicing oral summaries, and they may need support to stay on topic and keep their remarks concise.

Building on the Single-Paragraph Outline (SPO)

If your students have had practice creating the SPO, described in Chapter 4, they'll find that many of the same skills are involved in developing summaries:

- Distinguishing between essential and nonessential information

- Reducing text to notes or paraphrases

- Organizing the points they want to make

- Rephrasing a topic sentence as a concluding one

You can also have your students use the SPO to plan a paragraph that provides a summary.

Four Questions to Ask Before You Begin

Before you ask your students to start summarizing, there are four questions you'll need to answer first.

- *Do your students have sufficient knowledge of the topic to summarize it?* As always, it's best to embed summarizing activities in the content you're teaching and to ensure that you have spent **enough time on that content** to enable students to write about it intelligently.

- *Who is the audience for the summary?* Are you asking students to write the summary for you or for themselves?

- *What is the purpose of the summary?* Is it a comprehension check you'll collect or a study aid for the students? Is it an exercise in close reading or an effort to get the text's main points?

- *What is the format?* Will the summary be a single sentence or an outline for a paragraph? Another possibility is what we call the Combined Outline, which we'll introduce in the next section.

The Structure of Summaries: Three Choices

The following three formats will help your students to structure their thoughts about the information they have read, heard, or collected. Which one you use will depend on the text to be summarized, the audience, the purpose of the summary, and the ability level of your students. As always, it's a good idea to complete these activities collectively, as a class, before asking students to try them on their own. All three formats will require your students to go back into the text, read closely, and find the main idea and most important points.

Concise and Coherent: The Summary Sentence

The first format, the **Summary Sentence** template, looks a lot like the format your students will have used for sentence expansion. The question words are the same, but when filling in the answers for a summary sentence, students will be referring to a specific text. In addition, they won't be relying on a kernel sentence that is provided at the top as a starting point.

When you give your students a text to summarize, you may need to clarify what you want them to focus on when they create their summaries. When students are expanding a brief kernel sentence, the focus is clear. But a paragraph or an article may cover a range of subjects. If there's just one aspect of the text that you want your students to zero in on in their summary sentences, you'll need to make that explicit. Be sure students are writing their answers to the question words in the form of notes on the dotted lines.

The end product of the summary sentence activity is an informative, coherent sentence that could work as the topic sentence of a paragraph. Standing alone, it serves as a way of identifying the main idea of a text.

EXHIBIT 6.1

Summary Sentence

Name:_____ Date:_____

who/what: ....

(did/will do) what: ....

when: ....

where: ....

why: ....

how: ....

Summary Sentence

_____

_____

_____

_____

Source: Copyright © 2017 The Writing Revolution.

Many newspapers and magazines summarize their articles in a single sentence at the beginning, as a way of letting readers know what is to follow. Often, book and movie reviews and television shows are summarized in a single sentence. Consider showing your students how often summaries appear.

As with the sentence expansion format, students should begin their summary sentences with the answer to the *when* question. This is a handy formula that provides them with a clear starting point. It also guides them to use a sentence structure that is often found in writing but appears less frequently in spoken language.

Exhibit 6.1 provides the Summary Sentence template, also available full-size in Appendix J.

Longer and Deeper: The SPO

The SPO will be familiar to students who have already been introduced to that format. When they use it for a summarizing activity, they will be referring to a specific text and mining it for the information they'll need to complete the outline. Students will need to do the following:

- Identify details that support the topic.

- Generate a topic sentence.

- Select and sequence supporting details.

EXHIBIT 6.2

Single-Paragraph Outline

Name: _____ Date: _____

T.S. _____

_____

_____

1. ....

2. ....

3. ....

4. ....

C.S. _____

_____

Source: Copyright © 2017 The Writing Revolution.

- Write the details as notes on the dotted lines.

- Generate a complete concluding sentence.

    Exhibit 6.2 provides the template for the SPO.

Longest and Deepest: The Combined Outline

The **Combined Outline,** which combines the summary **sentence and** the SPO, is the most challenging of the three formats—and **therefore not** appropriate for Level 1 students. The Combined Outline **first requires** students to create a sentence that encapsulates a text's main **idea, using** the question words. That summary sentence becomes the topic **sentence** of an SPO.

    To complete the Combined Outline, students need to comb **through** the article again to find additional salient details, which they **must then** categorize and convert into notes on the dotted lines—without **repeating** information they've used in the topic sentence they've already **created.** Students must then craft a concluding sentence that doesn't simply **repeat** the topic sentence but tells the reader why the text they're summarizing is important. To complete the Combined Outline successfully, your **students** will find it very helpful to carefully annotate and underline the text **while** they read—or reread—it.

EXHIBIT 6.3

Combined Outline

Name:_____ Date:_____

Title:_____

who/what:...

(did/will do) what:...

when:..

where:...

why:..

how:..

T.S. (summary sentence): _____

_____

_____

Details:

1:...

2:...

3:...

4:...

C.S. _____

_____

_____

Source: Copyright © 2017 The Writing Revolution.

The template for the Combined Outline can be found in Exhibit 6.3 and Appendix K.

See It in Action: Examples of the Three Summarizing Formats

We've provided examples of the summary sentence and an SPO used for summarizing for Level 1 and Level 2 students. As for the Combined Outline, we're only providing an example for Level 2, because it's not appropriate for Level 1 students.

Level 1 Examples

The Level 1 summary sentence shown in Exhibit 6.4 was developed by a second-grade class that was studying three-toed sloths.

Exhibit 6.5 shows an example of an SPO used for summarizing. It's about Squanto and was done by a third-grade class.

EXHIBIT 6.4

Summary Sentence

Name: _____   Date: _____

~~who~~/what: _3-toed sloths_ ....

(did/will do) what: _considered world's slowest animals_ ....

when: ....

where: _Costa Rican jungle_ ....

why: _rarely move/rest a lot_ ....

how: ....

Summary Sentence

The three-toed sloths in the Costa

Rican jungle are considered the world's

slowest animals because they rarely

move and rest a lot!

Source: Copyright © 2017 The Writing Revolution.

EXHIBIT 6.5

Single-Paragraph Outline

Name: _____   Date: _____

T.S. _Squanto, a Patuxet Indian, had a fascinating_
life and was very important to the Pilgrims
in Plymouth.

1. _b. 1585 / kidnapped / taken to Eng. / learned English_

2. _1619 / back to Plymouth / live with Wampanoag_ ....

3. _1621 / translated for Pilgrims + Indians / lost boy_ ...

4. _taught Pilgrims to farm + fish_ ....

C.S. _____ _Without Squanto's help, the Pilgrims_
might not have survived!

Source: Copyright © 2017 The Writing Revolution.

Level 2 Examples

The following article, adapted from actual news reports, is about a devastating tornado. It's an example of how articles about current events can be excellent prompts for summarizing, especially if they relate to the content of the curriculum. The assigned article, for example, could be woven into a unit on weather and science. In the examples (Exhibits 6.6, 6.7, and 6.8), you can see how a single text can be adapted to practice all three summary formats.

Tornado Rips Through State

Oklahoma City Beacon Online

May 10, 2016—A devastating tornado hit an area on the southwest border of Oklahoma City this afternoon, causing widespread damage. Two miles wide, the twister began at 3:24 p.m., lasted for 40 minutes, and left behind a 20-mile path of devastation.

The powerful storm's extremely high winds destroyed hundreds of homes and buildings and tossed cars through the streets.

"We've had quite a few neighborhoods completely wiped out," said Sergeant Edward Olson of the Oklahoma City Police Department. "There's just nothing left there."

More than 20 people were killed and dozens were injured, including students at Clement Elementary School in Elwood, a suburb that was hit particularly hard. Although the school was destroyed, emergency workers were able to bring many of the children and other injured individuals to hospitals.

The rescue effort continues as emergency crews clear debris and search for missing people. The work is being hampered, however, by thunderstorms and damaged roads.

"We haven't given up hope that we'll find survivors," said a spokesperson for Oklahoma Highway Patrol. "We'll keep searching as long as possible."

The federal government has declared the counties affected by the tornado a federal disaster area, opening up the way for federal money to help with the rescue and rebuilding effort.

TWR's summarizing activities enable students to find the main points of a text, categorize them, and sequence them according to their importance or chronology. As with all TWR activities, you'll find you can

EXHIBIT 6.6

<table>
<tr><td colspan="2" align="center">**Summary Sentence**</td></tr>
<tr><td colspan="2">Name: _____ Date: _____</td></tr>
<tr><td colspan="2">~~who~~/what: tornado ....</td></tr>
<tr><td colspan="2">(did/will do) what: caused destruction ....</td></tr>
<tr><td colspan="2">where: OK City ....</td></tr>
<tr><td colspan="2">when: 5/10/2016 ....</td></tr>
<tr><td colspan="2">why: high wind speeds ....</td></tr>
<tr><td colspan="2">how: n/a ....</td></tr>
<tr><td colspan="2">Summary sentence: On May 10, 2016, a tornado caused
destruction in Oklahoma City due to its high wind speeds.</td></tr>
</table>

Source: Copyright © 2017 The Writing Revolution.

EXHIBIT 6.7

<table>
<tr><td align="center">**Single-Paragraph Outline**</td></tr>
<tr><td>Name: _____ Date: _____</td></tr>
<tr><td>T.S. On May 10, 2016, a major tornado hit
Oklahoma City.</td></tr>
<tr><td>1. homes + buildings destroyed ....</td></tr>
<tr><td>2. 20 killed / dozens injured ....</td></tr>
<tr><td>3. emergency crews remove debris / search + rescue ....</td></tr>
<tr><td>4. fed. gov't / "fed. disaster area" → $ ....</td></tr>
<tr><td>C.S. Clearly, this tornado was a devastating
event.</td></tr>
</table>

Source: Copyright © 2017 The Writing Revolution.

EXHIBIT 6.8

Combined Outline

Name: _____   Date: _____

Title: _"Tornado Rips Through State"_____

who/what: .tornado...

(did/will do) what: .caused destruction...

when: ...5/10/2016...

where: OK City..

why: .high wind speeds..

how: .n/a..

T.S. (summary sentence): On May 10, 2016, a tornado caused _____

destruction in Oklahoma City due to its high wind speeds. _____

Details:

1. .homes + buildings destroyed...

2. .20 killed / dozens injured...

3. .emergency crews remove debris / search + rescue.....................

4. .Pres. Obama / "fed. disaster area" → $.....................................

C.S. ___ Although tornadoes are devastating events, their _____

 impact would be even worse without emergency workers and ___

 government aid. _____

---

accomplish these objectives without necessarily requiring your students to turn their outlines into finished products.

Whether or not it results in a final, polished copy, summarizing will help ensure that your students absorb and retain information about whatever content they're studying. Far from being a low-level skill, summarizing can be a challenging and rigorous activity that provides powerful benefits.

By the end of first grade, Ana—the girl who provided a blow-by-blow account of her field trip to the amusement park—had learned how to write a coherent summary sentence that omitted extraneous information. Here's the summary she wrote about a class visit to the Statue of Liberty:

Who: *our class*
(did) What: *visited Statue of Liberty*
When: *Tuesday*
Where: *Liberty Island*
Why: *learn about its history*
Expanded sentence: *On Tuesday, our class went to Liberty Island to see the Statue of Liberty and learn about its history.*

And Mario—the boy who preferred to answer in monosyllables—was able, with prompting, to provide this extended response following the same visit:

On Tuesday, our class visited the Statue of Liberty on Liberty Island and we learned how happy the millions of immigrants were when they saw it.

TO SUM UP

- Summarizing builds on skills students have developed in sentence-expansion activities and in creating SPOs.

- Before asking students to summarize, make sure they have sufficient knowledge of the topic to understand the text you're asking them to summarize and that they understand the intended audience, purpose, and format.

- Once students are familiar with sentence expansion, you can have them summarize a text in a summary sentence.

- Students who have been introduced to the SPO can use it to summarize a specific text.

- Level 2 students can create summaries using the Combined Outline, which uses the summary sentence on the top half of the template as its topic sentence and requires students to provide additional information for the detail lines.

Notes

1. B. S. Bloom, M. D. Englehart, E. J. Furst, W. H. Hill, and D. R. Krathwohl, *Taxonomy of Educational Objectives: The Classification of Educational Goals; Handbook I: Cognitive Domain* (New York: Longman, 1956).

2. Immanuel Kant, *Kant's Critique of Judgement,* translated with Introduction and Notes by J.H. Bernard, 2nd ed. revised (London: Macmillan, 1914), http://oll.libertyfund.org/titles/kant-the-critique-of-judgement.

3. S. Graham and M. Hebert, *Writing to Read: Evidence for How Writing Can Improve Reading. A Carnegie Corporation Time to Act Report* (Washington, DC: Alliance for Excellent Education, 2010).

4. P. C. Brown, H. L. Roediger III, and M. A. McDaniel, *Make It Stick: The Science of Successful Learning* (Cambridge, MA: Harvard University Press, 2014).

CHAPTER 7

Moving on to Compositions
The Multiple-Paragraph Outline

When Toni-Ann Vroom and Dina Zoleo were social studies teachers at New Dorp High School on Staten Island, no one looked forward to the days when the state Regents exams were given. Some of the exams, such as the one in Global History and Geography, required students to compose multiple-paragraph responses—compositions that had to be written under time pressure. Back then, students had trouble writing at length even when they had unlimited time.

"Write a well-organized essay that includes an introduction, several paragraphs, and a conclusion," the directions for the exam might say. "Use evidence from at least four documents in your essay. Support your response with relevant facts, examples, and details. Include additional outside information."

Most students at New Dorp quickly scribbled a few random sentences. Some just left the pages blank. Teachers who were proctoring the exams knew they could count on leaving well before the allotted time was up.

Expectations for student writing have never been higher than they are today. Spurred by the dismal state of writing in college classrooms and the workplace, the Common Core standards demand that students at even the elementary level write at length and in a variety of genres: informational and opinion or argumentative essays as well as narratives. No longer is it enough for a fourth-grader to write a paragraph about his summer vacation or a trip to the zoo. The standards require him to be able to write, for example, compositions that "introduce a topic or text clearly, state an opinion, and create an organizational structure in which related ideas are grouped to support the writer's purpose."

Whatever people may think about the Common Core, most would agree that students need to learn how to write well about subjects beyond their personal experiences. But what is the most effective way to teach that skill? The Common Core writing standards tell us where students need to end up without explaining how to get them there. Especially when asked to write at length in an expository mode, students at all grade levels often struggle with organization, sentence structure, clarity, and coherence.

Simply handing out longer and more challenging writing assignments doesn't magically give students the skills they need to compose them. But chances are that in your teacher training programs most of you—like me—learned *what* should be assigned but not *how* to provide instruction that would result in unified, well-developed compositions.

Over the course of many years, my colleagues and I have analyzed countless compositions, research papers, and essays. After looking at long-term assignments and responses to essay questions on tests, we realized that a structured, sequenced method for guiding students to compose longer pieces of writing was needed. The **Multiple-Paragraph Outline (MPO)** is designed for students who are ready to write compositions of three or more paragraphs.

Organize and Build Knowledge: The Benefits of Outlining

Having your students practice making MPOs does the following:

- Develops organizational skills
- Helps in categorizing information
- Reveals gaps in knowledge or comprehension
- Guides students to a logical sequence for expository, narrative, and argumentative **text structures**
- Enables them to avoid repetition and irrelevant information
- Promotes cogent introductions and conclusions
- Helps them take notes efficiently
- Develops the ability to create transitions between ideas and **paragraphs**

Bear in mind that your students must know a topic well before they'll be able to create an MPO about it. Ideally, the topic will be one that is embedded in the curriculum and that they have been studying in class for some time. Book reports and biographies make good topics for Level 1 students. Some Level 2 students may be ready to tackle MPOs that require guided or independent research.

Creating an MPO will help your students cement knowledge they've already acquired and gather new information that builds on it. It's important to remember that, as with other TWR activities, *creating* the outline is a powerful activity in itself, regardless of whether a student turns it into a draft or a finished product.

Be sure to have students fill in an MPO before attempting to write any composition. Once students have completed an MPO, converting it into a draft will be a much easier task than simply plunging into a composition without a plan.

Prepping for the MPO

Your students will need to acquire a number of skills before they can develop an MPO on their own. If you've given them ample practice creating Single-Paragraph Outlines (SPOs) and drafting and revising paragraphs based on them, they will have already acquired some of the prerequisite skills. Specifically, they will have learned how to do the following:

- Develop a topic sentence that reflects the main idea of a paragraph.
- Write supporting details in note form, using key words and phrases, abbreviations, and symbols.
- Construct a coherent paragraph.

Most Level 1 students, including third- and fourth-graders, will be able to write simple multiple-paragraph compositions using these skills.

To create coherent, thesis-driven multiple-paragraph compositions, students will need to acquire some new skills through repeated practice. These skills are complex, and we recommend that you introduce them only to Level 2 students. They include the abilities to do the following:

- Distinguish among general, specific, and thesis statements.
- Generate a thesis statement that conveys the main theme of the composition, and incorporate it into the introduction and conclusion.
- Provide transitions between paragraphs.

In this chapter, we'll show you how to guide your Level 1 students to create multiple-paragraph compositions that can take the form of book reports and biographies. We'll also guide you through activities that will develop the new skills your Level 2 students need in order to create unified, coherent compositions of three or more paragraphs.

Take It Slow: Introducing the Level 1 Student to the MPO

Even if your students are still inexperienced writers, you may feel pressure to assign them multiple-paragraph argument essays or even research papers. We would urge you to resist that pressure. Your students' efforts will ultimately be far more successful if you first give them the practice they need to consolidate their skills at the paragraph level.

That's not to say, however, that they can plan or write only one paragraph at a time. Although they may not be ready to do the challenging work required to construct a sophisticated essay, they can still write straightforward compositions of three paragraphs—or possibly four or five. They don't necessarily have to start with three paragraphs and then progress to four or five. The length should be determined by the topic and content of the composition.

If, for example, a student is critiquing a book and the composition includes only an introduction, a plot summary, and an analysis of the book's strengths and weaknesses, three paragraphs may be sufficient. If the student also wants to compare certain characters in the book or describe conflicts, she could use the four- or five-paragraph MPO to plan the book report. (See Appendices O, P, and Q for three-, four-, and five-paragraph MPO templates and Appendix R for a three-paragraph book report MPO template.)

As with all MPOs, the MPO for Level 1 students will have a column on the left side headed "Main Idea" and a broader column on the right, headed "Details." Underneath these headings are a series of boxes. The Main Idea boxes are for words or phrases indicating the topic of each paragraph. The Details boxes have dotted lines where students write notes, using key words and phrases, abbreviations, and symbols that will form the basis of their body paragraphs. You'll need to make sure students have sufficient background knowledge to provide at least three details for each paragraph.

HOW TO DIFFERENTIATE MPO ACTIVITIES

Sometimes students have become comfortable creating an SPO and using it to draft a paragraph, but they aren't quite ready to jump to the MPO. For students who are ready to start writing multi-paragraph compositions but need more support than the MPO provides, we've devised something we call the Transition Outline.

Like the simple MPO for Level 1 students, the Transition Outline doesn't require a thesis statement. At the same time, it does require students to write a complete topic sentence for each paragraph, providing them with more structure. They also need to write a concluding sentence that applies to the entire composition.

Exhibit 7.1 shows a sample Transition Outline on the topic of national identification cards.

EXHIBIT 7.1

Transition Outline (3 Paragraphs)

Name: _____   Date: _____

Topic: **National ID Cards** _____

1st ¶ —T.S. **Will national identification cards keep us safe or invade our privacy?**

1. most → + about ID cards / 70%

2. gov't = fingerprinting/photos/pers. info

3. on database → easy chk. identity / track people?

2nd ¶ —T.S. **Many people think that an official card to identify people will create a safer nation.**

1. all states = same / making fakes → harder

2. thumb print ≠ stolen by criminals

3. help police / people present @ crime scene

3rd ¶ —T.S. **Although most Americans like the idea of national ID cards, there ae drawbacks.**

1. cards for citizens / criminals can = non-citizens

2. innocent people → feeling like criminals

3. checking IDs → slow down everything / lateness

C.S.: **National ID cards is a topic that clearly has two sides!**

_____

Level 1 students will need support in deciding on the main idea for each paragraph. For a simple three- or four-paragraph book report, provide them with the following cues in the Main Idea boxes:

- "Introduction" for the first paragraph
- "Plot Summary" for the second (or "Book Summary," if the book is nonfiction)
- "Opinion" for the third

Although some students will be able to fill in the Details boxes on their own, others will need you to provide appropriate cues and question words.

EXHIBIT 7.2

Multiple - Paragraph Outline (Book Report)	
Name: _____ Date: _____	
Title of Book: _____	

Main Idea	**Details**
Introduction ¶ 1	title author setting (place / date) main idea
Book Summary ¶ 2	who what where when why how
Opinion ¶ 3	audience? why?

Unlike the SPO, a Level 1 MPO doesn't require students to write out the topic sentences for their paragraphs—or any sentences at all. They'll do all the work of converting their notes into sentences at the **drafting and revising** stage. If you feel your students still need to write out their topic sentences in the planning and outlining stage, you may want give them the intermediate step of a **Transition Outline** (see "How to Differentiate MPO Activities").

Level 1 Example

After Ms. Franklin's Level 1 class had spent enough time working with SPOs that they had become comfortable with them, she decided to have her students plan a multiple-paragraph book report using the MPO. Because the students' skills were still developing, she decided to provide them with cues and question words for their Details boxes.

Ms. Franklin gave her students the MPO shown in Exhibit 7.2.

One student, Marta, after writing about the book *Rachel Carson: Pioneer of Ecology*, filled out the MPO and it looked like the one shown in Exhibit 7.3.

The Next Step: An Overview of the MPO for Level 2 Students

Unlike a Level 1 MPO, the Level 2 MPO requires students to generate a thesis statement, which they'll use as the last sentence of their introduction. When you teach your Level 2 students to create an MPO, guide them through that process and five other steps, which we discuss in more detail further on in this chapter. The numbers of the steps correspond to the numbers that appear on the sample MPO template in Exhibit 7.4:

1. Select a topic and identify the composition's purpose and audience.

2. Develop the thesis statement as a complete sentence. *This is the only complete sentence that should appear on the MPO.*

3. Write the main idea of each paragraph as a phrase or category in the Main Idea boxes on the left-hand side of the MPO.

4. Write the supporting details for each main idea in the Details boxes in the right-hand column of the MPO.

EXHIBIT 7.3

Multiple-Paragraph Outline (Book Report)

Name: __Marta_____ Date: _November 22_

Title of Book: __Rachel Carson: Pioneer of Ecology by Kathleen V. Kudlinski__

_____

Main Idea	Details
Introduction ¶ 1	.... title: Rachel Carson: Pioneer of Ecology .... author: Kathleen V. Kudlinski setting: PA & MD main Idea: RC=introduced ecology to world ....
Book Summary ¶ 2	.... who: RC what: writer, scientist, ecologist /activist anti .... pollution when: 1907–1964 why: wanted to save planet how: by camping + studying + writing ....
Opinion ¶ 3	.... audience: students opinion: liked learning about RC / events in her .... life / ecology

Source: Copyright © 2017 The Writing Revolution.

5. Develop the introduction by writing a general statement (G), specific statement (S), and thesis statement (T) using notes for the general and specific statements and a *T* to indicate the placement of the thesis statement.

6. Develop the conclusion by inverting the order of the *G, S,* and *T* statements in the introduction and rewording them.

As with the SPO, you should spend a lot of time modeling the MPO for the whole class and have students practice trying to create the outlines collectively before expecting them to develop an MPO independently.

EXHIBIT 7.4

Multiple-Paragraph Outline (5 Paragraphs)

Name: _____ Date: _____

Topic: _____**1**_____

Thesis Statement: _____**2**_____

_____

Main Idea	Details
Introduction ¶ 1	....**5**.............................. ....
¶ 2 **3**	....**4**.............................. ....
¶ 3 **3**	....**4**.............................. ....
¶ 4 **3**	....**4**.............................. ....
Conclusion ¶ 5	....**6**.............................. ....

Source: Copyright © 2017 The Writing Revolution.

If the topic for Level 2 students requires independent research, you'll need to guide them to use reliable sources and tell them specifically which ones are acceptable. For example, you may want to warn them against using *Wikipedia* because much of the information may not be objective or verified. (See the next Be Careful box.)

MPOs can have three, four, five paragraphs and can use a variety of formats. For a compare-and-contrast MPO, or one that presents two sides of a topic, a student could use the following categories:

- Introduction (identify the topic/why it will be discussed/two sides will be presented)

- Similarities (advantages/pro)
- Differences (disadvantages/con)
- Conclusion

A **problem-solution** MPO might look like this:

- Introduction (identify the topic/explain its importance or reasons for writing about it)
- Problem
- Solution
- Conclusion

An MPO for a biographical composition follows this format:

- Introduction (identify subject/why she or he is important)
- Early life
- Major accomplishment(s)
- Legacy
- Conclusion

An MPO for a major event would be set up in the following format:

- Introduction (identify event/explain importance)
- Background
- Event
- Impact
- Conclusion

An MPO for a five-paragraph argumentative essay, which we'll discuss in more detail in Chapter 8, would have the following structure:

- Introduction (state position and acknowledge counterclaim)
- Background and introduction of claim
- Counterclaim and evidence
- Claim and strongest evidence
- Conclusion

BE CAREFUL

Teaching students effective research skills is an important but challenging task—especially in the era of the Internet. It's all too easy for students to stumble on a website that looks reliable but is riddled with misinformation. Students may also mistake personal opinions they find online for fact. They simply may be overwhelmed by the amount of information they find.

A full discussion of the topic is beyond the scope of this book, but we can offer a few suggestions for how to help your students develop online research skills:

- Help your students use precise keywords in their online searches. If they type in *Kennedy assassination,* they may get results about both the assassination of John F. Kennedy and that of Robert Kennedy.
- It's a good idea to skim search results for words that pop up frequently and add those to the search terms. That's especially true for more sophisticated words, which can yield more scholarly or academic results. If a student is researching immigrants who send money back home, for example, adding the term *remittances* could be helpful.
- Let students know about words and symbols they can use to refine their online searches. They can use quotation marks around search terms to get the exact wording, insert *and* between search terms to produce results that focus on both subjects, and include a space followed by a minus sign to eliminate a particular meaning of a term (for example, a student searching for information on the planet Saturn could type *Saturn -car* to eliminate results relating to the Saturn vehicle).
- Rather than just having students use Google, you can encourage them to use databases that specifically direct them to academic or scholarly sources, such as Google Scholar. For students who need information that is written in a less complex style, you might have them add the word *kid* to their Google search to pull up more accessible texts. Some states, such as Kentucky, provide residents access to reliable online databases that are geared to children, like Searchasaurus and Grolier Online.
- Encourage your students to check whether a website's URL ends in a .com, .org, .gov, or .edu. Websites connected with a government agency (.gov), university (.edu), or museums (often .org) are generally more trustworthy than someone's personal website.
- Have your students evaluate websites with a critical eye. They should be asking questions such as: Who wrote this? What is his or her perspective? What are his or her credentials? Who is sponsoring this site? Are there links and references to other sources that corroborate the information?
- Model the process of searching online for the class, just as you model TWR strategies and activities.

Your school librarian can be a valuable resource in helping your students develop research skills. Without these skills, they may find themselves investing a lot of effort in a project that relies on information that is questionable or just plain wrong.[1]

What to Write About: Selecting a Topic

When your students are still learning to create MPOs, the entire class should be writing about the same topic, which you will choose. You'll be better able to control the research they'll need to do and the progress they're making on their drafts, and the feedback you give them will be more targeted. If each student in a large class is working on a different topic, the teacher can't become enough of an expert on each subject to provide effective guidance and check all the sources students are using.

Once students have become adept at developing MPOs, they'll be able to begin selecting their own topics. Still, they'll need practice before they can confidently refine a topic on their own so that it's the right size for a composition—neither too narrow nor too broad. The Civil War, for example, is too broad, and a discussion of a specific minor battle might be too narrow. A review of the military career of Robert E. Lee or an analysis of the Battle of Gettysburg would work better.

Even students who have had experience with MPOs may need guidance in selecting an appropriate topic. You'll want to be sure that you approve each student's topic before the work of research or planning gets underway.

Research Papers: Sticking to a Schedule

If the compositions you've assigned require research, make sure your students are staying on track over the days or weeks that they're working on their projects. Once students have their topics, it's best to set up a detailed schedule listing due dates for each stage of the process: gathering material, developing a thesis, coming up with a bibliography, making note cards, and so on. We suggest that you require students to get your approval for each section before moving on to the next step.

In Appendix F you'll find a Research Plan Time Sequence Sheet, adapted from one developed at The Windward School in White Plains, New York. This sheet can be used for research papers, including argumentative essays. You'll find it extremely helpful in guiding your students to manage their time and understand your expectations.

Settle on a Theme: Develop a Thesis Statement

Once your students are ready to tackle developing a **thesis statement,** first explain what it is: a statement that conveys the main theme of the entire composition—just as a topic sentence conveys the main idea of a single paragraph. A thesis statement often contains what is known as a *plan of development*. Essentially, that means that the thesis statement presents the main points of the composition in the order in which they will be addressed.

For example, here's a thesis statement that might be used for a composition on the Civil War:

The impact of the economic, social, and political effects of the Civil War lasted for generations.

This sentence signals to the reader that after the introduction, the next paragraph of the essay will focus on the economic effects of the Civil War. Then there will be a paragraph on the social effects and finally a paragraph on the political effects.

Not all thesis statements need to spell out the plan of development so precisely. For example, a thesis statement could simply say, "Theodore Roosevelt's presidency marked the beginning of the United States as a world power." The essay could then address the specifics—the Panama Canal, the Roosevelt Corollary—contained in that general idea.

Constructing a thesis statement requires that students understand the main points they will be making in a composition and the tone or text structure they will adopt. At the same time, they'll need to be able to state their thesis in a single sentence—and one that is not overstuffed.

You may find it helpful to provide students with examples of different approaches they can use when developing their thesis statements:

- A personal judgment:

  It is urgent that problems associated with rising sea levels as a result of global warming be addressed in the next decade.

- Advice or directions:

  There are a number of effective strategies to combat the effect of rising sea levels.

- A statement of consequences (cause and effect):

  If global warming is not taken seriously worldwide, coastal cities will be in danger.

- An argument for or against an issue. When students are writing pro-con or argumentative essays (see Chapter 8), it's often a good idea to begin a thesis statement with a subordinating conjunction that sets up an opposing argument. For example:

  Although most scientists believe there is persuasive evidence that global warming is caused by human actions, some critics disagree.

- An interpretation (usually of fiction or poetry):

  The endless legal morass described by Charles Dickens in *Bleak House* is as relevant today as it was over a century ago.

- Compare and contrast:

  There are significant differences between the immigration policies of the candidates.

Once your students have crafted their thesis statements, they'll write them at the top of the MPO. Tell students that this is the *only* time they'll write a complete sentence on the MPO. Eventually, they will use their thesis statements as the final sentences of their introductory paragraphs, where the statements will have the most impact on the reader. Later students will rephrase their thesis statements as the first sentences of their concluding paragraphs.

As students go on to construct their body paragraphs, they'll be able to refer back to their thesis statements to keep them on track. Every paragraph in the composition should relate to the theme contained in the thesis statement.

Writing a Biographical Essay: A Level 2 Example (Part 1)

After Mr. Miller's class had been studying the Progressive Era for a couple of weeks, he asked his students to write a biographical essay about a figure from the period. One student, Diana, was particularly intrigued by Theodore Roosevelt and wanted to learn more about him. Mr. Miller approved the topic and helped her locate some reliable articles about Roosevelt online. Diana also found a brief biography of him in the school library.

According to the schedule she and Mr. Miller had agreed on, Diana had a week to read about Roosevelt and take notes before turning in her thesis statement. When she showed her MPO to Mr. Miller for his approval, it looked like this:

Topic: *Theodore Roosevelt*

Thesis Statement: *Theodore Roosevelt's early life and political career prepared him to have a major impact on 20th-century events in the United States and abroad.*

Diana knew she would be able to refer to the thesis statement for guidance as she constructed the rest of her outline.

Main Ideas and Details: Planning Body Paragraphs

After your students have settled on a thesis statement, they'll move on to plan their body paragraphs. This is actually a two-step process. First, they will need to decide on a word or phrase that describes the main idea of each paragraph. Once they have their main ideas in the boxes on the left, they'll use their notes to fill in the details of each paragraph on the dotted lines. The MPO does not require students to create topic sentences for their body paragraphs, as they did on the SPO. That will come later, at the drafting and revision stage.

What's the Big Idea? Filling in the Main Idea Boxes

The Main Idea boxes for each body paragraph appear in a column along the left-hand margin of the MPO. Each main idea should be a word or brief phrase that signifies the topic of the paragraph and supports the composition's thesis. Although students won't be writing topic sentences on the MPO, tell them to write a T.S. in each Main Idea box to remind them to include the sentences when they compose their drafts.

Listing the main ideas helps students avoid repetition and ensures that each paragraph relates to the composition's overall theme. If a thesis statement contains a plan of development, stating each of the main points the composition will make, the student can use it as a guide when filling in the Main Idea boxes.

Different types of compositions call for different kinds of main ideas for the body paragraphs, as you can see from the examples we provided in the section of this chapter called "The Next Step: An Overview of the MPO for Level 2 Students." The order of the paragraphs also will depend on the type of assignment. In a biographical composition, for example, the order would be chronological.

The Nitty Gritty: Filling in the Details Boxes

After your students have filled in the Main Idea boxes, they're ready to start filling in the Details boxes on the right side of the outline. Make sure students understand that the details for each paragraph will relate to its main idea and will be written in note form rather than full sentences. Although students need to settle on the order of the paragraphs when creating the MPO, the order of the details doesn't matter at this point. They can decide on that when it's time to write their drafts.

If your students have done research on their topic, they may need to transfer information from their notes to the appropriate Details box on the outline. They can abbreviate citations to documents, examples, or quotations.

Writing a Biographical Essay: A Level 2 Example (Part 2)

Diana had already presented her preliminary bibliography and her note cards on Theodore Roosevelt to Mr. Miller for his approval. Now she was ready to tackle coming up with the main ideas for her body paragraphs. Her first step was to look closely at her thesis statement: "Theodore Roosevelt's early life and political career prepared him to have a major impact on 20th-century events in the United States and abroad."

Because this was a biographical essay, Diana knew she would proceed chronologically. Her second paragraph would focus on Roosevelt's early life, her third on his political career, and her fourth on his legacy, domestic and foreign. She wrote each of those phrases in the appropriate Main Idea box—being careful to also write T.S. in each box to remind her to write a topic sentence when she got to the stage of composing her draft.

Then she went through her notes to find details that matched up with the main idea of each paragraph. Exhibit 7.5 shows what her MPO looked like when she had finished planning her body paragraphs.

Back to the Beginning: Planning Introductions

Once students have their thesis statements and the outline of their body paragraphs, they're ready to turn their attention to their introductions. Introductions set forth the topic of the composition and engage the reader's interest. Writing introductory paragraphs, like writing concluding ones, requires the ability to summarize information and make generalizations. Although students have had practice with these skills at the paragraph level, in creating topic sentences, undertaking them at the multiple-paragraph level is a bigger challenge. They'll need to extract the essential idea from a greater volume of information. And they'll be creating three sentences for their introductory paragraphs, not just one introductory sentence. Before you have students tackle creating their own introductory paragraphs, make sure they've had plenty of practice with the preparatory activities we describe in the next sections.

EXHIBIT 7.5

Multiple-Paragraph Outline (5 Paragraphs)	

Name: _____   Date: _____

Topic: <u>Theodore Roosevelt: His Life and Legacies</u>

Thesis Statement: <u>Theodore Roosevelt's early life and political</u> <u>career prepared him to have a major impact on 20th-century</u> <u>events in the United States and beyond.</u>

Main Idea	Details
Introduction ¶ 1	G.. S.. T..
Early Life ↓ T.S.	D.O.B. 10/27/1858 / NYC sickly / homeschooled Harvard / Columbia Law / historian 1st marriage / Badlands
¶ 2 Political Career ¶ 3 ↓ T.S.	'81 NYS Assembly '95 NYC Police Commissioner '97 Asst. Sec. Navy / Rough Riders / '98 / NY Gov. '00 VP → '01 Pres
Legacies ¶ 4 ↓ T.S.	laws / anti-trust / consumer & work safety environment / parks / Nat'l Forest Service / reserves Panama Canal / Roosevelt Corollary Russo-Japanese War / Nobel Prize '06
Conclusion ¶ 5	T.. S.. G..

Source: Copyright © 2017 The Writing Revolution.

No More Plodding Introductions: The GST Formula

Over the years, we have seen that students often have trouble writing introductions and conclusions. Here is how Kevin, one of Dina Zoleo's 10th-grade students, began his essay about the impact of absolute rulers in Russia and France. It may look all too familiar to you.

In the 15th and 18th centuries, absolute rulers were very common. In this essay, I will tell you about the leadership of Louis XIV and Peter the Great.

Although Kevin provides the requisite information, he also tells us—unnecessarily—that he is *going* to tell us something, but it's not clear what. He could instead engage the reader's interest by indicating the substance of what he's going to say. He might, for example, have begun with something like this:

Although they lived in different eras and countries, Louis XIV and Peter the Great shared many of the strengths and weaknesses common to absolute rulers.

How can your students avoid the type of plodding introduction that Kevin initially produced? We have found that the format suggested in *The St. Martin's Handbook*[2] is an excellent one for developing writers. According to the handbook, introductory paragraphs should unfold in this order:

1. First sentence: general statement (G)

2. Second sentence: specific statement (S)

3. Third sentence: thesis statement (T)

Teachers sometimes tell us they think that the GST format makes students' introductions too formulaic. But the fact is that most students actually need and appreciate a formula to help them structure coherent introductions and conclusions.

"Over the years, many of my high school students told me they struggled with writing introductions and didn't know how to begin," says Dina. "GST really helped them figure out how to create an introduction and made it much easier for them."

By providing a structure, the GST formula frees up students' brain power so they can focus on figuring out what's important and what they want to say. And just as an experienced cook eventually begins to depart from strictly following a recipe, students who have become comfortable with the GST formula can experiment with other structures when they're ready.

TECHNICAL TIP

Here's how to structure an introductory paragraph:

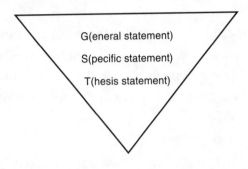

G(eneral statement)

S(pecific statement)

T(hesis statement)

Your students will need practice to be able to recognize the differences among these three kinds of statements—and they'll need to practice recognizing that differences in sentences you provide before they can create Gs, Ss, and Ts of their own. As with other challenging aspects of writing, we've broken the process of developing these skills into manageable chunks that will eventually enable students to create effective and coherent multiple-paragraph compositions.

The next three sections provide examples of introductory paragraphs that follow the GST format. The words in bold indicate elements of the plan of development that are embedded in the thesis statement.

Book Report

[G] Countless books are published each year, but only a few become classics. [S] William Golding's novel about a group of British school boys stranded on an island after a plane crash has been required reading in many schools for decades. [T] *Lord of the Flies* has intrigued readers because of its **plot, characters,** and **the lessons** that can be learned from this compelling tale.

Opinion-Argumentative

[G] Penguins are among the most popular animals. [S] However, they have become an endangered species as sea ice disappears from their habitats. [T] **Rising sea levels** are among the most dangerous effects of climate change and should be viewed as an **urgent issue**.

Significant Event

[G] All great presidents have a signature achievement that profoundly affected future generations. [S] Many historians consider the acquisition of the Louisiana Territory from France as Thomas Jefferson's outstanding accomplishment. [T] As a result of the Louisiana Purchase, he significantly **increased the size of the United States, extended its borders, and opened up new trade routes.**

Practice Makes Perfect: Constructing General, Specific, and Thesis Statements

To help your students understand the distinctions among G, S, and T sentences, first have them distinguish each type from the others. Once they've become familiar with the concepts, you can have them practice writing each of the three types. To do that, provide them with two sentences and have them create a third—for example, give them a general and a specific statement and have them write a thesis statement that goes with them. Do these activities orally and as a class before having students try them independently.

The next sections provide examples of activities for each of these steps. For most of these activities, students will need to have background knowledge about the subject they're writing about. As always, it's best to embed the activities in the content of your curriculum.

Distinguishing Among General (G), Specific (S), and Thesis Statements (T)

If your class has been studying the history of slavery in the United States, you might give students these three sentences and ask them to mark them G, S, or T (as shown).

The abolitionists wanted to end this disgraceful practice. (S)

Frederick Douglass, a former slave, was one of the most important members of this group. (T)

Slavery is a tragic part of United States history. (G)

Writing a G When Given an S and a T

Next, provide your students with a specific statement and a thesis statement and have them supply a general statement. Keep the order of the sentences—G, then S, then T—but leave the first line blank for your students to fill in. (This example shows how a student might fill in a general statement.) Remember to provide a solid line for them rather than a dotted one, because you're asking them to write a complete sentence.

> **G:** *Sometimes adversity can lead to positive historical developments.*

> **S:** After the War of 1812, the United States, a new nation, was forced to rely on its own resources when England blockaded American ports.

> **T:** The resulting acceleration of the Industrial Revolution led to numerous changes in American society.

Writing a S When Given a G and a T

The next step is to provide students with a general statement and a thesis statement and have them create a specific statement. (This example also shows how a student might fill in a specific statement.)

> **G:** Scientific research has often been embroiled in controversy.

> **S:** *Stem cell research provides valuable insights into curing many diseases.*

> **T:** Although research in this area holds great promise, ethical, religious, and political concerns need to be addressed.

Writing a G and an S When Given a T

Now you'll ask your students to write *two* sentences: Provide them with a thesis statement and have them write a general statement and a specific statement to go with it. (This example shows how a student might fill in a general statement and a specific statement.)

> **G:** *Social networking sites are extremely popular.*

> **S:** *However, online bullying and inappropriate messages have led to depression and isolation among teenagers.*

> **T:** Social media can be dangerous, especially to adolescents.

Writing a T When Given a Topic

A more challenging activity is to give students a topic and have them write a thesis statement for it. (This example shows how a student might fill in a thesis statement.)

> Topic: Causes of Homelessness

> **T:** *Mental illness and substance abuse are two of the leading causes of homelessness.*

Adding Specifics to the Introductory Paragraph

As students become more proficient, there is no need to limit their introductions to three sentences. Typically, the fourth or fifth sentences are specific statements, often facts or statistics. You can have them practice adding specific statements by giving them a G, S, and T and asking them to add another S. (This example shows how a student might fill in an additional specific statement.)

> **G:** As the United States grew in industrial and economic power, two controversial figures emerged.
>
> **S:** _By the end of the 19th century, Carnegie controlled almost the entire steel industry and Rockefeller's Standard Oil Company controlled 90% of the refining business._
>
> **S:** Both men made tremendous philanthropic contributions that made them heroic in the views of many.
>
> **T:** However, should these early builders of big business in America be considered robber barons or captains of industry?

Take Off the Training Wheels: Writing Introductions Independently

The amount of time you spend on the practice activities we've just described will vary depending on the abilities of your students and the complexity of the content they're studying. You'll need to use your own judgment about when they're ready to try writing their own introductions.

Once you decide that they're sufficiently prepared, first have them practice different ways of beginning an introduction: with an example, a question, a fact or statistic, or a description.

Wrap It Up: Crafting Conclusions

After students have had ample in-class practice with the activities that will help them plan their introductions, it's time to begin working on conclusions. The function of a conclusion is to restate and reinforce the thesis statement of the composition. To do this, a concluding paragraph should do at least some of the following:

- Summarize.
- Offer a solution or recommendation.
- Pose a question.

- Justify a position.
- Present a point of view.

The structure of the concluding paragraph reverses the structure of the introductory one: instead of GST, the concluding paragraph follows a TSG pattern. The thesis statement should be rephrased and positioned as the first sentence instead of the last.

TECHNICAL TIP

Here's how to structure a concluding paragraph:

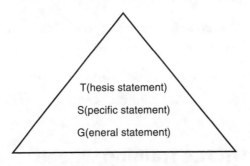

T(hesis statement)

S(pecific statement)

G(eneral statement)

Remind students that the last words in a paragraph or a composition will have the most impact on the reader; therefore, the concluding paragraph should contain its key points. After the thesis statement, students should write a specific statement that differs from the one they used in the introductory paragraph, followed by another general statement. Both should relate to, but expand on, statements in the introductory paragraph.

If students are having trouble rephrasing the thesis statements in their conclusions, you can provide them with some sample thesis statements and have them practice rephrasing them. You can also provide them with a list of synonyms for commonly used terms—if they've used *effect* in the original thesis statement, for example, they could use *impact* or *result* when they rephrase it. Another excellent way to convert an introductory thesis statement to a concluding one is to introduce it with a transition word or phrase such as *in conclusion* or *clearly*.

Here are examples of an introduction and conclusion following the GST and TSG formats on the topic of the monarch butterfly.

Introductory Paragraph

The beautiful colors and migration of the monarch butterfly have always been fascinating to scientists. Currently, there are both habitat and environmental factors that pose threats to this favorite flying insect. Even though historically the monarch butterfly population has come back from winter storms that threatened its existence, recovering from thoughtless actions of humans might prove to be more problematic.

Concluding Paragraph

Although monarch butterflies have bounced back from past threats caused by nature, the hazards caused by people may be too monumental for this favorite butterfly population to overcome. Concerns about the future of the monarch are valid and serious. It is imperative to address the dangers confronting this remarkable butterfly before it becomes extinct.

HOW TO DIFFERENTIATE MPO ACTIVITIES

If some of your students are struggling to complete an MPO, try providing them with the main ideas they'll use to organize their paragraphs. You can also provide some students with a thesis statement or the general or specific statements they'll use in their introduction and conclusion.

Writing a Biographical Essay: A Level 2 Example (Part 3)

Mr. Miller's class had spent several days on the G, S, and T activities, first as a whole class and then in small groups and individually. Diana was now ready to plan her own G and S about Theodore Roosevelt. She made some notes, using key words and phrases and abbreviations, for her G and S, using the dotted lines in the Details box for her Introduction. She already had her T, of course. Rather than copying it into the Details box for the Introduction, she only needed to put a *T* on one of the dotted lines.

When she was done, the Details box for her Introduction looked like this:

G: *powerful/exciting*

S: *26th pres./youngest (42)*

T:

The Details box for her concluding paragraph looked like this:

Rephrase T

S: *crusader/challenger*

G: *role model → 20th cent. pres.*

Make It a Composition: Drafting and Revising MPOs

Converting an MPO into a multiple-paragraph composition is a more challenging undertaking than turning an SPO into a single paragraph. When converting the MPO into a draft, students will need to use their notes to create general and specific statements for their introductions and conclusions, topic sentences for each of their paragraphs, and detail sentences. (Students will not be writing concluding sentences for each paragraph in a multiple-paragraph composition.)

Nevertheless, if you've helped them develop a well-thought-out MPO by following the steps in this chapter, converting it to a draft should be an efficient process. Students will already know what their topic is, the basics of what they want to say, and the order in which they want to say it. In the revision process, they can devote their mental energy to crafting interesting and varied sentences and using transitions to create a coherent and effective composition.

Students sometimes have trouble using transitions to create links between paragraphs. If that's the case for your students, remind them that they can use the different categories of transitions to connect their paragraphs, just as they've used them to connect sentences within a paragraph. See Table 5.1, "Transitional Words and Phrases," and our discussion of how to use transitions to link one paragraph to the next in the section called "Smoothly Flowing Compositions: Using Transitions to Link Paragraphs" in Chapter 5.

BE CAREFUL

As students convert their outlines into drafts and revise them, they may want to incorporate quotations from text they have read. For many students, figuring out how to integrate quotations appropriately and smoothly is a major challenge. If your students are having difficulty incorporating quotations into their multiple-paragraph compositions, review our discussion in the section of Chapter 5 called "Bring in the Authorities: How to Incorporate Quotations."

After teachers at New Dorp High School had been implementing TWR strategies for several years, the day of the Global History and Geography Regents exam suddenly looked very different. No longer did students simply write a few sentences, close their text booklets, and leave.

Toni-Ann and Dina remember their amazement—and that of their colleagues—when they saw their students spontaneously drafting outlines before starting to write their essay answers. Even more amazing was the fact that the students kept writing for the entire allotted time. Teachers who were used to leaving early on exam days, because students gave up so quickly, found they had to stay much longer than they'd planned.

Teachers were thrilled to see students putting the planning skills they'd learned in class to such good use and composing their answers with such confidence. When the scores on that year's Regents exam came back, there was a marked increase in the number of students who passed.

Three years after New Dorp adopted TWR strategies, the pass rate on the Global History and Geography Regents had risen from 64% to 75%. The pass rate on the English Language Regents had gone up from 67% to 89%. And the number of students who had to take the Regents repeater course—a cram course designed to help struggling students collect a graduation requirement—dropped by 89%, going from 175 students to only 20.

TO SUM UP

- Before trying to create MPOs, students need ample experience developing topic sentences, writing supporting details in note form, and constructing coherent paragraphs.

- Level 1 students can use these skills to create simple three- or four-paragraph MPOs for book reports and biographies.

- Students who are ready for multiple-paragraph writing but still need more support can use the Transition Outline, which has them write topic sentences for each paragraph.

- Introduce students in Levels 1 and 2 to MPOs by modeling the process of creating one.

- Assign topics to students who are still learning to create MPOs and provide guidance in selecting a topic for more experienced students.

- If students' MPOs require independent research, have them commit to a schedule with deadlines for each step of the process.

- Provide students with models of thesis statements that fit the type of MPO they're constructing, and have them include a plan of development that maps out the structure of the composition.

- Have students fill in the Main Idea and corresponding Detail boxes for each paragraph of the MPO in note form.

- To prepare students to write introductory paragraphs, introduce them to the GST formula—incorporating general, specific, and thesis statements—and have them practice distinguishing among and creating the three types of statements.

- Have students reverse the formula to TSG for the conclusion.

- Have students convert their completed MPOs to drafts, revise them by varying sentence structure, and use transitions to link paragraphs and sentences.

Notes

1. L. H. O'Hanlon, "Teaching Students Better Online Research Skills," *Education Week* (May 22, 2013), www.edweek.org/ew/articles/2013/05/22/32el-studentresearch.h32.html.

2. A. Lunsford and R. Connors, *The St. Martin's Handbook* (New York: St. Martin's Press, 1995).

CHAPTER 8

Take a Stand
Writing Opinion, Pro-Con, and Argumentative Essays

Ms. Randolph had asked her 10th-grade history class to write an essay taking a position on the Industrial Revolution: On balance, was it a positive or a negative development? She had asked students to consider both sides of the issue, choose one, and explain why they had done so.

Ms. Randolph noticed that one of her students, David, was looking particularly glum. He had been working on his essay for half an hour but had only managed to write three sentences, plus a quotation he'd taken from the textbook:

> *The Industrial Revolution was a positive development. There were new inventions and people could take railroads to places they wanted to go. Children had to work long hours and the workers couldn't take vacations. "The Industrial Revolution resulted in the most profound, far-reaching changes in the history of humanity."*

"David," Ms. Randolph said, "the first sentence is fine. But do these facts about child labor and workers not taking vacations support your argument that the Industrial Revolution was a positive development?"

David shrugged. "I guess not," he admitted.

"And what about this quotation?" Ms. Randolph asked. "It says the Industrial Revolution brought big changes, but does it say they were *positive* changes?"

David examined the quotation for a few seconds and then shook his head.

"How about putting the sentence about child labor in a different paragraph?" Ms. Randolph suggested. "And if you want to use a quotation, can you find one that supports your argument?"

David sighed heavily and took out a clean piece of paper to start over. Ms. Randolph hoped he'd figure out a way to organize his essay so that it clearly made a case for the Industrial Revolution as a positive development, summarized and rebutted the case on the other side, and smoothly integrated relevant evidence and quotations. But she wasn't particularly optimistic.

These days, teachers frequently assign opinion and argumentative essays to satisfy the requirements of the Common Core and other state writing standards. Children as young as third grade are expected to present their claims and convince a reader of their point of view. By sixth grade, they're supposed to be supporting their claims with evidence, and by seventh grade they should be acknowledging arguments on the other side. As we have discovered, even older students often struggle to write these kinds of essays if they haven't learned the appropriate language and structure.

Often opinion or argumentative writing is treated as a separate category that can be addressed only by having students take and defend positions on topics beyond the school curriculum—such as the pros and cons of school uniforms, video games, or chocolate milk. The best way to ensure that students have sufficient knowledge of the topic they're writing about, however, is to choose a topic they've already been studying. So stay alert for topics in the curriculum, at whatever grade level you're teaching, that lend themselves to pro-and-con treatments.

It's true that argumentative writing poses some distinct challenges, which we'll address in this chapter. But the strategies your students have been practicing—whether in the context of argumentative writing or not—are already building the skills they'll need to craft effective arguments:

- Completing sentence stems using *because, but,* and *so* develops students' ability to connect a **claim** to evidence, introduce a **counterclaim,** and describe cause-and-effect relationships.

- Using subordinate conjunctions such as *while* and *although* at the beginnings of sentences enables students to acknowledge or make a claim while simultaneously bringing in an opposing claim.

- Creating topic sentences and thesis statements enables students to identify the main points they want to make in an argument.

- Summarizing develops the ability to succinctly describe claims on both sides.

- Creating Single-Paragraph Outlines (SPOs) and Multiple-Paragraph Outlines (MPOs) helps students logically organize claims and evidence.

- Incorporating quotations and paraphrases during the revision process teaches students how to cite evidence for claims in an effective way.

As we emphasize throughout this book, however, these strategies will help students write well only if they have knowledge of what they're writing about. That applies to argumentative writing at least as much as to any other genre.

The Three Steps to Argumentative Writing: Opinion Pieces, Pro-Con Paragraphs, and Pro-Con Essays

Practicing writing opinion, pro-con, and argumentative pieces does the following:

- Develops analytical and logical thinking skills
- Helps students distinguish reliable sources from unreliable ones
- Improves organizational skills
- Teaches students to cite textual evidence effectively
- Develops the ability to assess and rank stronger and weaker arguments

As with other TWR strategies, these benefits will accrue whether or not students create a finished product. Planning and outlining an opinion, pro-con, or argumentative essay is a valuable exercise in itself—especially if it's embedded in the content of the curriculum.

In opinion and argumentative writing, the author is trying to convince a reader to adopt a certain point of view. In **pro-con** writing, the author lays out two sides of an issue and the evidence to support each but doesn't take a position. In terms of the skills required, opinion writing is the easiest—and generally assigned only to elementary students—followed by pro-con paragraphs and then pro-con essays. When you guide your students through these three types of writing, which we outline in the next section, you'll be preparing them for the considerable challenge posed by argumentative writing.

Working Up to Argumentative Writing

Opinion pieces are the least demanding of these types of writing because they allow students to present only one point of view on a subject, without bringing in arguments on the other side. Students must do more than simply state their opinions, however. They need to back up their opinions with reasons, although their reasons can be based on personal experience rather than evidence. For example, a student might write an opinion piece arguing that dogs make better pets than cats. He might talk about how loyal, affectionate, and obedient his own dog is. He wouldn't need to bring in and evaluate arguments against dogs (they need to be walked) or in favor of cats (they keep themselves clean).

Pro-con paragraphs are a significant step up: Each paragraph presents one side of an issue and the evidence that supports it. A student might write a pro paragraph arguing that the ambition of Alexander the Great was a positive trait, because he brought the benefits of Greek civilization to other lands. Then he could write a con paragraph arguing that it was a negative trait, because Alexander's conquest of foreign lands caused so much suffering.

In a pro-con essay—essentially, pro and con paragraphs with the addition of an introduction and a conclusion—students take a neutral stance, simply presenting the claims and evidence on each side. The thesis statement for a pro-con essay might say something like "Although some argue that Alexander's ambition was a positive trait, others say it led him to take actions that caused a great deal of suffering."

In an argumentative essay, students evaluate the evidence on both sides of a question, adopt the position they feel is stronger, and demonstrate why the evidence supports their position rather than the opposing point of view. The thesis statement might be the same as the one in the previous paragraph, except that the words *others say* would be omitted—if, that is, the student had decided that the bulk of the evidence supported a negative view of Alexander the Great.

The first three types of writing just discussed constitute a scaffold leading to the argumentative essay. In writing opinion pieces, younger students get practice listing reasons that support a claim. When crafting pro-and-con paragraphs, students learn to state opposing positions and present evidence that supports each one. If they actually agree with one side rather than the other, they get practice suspending their own opinions and putting themselves in the shoes of someone on the other side—a skill that will serve them well when they turn to argumentative writing and need to summarize an opposing viewpoint fairly.

When students adopt a neutral stance in a pro-con essay, they're developing the skill of distancing themselves from claims on each side, which will also come in handy in argumentative writing. The success of an argument depends on adopting a tone that is neutral but subtly persuasive to convince a reader that you've considered all the evidence fairly before taking a position.

Challenges of Argumentative Writing

When students ultimately engage in argumentative writing, it may seem that they're returning to the world of opinion writing in that they're stating what *they* believe. But there's a crucial difference between opinion and argumentative writing: Rather than starting with an opinion and finding reasons to back it up, students first need to consider the evidence on both sides and decide which is more convincing and why. This can be a challenge, but their practice in dealing with claims and evidence in their pro-con paragraphs and essays will help equip them for the task.

It may be difficult for students to come up with evidence to dispute every claim on the other side of an issue—for good reason. It's rare to find a question for which there are *no* good arguments on the other side. In real life—and in college—arguments can, and often should, take the form of agreeing in part and disagreeing in part. One popular text on college argumentative writing lists three ways of responding to others' ideas: *yes, no,* and *okay, but.*[1] We understand, however, that middle and high school students may be required to take a stance in an argumentative essay that doesn't allow for a nuanced *okay, but* position.

As challenging as it is to learn to write an argumentative essay, it's a skill that will serve your students well. It's the kind of writing that is most frequently assigned in college, and if students are encountering it there for the first time they'll be at a serious disadvantage. It's also a skill your students will generally find useful in later life in the workplace and personally. Of all the writing genres, it's the most effective at sharpening their analytical faculties. Learning to construct and defend an argument will force your students to think logically and critically.

Fact Versus Opinion: Introducing the Distinction

If you're teaching Level 1 students who are older—in middle or high school—you'll always want them to connect their claims to evidence. Allowing them to defend claims on the basis of their opinions rather than evidence could lead to bad habits that will be hard to break.

Elementary students may not be ready to bring in evidence to support their reasons. Nevertheless, it's important for younger students to develop an understanding of the difference between opinion and fact, because opinions won't be enough to support their arguments later on when they're writing argumentative essays. They'll need evidence.

Some topics don't lend themselves to reasons beyond the author's personal experience. If you ask your students to write an opinion piece about what the best holiday is, they're probably going to list the reasons *they* like Christmas or Thanksgiving. To help your students develop the skills that will help them write argumentative essays, you'll need to choose topics that lend themselves to reasoned debate, based on facts. And your students will need to have factual information they can draw on to support their opinions.

You can start introducing students to the fact-opinion distinction in the early elementary grades. In one of our partner schools, for example, a first grade teacher had her class collectively plan an opinion paragraph explaining why Play-Doh is an excellent product. As they came up with a topic sentence and details for the body, the teacher listed them on a whiteboard. Then she guided them through the process of coming up with a concluding sentence, producing an outline that looked something like this:

T.S. Why is Play-Doh a popular product?

1. easy to form shapes

2. doesn't stain or ruin clothes

3. not expensive

4. lots of new colors

C.S. Play-Doh is great!

During this kind of activity, a teacher can point out that the concluding sentence is an opinion, and the details on the numbered lines are facts that support it.

Conjunctions, Transitions, and Kernels: Laying the Foundation for Argumentative Skills

As the Play-Doh example demonstrates, you can introduce students to the fundamentals of opinion and argumentative writing at any skill or grade level. When students are working on sentence-level activities, activities with sentence stems—using conjunctions such as *because*, *but*, and *so*—give them practice in connecting claims to reasons, introducing an opposing view, and tracing cause and effect. Activities with transition words produce the same kinds of benefits.

When you have students practice argumentative skills, choose a topic that has two debatable sides. If the topic is also embedded in the content students are studying, conjunction and transition activities will deepen students' comprehension and spur them to think analytically about what they've learned.

All five categories of transition words and phrases can be helpful in presenting and evaluating reasons and claims (see Table 5.1) Students can learn to use the following types of transitions:

- Time and sequence transitions such as *in addition* and *finally* to list reasons and claims on each side

- Illustration transitions such as *for example* and *specifically* to provide examples of a general claim or introduce evidence

- Emphasis transitions such as *most important* or *certainly* to highlight their most important claims or underscore an argument

- Change-of-direction transitions such as *however* and *in contrast* to introduce or acknowledge opposing claims

- Conclusion transitions such as *thus* or *in the end* to signal that they're wrapping up an argument

Another sentence-level activity that can be adapted to build argumentative skills is sentence expansion: giving students a simple, active, declarative sentence with only one verb, along with question words to help them expand it. To make sentence expansion into an argumentative activity, make the kernel sentence you give students one that that takes a position. For example:

The Emancipation Proclamation helped them.

Whom? ....

When? ....

Where? ....

Why? ....

A student's expanded sentence might be as follows:

In 1863, the Emancipation Proclamation helped slaves because it changed the focus of the Civil War to include the abolition of slavery.

You might also give them a kernel that takes the opposite position. For example:

The Emancipation Proclamation didn't help them.

Whom? ....

When? ....

Where? ....

Why? ....

In 1863, the Emancipation Proclamation didn't help slaves because it applied only to slaves in states where the Union government had no control.

TECHNICAL TIP

Transition words and phrases that signal a change of direction are particularly useful when introducing a contrasting point, example, or argument. Change-of-direction transitions can come in the middle of sentences, as with *but,* or at the beginning of a new sentence, as with *however.* When one paragraph is devoted to a claim and the next to a counterclaim, tell your students they can introduce the first paragraph with *on the one hand* and the second paragraph with a change-of-direction transition such as *on the other hand.*

One type of change-of-direction transition—subordinating conjunctions—is particularly useful for thesis statements in pro-and-con or argumentative essays. If students learn to begin their thesis statements with words such as *although* and *while,* they'll be able to acknowledge two opposing claims. They'll also be able to avoid using the first person, which can detract from the authority of their argument.

For example, here's a claim stated in the first person, without acknowledging that there's another side to the argument:

> I believe that the minimum wage should be raised in every state.

Compare that to this thesis statement for a pro-con or argumentative essay that makes use of a subordinating conjunction:

> Although some argue that increasing the minimum wage would have a negative impact on the US economy, an increased wage would be very beneficial to lower-middle-class households.

Level 1 Example

Mr. Williams's elementary Level 1 class had been reading about the advantages and disadvantages of keeping animals in zoos as opposed to their natural habitats. To help students understand the debate and work on their writing skills, Mr. Williams gave them sentence stems that required them to supply a logical or evidence-based reason to support the pro-zoo side and explain what followed from that position. (The examples show sample student responses.)

Zoos are good for animals **because** _they protect endangered species from extinction._

Zoos are good for animals, **so** _people should continue to support them._

Since zoos educate visitors about conservation, _people learn to respect the environment._

Then he made the activity more challenging by asking them to consider an argument on the other side:

Zoos are good for animals, **but** _many people oppose taking them out of their native habitats._

Although some people believe that animals should not be captive, _others argue that zoos help some species survive._

Next Mr. Williams wanted his students to practice using transition words between sentences. Although the students weren't yet ready to write pro-and-con paragraphs about zoos, he wanted them to have experience creating the kinds of connections between thoughts that they would need to use during the drafting and revising stage.

Mr. Williams gave his students pairs of sentences that had no transition words connecting them. The students needed to choose an appropriate transition word for each pair and write it in the blank. To provide additional support, Mr. Williams provided a word bank of transition words for his students to choose from. (In the following examples, italicized words represent the students' responses.)

If zoos are closed, many animal species may become extinct. _For example,_ the numbers of gorillas and elephants have decreased because of poachers.

Zoos have improved over the years. _However,_ many animals show signs of distress.

Zoos have improved over the years. _As a result,_ animals live longer in them and are healthier.

Zoos can be good for animals. _On the other hand,_ zoos can't always replicate life in the wild.

Level 2 Example

When Ms. Alvarez's Level 2 history class was studying the presidency of Andrew Jackson, she gave them the following sentence stems to develop their argumentative writing skills. (Sample student responses are provided.)

> Andrew Jackson's opponents called his approach to government employment "the spoils system" **because** _it rewarded his supporters with government jobs for which they weren't qualified._

> Jackson threatened to use force if South Carolina disobeyed federal tariff law, **so** _he was able to preserve the union._

Ms. Alvarez then made the activity more challenging by introducing stems that required students to consider both pro and con considerations.

> **Although** Jackson railed against government corruption, _he ignored the corrupt actions of government officials during the relocation of Indians on the Trail of Tears._

> **While** Jackson's presidency pushed the nation further toward democracy, _his many vetoes made him appear power-hungry and dictatorial._

As Mr. Williams did with his Level 1 class, Ms. Alvarez also had students supply transition words to link sentences about Jackson's administration. Because her Level 2 students were more experienced writers, she had them come up with their own transition words rather than giving them a word bank to choose from. (Sample student responses are provided).

> Before Jackson, presidents had only vetoed legislation they believed to be unconstitutional. _However,_ Jackson vetoed legislation as a matter of policy.

> Jackson believed that it would be impossible to assimilate Indian tribes into white society. _Moreover,_ he knew that whites wanted Indian lands.

> Jackson was the first president who did not come from a wealthy family. _For example,_ he was born in a log cabin.

Short Takes: Using Pro-and-Con SPOs as Stepping-Stones

Before asking your students to undertake an entire argumentative essay—which would raise two points of view and present evidence for and evaluate each—give them ample practice planning a single paragraph that takes a position backed by evidence. Then they can practice planning another single paragraph that takes the opposing view—again, backed by evidence. These activities will prepare them to write a pro-con essay neutrally presenting two points of view. They will also equip students for the more difficult task of deciding which position is stronger and why, which they'll confront when they write argumentative essays.

Identify and Rank the Reasons: Matching Opposing Topic Sentences With Details

A great way to introduce the skill of constructing arguments on two sides is to provide two SPOs that have only the topic sentences filled in, one pro and one con. At the bottom, provide a list of details, in note form, and ask students to match each detail to the appropriate topic sentence.

Level 1 Example

Mr. Williams gave his class an activity on zoos shown in Exhibit 8.1. One topic sentence took a pro-zoo position and the other an anti-zoo one. Students had to look at the list of details provided and copy them onto the appropriate dotted lines.

EXHIBIT 8.1

Select appropriate details from the list to support each topic sentence.

T.S. Zoos provide benefits to both animals and people.

1. ....
2. ....
3. ....
4. ....

T.S. Zoos are harmful to animals and should be abolished.

1. ....
2. ....
3. ....
4. ....

provide food + water + shelter
small exhibits / little room to roam (ex. elephants)
captivity → distressed
natural animal behavior / could never survive in wild
care for injured + abandoned
protect endangered species → ↓ animals extinct
visitors tease
educate visitors / conservation

Source: Copyright © 2017 The Writing Revolution.

Level 2 Example

Ms. Alvarez gave her history class the activity about the presidency of Andrew Jackson shown in Exhibit 8.2.

Since you're essentially doing the research for them, your students can focus on deciding which evidence supports which claim. When embedded in the content of the curriculum, this activity will also encourage your students to engage in close reading of texts. They'll need to think carefully to decide which details from the text go with which topic sentence.

Tell your students they should list the strongest reason or evidence last, where it will have the most impact on the reader. That means they'll need to decide which detail provides the strongest argument in support of each claim. We've seen the activity of creating pro-and-con SPOs spark great classroom debates about which piece of evidence is strongest and why. This practice evaluating the strength of claims will also prepare students for deciding which position they want to take when it's time to write argumentative essays.

EXHIBIT 8.2

Select appropriate details from a list to support T.S.

T.S. Andrew Jackson, the seventh U.S. president, was a <u>hero</u> of the common man.

1. ....
2. ....
3. ....
4. ....

T.S. President Jackson should be remembered as an <u>unjust leader</u>.

1. ....
2. ....
3. ....
4. ....

spoils system = rewarded unqualified supporters
nullification crisis/preserved union
relocation of Native Americans → Trail of Tears
many vetoes = power-hungry/dictatorial
Tariff of Abominations
voting ↑→ spirit of equality
self-made man
born in log cabin

Source: Copyright © 2017 The Writing Revolution.

Both Sides Now: Creating Pro-and-Con SPOs From Scratch

Once students have become familiar with matching details to the appropriate topic sentence and evaluating their strength, they can start creating their own SPOs. They'll need to come up with a topic sentence and a concluding sentence for each paragraph—pro and con—and write supporting details in note form on the dotted lines of each outline.

Level 1 Example

Mr. Williams decided his class was now ready to build on their previous activities by creating their own SPOs on the subject of zoos—one pro and one con. To do this, they would need to create topic and concluding sentences.

Because they were still in the early elementary grades, the students hadn't yet been introduced to all three strategies for creating effective topic and concluding sentences—using one of the sentence types, using an appositive, and using a subordinating conjunction. Mr. Williams had taught them only the first strategy, using one of the four sentence types: a command, a question, an exclamation, or a statement. He reminded them of each type before they began filling out their SPOs.

Exhibits 8.3 and 8.4 show examples of the SPOs students produced.

EXHIBIT 8.3

Single-Paragraph Outline

Name:_____   Date:_____

T.S. _Zoos benefit animals in many ways._____

_____

_____

1. provide food + water + shelter

2. care for injured + abandoned animals

3. protect endangered species → ↓ animals extinct

4. educate visitors / conservation

C.S. _Let's keep animals safe in zoos!_____

_____

Source: Copyright © 2017 The Writing Revolution.

EXHIBIT 8.4

Single-Paragraph Outline

Name: _____ Date: _____

T.S. __It is cruel to keep animals in zoos.__ _____

_____

_____

1. small exhibits / little place to roam (ex. elephants) ....

2. captivity → animals distressed ....

3. natural animal behavior / could never survive in wild ....

4. visitors tease animals ....

C.S. __Boycott the zoos!__ _____

_____

Source: Copyright © 2017 The Writing Revolution.

Level 2 Example

Ms. Alvarez also had her history students plan their own pro-and-con SPOs on Andrew Jackson. She required most students to come up with different topic sentences than the ones she had supplied for the matching activity, and she reminded them of all three ways to create one. But she allowed those who needed more support to reuse the topic sentences she had provided.

Similarly, she required some, but not all, students to come up with some different details than the ones she had provided. She reminded them to write in the sources for the details in note form, so that they would be able to provide citations or incorporate quotations from the text if and when they turned their SPOs into paragraphs.

Consider the Alternatives: Planning and Writing Four-Paragraph Pro-Con Compositions

The next phase in developing the skills necessary for the argumentative essay is to have students turn each of their pro-and-con SPOs into a single MPO that considers both sides but doesn't take a position. To do that, students need to add introductory and concluding paragraphs.

As we discussed in Chapter 7, the first steps in creating an MPO are to select a topic and develop a thesis statement. If students are choosing a new topic at this point, make sure that it's both debatable and manageable—neither too broad nor too narrow. Ask yourself if students will be able to handle the amount of evidence or research required.

As we mentioned previously, in a pro-and-con MPO the thesis statement simply acknowledges that there are arguments on both sides. If the topic is, for example, the pros and cons of zoos, a simple Level 1 thesis statement might be:

There are arguments for and against zoos.

If the topic is the presidency of Andrew Jackson, a Level 2 thesis statement might be:

Although some observers have praised Andrew Jackson as a hero of the common man, others have denounced him as a corrupt tyrant.

As with any MPO, students will also need to come up with general and specific statements to go along with their thesis statements. Their introductions will follow the GST formula:

1. General statement

2. Specific statement

3. Thesis statement

Their concluding paragraphs will reverse the order so that it becomes TSG: first a rephrasing of the thesis statement, followed by a new specific statement, and then a new general statement.

The body paragraphs of the MPO can be based on the pro-and-con SPOs that students have already completed. If they took sides when drafting their pro-and-con SPOs, of course, they may need to modify the language they used. For example, the concluding sentence of the con SPO on zoos—"Boycott the zoos!"—wouldn't work as part of a neutral discussion of the arguments for and against zoos in a pro-con essay. Instead, the sentence would need to say something such as "Opponents of zoos have urged people to boycott them."

This would be a good point to introduce your students to words that will come in handy in presenting arguments that are made by others. For example, they can describe those on one side as *proponents* and those on the other as *naysayers.* Instead of simply using the verb *said,* they can use verbs such as *argue* and *maintain.* Before students create their MPOs, have them practice constructing thesis statements that use words such as these to introduce two sides of an argument.

Table 8.1 Argumentative Nouns and Verbs

Nouns	Verbs
advocates	advocate
adversaries	argue
challengers	believe
critics	claim
defenders	criticize
naysayers	debate
opponents	defend
proponents	propose
supporters	support

Examples:

Proponents of imperialism argue _____.

Critics of Andrew Jackson believe _____.

Advocates of US expansion claim _____.

Source: Copyright © 2017 The Writing Revolution.

Table 8.1 provides a list of terms teachers at one of our partner high schools posted in their classrooms to help students craft their pro-con thesis statements. It also came in handy when students were drafting and revising their MPOs into pro-con compositions and later on when they wrote argumentative essays.

Level 1 Example

Mr. Williams introduced his class to the idea of creating a pro-con MPO by modeling the process as a whole-class activity. Exhibit 8.5 shows what the MPO looked like.

Level 2 Example

Ms. Flynn was teaching a Level 2 government class that was studying security, surveillance, and the issues associated with national identification cards. She had assigned her students several articles on the topic and led class discussions on the advantages and disadvantages of national ID cards.

EXHIBIT 8.5

Multiple–Paragraph Outline (4 Paragraphs)	

Name: _____   Date: _____

Topic: _Zoos_ _____

Thesis Statement: __Although some believe that it's cruel to keep__ __animals in captivity, others believe that zoos are beneficial for__ __animals and visitors.__ _____

Main Idea	**Details**
Introduction ¶ 1	....
Con ¶ 2 (Counter-claim) ↓ T.S.	....
Pro ¶ 3 (Claim) ↓ T.S.	....
Conclusion ¶ 4	....

To help students analyze the issues and prepare for a pro-con MPO and essay, she gave them the following sentence stems (examples shown with student responses):

Many Americans support the idea of a national ID card **because** _they believe national ID cards would keep Americans safer._

Proponents support the idea of a national ID card, **but** _critics fear it would be a violation of their rights._

She also gave them transition activities to help them practice linking sentences. Since Ms. Flynn's students were more experienced writers, she didn't just ask them to choose an appropriate transition and insert it into a blank. She gave them a transition word at the beginning of the second sentence and required them to complete the rest of the sentence.

Advocates support the idea of a national ID card, **so** _Congress should introduce legislation to create them._ National ID cards would benefit law enforcement. **For example,** _it would be easier for police to identify criminals._

EXHIBIT 8.6

Multiple–Paragraph Outline (4 Paragraphs)	

Name: _____   Date: _____

Topic: __National ID Cards_____

Thesis Statement: __The intense debate regarding national ID cards must evaluate the benefits of security versus the right to privacy.__

Main Idea	Details
Introduction ¶ 1	G .... S .... T ....
Security ↓ ¶ 2 T.S.	same for all / hard to fake w/hologram .... incl thumb print → prev. crim. from using .... will keep US safer / ↓ identity theft .... emerg. med. info. ....
¶ 3 Right to Privacy ↓ T.S.	for citizens / non-citizens? illegals? .... slow everything ↓ .... invasion of privacy / govt. .... ACLU = ↓ freedom / track ind. / cost $ $ ....
Conclusion ¶ 4	rephrase T .... S .... G ....

Critics of national ID cards strongly believe that the government should not have the ability to track it citizens. **On the other hand,** _supporters believe that the cards would be a deterrent for criminals._

Although national ID cards could decrease criminal behavior, _law-abiding citizens would be made to feel like suspects._

She then asked each student to create an MPO that presented the arguments on both sides. Exhibit 8.6 shows what one of her students produced.

Make Your Case: Planning and Writing the Five-Paragraph Argumentative Essay

If they wrote opinion pieces in elementary school, your students practiced taking a position and backing it up with reasons. In crafting pro-and-con SPOs, they learned to support their positions with evidence, and they also got experience switching sides. When they moved on to the pro-con MPO, they developed the ability to stand back and describe each side neutrally.

Now, with the argumentative essay, they'll have to take a position once again—but they'll need to consider the evidence on both sides before deciding which position to take. They'll also need to explain that decision convincingly by presenting evidence and quotations in ways that buttress their position.

Level 1 students are generally not yet experienced enough to plan and write argumentative essays. Therefore, have them keep practicing opinion and pro-con pieces until they've developed the skills necessary for argumentative writing.

Know Where You're Going: Using an MPO to Plan an Argumentative Essay

Before your students can start creating an MPO for an argumentative essay, they have to decide which position they're taking. To do that, they'll need to understand the facts and evidence on both sides quite well. You'll want to ensure that the class has spent ample time studying and discussing the topic first.

Let your students know that when creating a thesis statement for an argumentative essay, they should put the argument they're making last. For example, if a student wants to argue that the Industrial Revolution was essentially a positive development, she would *not* write, "Although the Industrial Revolution brought many benefits, its drawbacks cannot be ignored." Instead, she would end the sentence with the point that the Industrial Revolution brought benefits, as in this sentence: "Although the Industrial Revolution had its drawbacks, the many benefits it brought cannot be ignored."

The standard argumentative essay consists of five paragraphs. In addition to the introductory and concluding paragraphs—which will use the GST and TSG structures—the essay will have three body paragraphs:

- A first body paragraph that lays out the background of the issue accurately but in a way that tends to support the position the author is taking
- A second body paragraph that presents the counterclaim and the evidence to support it
- A third body paragraph that provides the strongest evidence for the author's point of view

Students should generally not attempt to raise a claim and **rebut** it in the same paragraph. In our experience, that approach often leads to a fragmented and confusing presentation of the information. Some teachers may be concerned that students will lose their train of thought if they need to wait until a separate paragraph to respond to a claim. If students have created an effective outline before writing, however, they won't have that problem.

The challenge of the argumentative essay is to be both persuasive and fair. Students will need to convince the reader that their own position is the stronger one but at the same time summarize the opposing point of view accurately. Their experience writing neutral pro-and-con paragraphs and essays will help them with the latter task.

Back Up Your Claim: Incorporating Evidence and Quotations

Because students themselves are unlikely to be experts in the topics they're writing about, they'll need to introduce citations, paraphrases, and quotations. Although they should cite authorities supporting both sides, they'll need to show why those who support their own side are more convincing.

Certain words are particularly well suited to framing quotations or paraphrases in argumentative writing. When introducing a quotation or summary that supports their claim, students will want to do whatever they can to make a case for their perspective. They should characterize the speaker in a way that indicates her authority and use stronger verbs than *says* or even *believes* to introduce the statement. More powerful verbs include *endorses, asserts, emphasizes, reminds us,* and *affirms.*

For example, a student seeking authority in arguing against harsh forms of juvenile justice could simply write the following:

Professor Owens said, "Programs like boot camps have been shown to be ineffective in preventing juvenile delinquency."

Think how much more mileage the student could get out of that quotation by framing it with an appositive that indicates the speaker's authority and using a verb that links the speaker's ideas to the student's own point of view:

Professor Owens, a nationally recognized expert on juvenile justice reform, endorses this view when she writes, "Programs like boot camps have been shown to be ineffective in preventing juvenile delinquency."

Illustration transitions are also effective ways to introduce textual evidence and quotations.

*Experts in the field of juvenile justice reform agree that harsh measures don't work. **For example,** Professor Owens has written that boot camps "have been shown to be ineffective in preventing juvenile delinquency."*

At the MPO stage, your students won't actually be incorporating citations and quotations, but they will be making notations on their outlines referring to them. Later, during the revising stage, they'll integrate that evidence when they convert their MPOs into drafts and final copies. To prepare your students for that task, it's a good idea to have them practice introducing quotations and other evidence in a way that supports a claim.

Level 2 Example

Ms. Flynn felt that her students were now ready not only to summarize the arguments on both sides of the debate on national identity cards but also to take a position and evaluate claims on the other side. She asked her students to think carefully about the arguments on each side and then choose the position they personally felt was stronger. Their next task was to craft a thesis statement that stated their chosen position and acknowledged a counterclaim.

She also wanted her students to start citing sources for their evidence and quotations, so she told them to be sure to note them on the details lines of their MPOs. Exhibit 8.7 shows the MPO that one of her students produced.

When your students are beginning to write argumentative essays, you may decide to limit them to four paragraphs. They'll omit the paragraph

EXHIBIT 8.7

Multiple–Paragraph Outline (5 Paragraphs)

Name: _____   Date: _____

Topic: __**National ID Cards**_____

Thesis Statement: _____ **Although National ID cards may provide**
more security, they will violate our right to privacy._____

Main Idea	Details
Introduction ¶ 1	G .... S .... T ....
violate privacy (claim) ↓ **T.S.** ¶ 2	ID card = "Band Aid" / misplaced "quick fix" (ACLU) cost billions / logistical nightmare (Wadhwa, Forbes) slow everything ↓ traffic jams + delays false sense of security / easily forged (Schneier, Minneapolis Star Tribune)
¶ 3 **security (counter-claim)** ↓ **T.S.**	will keep U.S. safer thumb prints on card → deter criminals (Washington Post) database → help law enforcement could safeguard voting (Washington Post)
¶ 4 **violate privacy (claim)** ↓ **T.S.**	invasion of privacy / govt. "internal" passports → lack of freedom / hurt law-abiding citizens (ACLU) easily monitor + track individuals → intrusiveness possible discrimination + harassment (ACLU)
Conclusion ¶ 5	Rephrase T S .... G ....

Source: Copyright © 2017 The Writing Revolution.

right after the introduction that lays out the problem and introduces their own argument. Instead they'll have only two body paragraphs: the first presenting the counterclaim and evidence and the second presenting their own claim and evidence.

Eventually, students will become experienced enough at planning and writing argumentative essays that they'll be able to produce them fairly quickly—even when asked to do so on a timed exam. We've seen students spontaneously sketch an outline before writing a well-crafted argumentative essay on the New York State Regents exam when they've been given articles that lay out pro-and-con positions on an issue.

If you're a middle or high school teacher, the following scaffold will help you guide your students through the activities that lead to the crafting of a five-paragraph argumentative essay.

Argumentative Writing Scaffold for Middle and High School

The following activities will enable students to organize their material more effectively, think more analytically, and write more coherently as they prepare to tackle argumentative assignments.

Sentence-Level Strategies

- Use *because, but,* and *so* activities to present students with a sentence stem that takes a position and have them:

  - Connect a claim to evidence (*because)*, introduce a counterclaim (*but*), and describe cause-and-effect relationships (*so*).

  - Use subordinating conjunctions (*while, although,* and *even though*) to write sentences that acknowledge a counterclaim and state a claim.

  - Use sentence expansion activities to present students with a kernel sentence that takes a position.

Single-Paragraph Outline

- Practice writing topic sentences for paragraphs that take a position, using the three ways of creating them:

  - Sentence type (e.g., a command can be used to make a call for action)

  - Subordinating conjunction

  - Appositive

- Match topic sentences taking opposing positions with appropriate details.

- Use an SPO to plan a paragraph that takes a position backed by evidence.

- Use an SPO to plan a paragraph that takes an opposing view, again backed by evidence.

Revision

- Practice using transitional words and phrases to present and evaluate reasons and claims:

  - Time and sequence: to list reasons and claims on each side

  - Illustration: to provide examples of a general claim or introduce evidence

  - Emphasis: to highlight important claims or underscore an argument

  - Change of direction: to introduce or acknowledge opposing claims

  - Conclusion: to signal wrapping up an argument

Multiple-Paragraph Outline

- Practice writing pro-con thesis statements that present two sides of an argument *without* taking a position.

- Write a four-paragraph pro-con MPO that lays out two sides of an argument *without* taking a position (e.g., "Although there are many who argue that an extended school year will benefit students, opponents believe that additional time will not produce meaningful student results.")

- Practice writing argumentative thesis statements that present two sides of an argument and take a position, placing the position the student is taking at the end of the sentence.

- Write a five-paragraph MPO that lays out two sides of an argument and takes a position:

  - **First body paragraph:** lays out problem and discusses its importance, while introducing author's argument

  - **Second body paragraph:** presents the counterclaim and the evidence that supports it

  - **Third body paragraph:** rebuts the counterclaim and provides evidence for the author's point of view

It should be clear by now what a monumental task David faced when Ms. Randolph asked him to write an argumentative essay on the Industrial Revolution. He hadn't been taught how to plan and write pro or con paragraphs or how to combine them into a pro-con essay. He hadn't had any practice assessing which arguments supported his position or evaluating which were stronger and weaker. He hadn't been shown how to construct a thesis statement that presented his position while also acknowledging an opposing argument. Nor had he learned how to create an MPO to guide him through this complex process. He didn't have an arsenal of transitions, nouns, and verbs to draw on to help him make his argument smooth and convincing.

David was just expected to somehow figure all of this out for himself. No wonder he had looked so discouraged.

TO SUM UP

To be able to plan and write an effective argumentative essay, your students will need to be able to do the following:

- Understand the difference between fact and opinion.

- Present a claim using emphasis, illustration, and conclusion transitions to underscore an important point, provide an example, or indicate they're coming to the end of their argument.

- Use conjunctions such as *but*, subordinating conjunctions such as *although*, and change-of-direction transitions such as *however*, to signal that they're introducing a different point of view.

- Use nouns and verbs that are well suited to argumentative writing (see Table 8.1).

- Integrate quotations with appropriate introductions and explanations.

- Determine which piece of evidence is the strongest and therefore should be mentioned last.

- Use the SPO to plan two paragraphs presenting opposing points of view and evidence to support them.

- Use the MPO to plan pro-con essays that present two points of view and supporting evidence in a neutral manner.

- Use the MPO to plan four- or five-paragraph argumentative essays that take a position backed by evidence.

Note

1. G. Graff, C. Birkenstein, and R. Durst, *They Say/I Say: The Moves That Matter in Academic Writing* (New York: W. W. Norton, 2012), p. 56.

CHAPTER 9

A Gauge and a Guide
Assessing Students' Writing

Yan Lin, a first-grader in a public school in New York City, is the child of Chinese immigrants who speak little English. Like the other 31 students in her class, she is still learning the language herself. And like every other child in her school, Yan Lin comes from a family whose income is low enough to qualify her for a free or reduced-priced lunch.

In September, Yan Lin's teacher asked her and her classmates to write a paragraph about school. The teacher did this partly to determine what kind of help students needed with their writing and partly to provide a benchmark for progress in the future. Exhibit 9.1 shows what Yan Lin wrote.

In May, after nine months of implementing TWR strategies, Yan Lin's teacher gave her another assessment, using the same prompt. Exhibit 9.2 shows what she wrote.

The difference between these two assessments—each of which Yan Lin wrote without teacher assistance—is dramatic. By the end of May, Yan Lin had learned where sentences should begin and end. She knew how to use conjunctions, expand sentences, and add relevant details. After developing many Single-Paragraph Outlines (SPOs) and practicing the scaffolding activities with her class, she had also learned how to begin a paragraph with a topic sentence and end with a concluding one.

Yan Lin's pre-assessment in September provided her teacher with guidance about what skills she already had and what skills she still needed to acquire. And her post-assessment in May revealed—to her and to her teacher—how far she had come in just one school year.

EXHIBIT 9.1

School: PS 20
Name: Yan Lin
Grade: 1-247
Date: Sept. 22, 2015

Writing Pre-Assessment

Directions: Please write a paragraph about school.

Today I go to school and teacher siad get the noetbook and I write my name, grade, and. I put the noetbook inside the, Table and teacher gif me the paper. And about the school seven sentenens, And I eat lucnh and. I go to the jam and come. To class to do homework and. Reid the book and soon I go home.

EXHIBIT 9.2

School: PS. 20
Name: Yan Lin
Grade: 1-247
Date: May. 31, 2016

Writing Assessment

Directions: Please write a paragraph about school.

A school is a place where we learn. I like school because, I can play with my friends. We do math in school and we write in school. We draw in school and we go to gym to play balls. Everyday we have homeworks. We need things to use in school. In my opinion school is great.

Finding the Right Yardstick

Assessing your students' writing does the following:

- Enables you to pinpoint skills individual students have or need to acquire

- Provides information about the skills you need to focus on for your class as a whole

- Helps you set goals for individual students and your class

- Tracks the progress your students make over the course of the year

Measuring the quality of student writing may be one of the most difficult tasks in all of educational assessment. Although it's easy to see the improvement in Yan's writing, that's not always the case. Give two teachers the same student essay, and it's possible you'll get two wildly different evaluations of its effectiveness.

True, some aspects of writing are easy to quantify—total number of words or sentences written, number of correctly spelled words, or proper grammar and usage—but others are highly subjective. Studies that have compared ratings of the same piece of writing by more than two readers have found little consistency in their scores.[1]

Even experts have disagreed on the best way to go about measuring writing quality. "Over the years," one such expert has written, "writing assessment research and practice has suffered from dissension at every point, on almost every feature of stimulating, producing, evaluating, and teaching writing."[2]

A number of factors can interfere with the accuracy of writing assessments:

- *Decoding.* When students are asked to write in response to a written prompt, some may have difficulty decoding it.

- *Background information.* Lack of knowledge about the topic causes some students to have trouble understanding the prompt.

- *Computers.* If students write their responses on computers, those who are comfortable using computers will have an advantage over those who aren't.

- *Mechanical errors.* There are questions about how much weight to give to errors in capitalization, punctuation, spelling, and grammar. Although students need to master these aspects of writing, technical mistakes can be distracting and lead teachers to overlook the progress students may have made in organizing their ideas or using complex sentence structures.

Difficult as the task may be, however, it's crucial that you assess the quality of your students' writing throughout the school year. Regular assessment will not only measure your students' progress, it will also inform your decisions about what to teach and where to focus your efforts.

Standardized tests are unlikely to give you the kind of feedback you need. They may not be measuring the writing skills you're trying to teach, and in any event the results of state tests are usually not available until months after they've been administered. Consequently, they'll provide little or no help in diagnosing your students' needs.

In evaluating student writing, many teachers use rubrics with a number of criteria rather than simply issuing a single grade or score. Standard rubrics can help you focus on specific elements of your students' writing, but even their criteria tend to be too broad. Typically, rubrics are more useful for ranking students as opposed to providing specific suggestions for moving them toward the objectives you have set.

TWR has developed assessment tools that are tied to the specific strategies we teach. Unlike other tests and rubrics, they will provide you with valuable information about how to use those strategies to help students progress from one level to the next.

ASK THE EXPERTS

Although there's been disagreement among experts about the best way to evaluate students' writing, one meta-analysis of 136 studies of writing assessment came up with some recommendations:

- Use assessments to provide students with feedback about the effectiveness of their writing.
- Teach students how to assess their own writing.
- Monitor students' progress in writing on an ongoing basis.

The report also listed six best practices in writing assessment:

- *Allow students to use either paper or computers to write—or have them use the medium you know they're used to.* Studies have shown that students who use computers score better that those who write by hand—unless they have little experience using a computer to write, in which case they score worse.
- *Try not to judge a writing sample on the basis of the students' handwriting.* Teachers tend to give lower scores to students with less legible handwriting.
- *Mask the students' identities when scoring papers.* Teachers may subconsciously give a student a higher or lower score depending on the quality of her previous work or her race, gender, or ethnicity. One easy way to guard against subconscious bias is to have students put their names on the back of a paper rather than the front.

- *Put students' papers in random order before scoring them.* Some studies have suggested that raters' scores will vary depending on the quality of the essays they've just read. If a rater has just read a series of high-quality essays, she's more likely to give the next piece of writing she reads a lower score—and vice versa.
- *Collect multiple samples of each student's work.* The quality of a student's writing often varies with the type of composition. Some are better at writing narratives, and others may excel at argumentative or informational essays.
- *Try to ensure the reliability of your scoring.* Much of what goes into scoring a piece of writing is subjective. To control for that, schools can offer training for teachers on how to assess writing. Administrators can provide benchmark descriptions or examples for each point on a scale, have multiple teachers score each paper, and base scores on more than one writing task.

The authors of the meta-analysis acknowledge that assessing writing—like teaching it—is a labor-intensive business. But they note that studies have found that briefer comments can be more effective than extensive feedback, because students are less likely to get discouraged. This is one area in which TWR strategies and abbreviations can come in handy: once a student knows what's expected and understands that a notation such as "app in TS" means "use an appositive in your topic sentence," it's relatively easy for a teacher to provide brief but effective feedback.[3]

Don't Guess—Assess!

What makes a piece of writing good? John Langan, the author of a popular series of high school and college textbooks on writing, has identified four criteria that are used by most of us, consciously or not, to answer that question.[4]

Structure

- Are the sentences in the paragraph and the paragraphs in a longer composition arranged appropriately?

Coherence

- Are the sentences (and paragraphs) logically related to one another?

Unity

- Does every sentence support the main idea of the paragraph?
- Does every paragraph support the main idea of the composition?

Sentence Skills

- Are the sentences grammatically correct and clear?
- Are there compound and complex sentences in addition to simple, active ones?
- Is there a variety of sentence starters?

As you've seen throughout this book, TWR strategies are designed to guide students to incorporate all of these elements into their writing.

But how will you know whether the strategies are actually working to move your students toward that goal? You'll probably have a general sense of how things are going, but to get a clear picture you'll need to measure your students' progress at regular intervals. We've created two basic types of assessments that are keyed to our strategies. You should give each kind of assessment to your students two or three times a year.

The first type, the **independent writing sample,** is designed to give you an overall sense of whether your students' writing is improving: Are they using run-on sentences? Repeating themselves? Remembering to include a topic sentence at the beginning of a paragraph? Do they go off topic and add irrelevant information?

The other type of assessment is **diagnostic worksheets** for Levels 1 and 2. These assessments generally provide students with a text to read and then ask them to perform a series of writing tasks based on the text, using TWR strategies. By using assessments that are tied to the specific TWR strategies you've taught, you'll be able to determine whether your students have mastered those strategies and are ready to move on or whether they still need more practice. The Level 1 and 2 diagnostic assessments can found online at http://twr-resources.thewritingrevolution.org/.

The independent writing and diagnostic assessments will help you decide which specific objectives you should focus on in the months ahead and which TWR strategies your students need to learn throughout the year. But you should also refer to the list of suggested grade-level objectives in Chapter 10 for guidance. They will give you an idea of what we've seen teachers cover during the course of a year. Depending on the ability of your class, you may choose to move slower or faster.

In middle and high school, where students have multiple teachers, English or social studies teachers may be the instructors who administer the assessments. If that's the case, those teachers should communicate their recommendations about which strategies and activities to focus on to other content area teachers, using the list of objectives in Chapter 10 as a guide. The Single Paragraph Checklist, available online at http://twr-resources.thewritingrevolution.org/, is helpful in summarizing the results for other teachers.

Get the Big Picture: Independent Writing Assessments

At the beginning, middle, and end of the school year, you should give your students an independent writing assessment. The teachers who partner with us have their students write a paragraph in response to a prompt, with no guidance or assistance—the way Yan Lin's first-grade teacher asked her to write about "school."

Another way of administering an independent writing assessment is to have students write in response to a text or multiple texts—or even a text and a video. At least one of our partner schools has experimented with this approach successfully. Each method of assessment has advantages and disadvantages.

Short and Sweet: Using a Free-Standing Writing Prompt

If you're going to use a simple prompt, be sure your students have sufficient background information to write about it coherently. Remember: People can only write well about subjects they know well. You'll need to give all students in the class or grade the same prompt to write about, so you have to ensure that all of them have the necessary background.

A prompt can consist of a single word or a brief phrase. Some prompts we have found to be useful are:

Our school (or school or how to survive in school)

Friends (or friendship or how to make / keep friends)

Hopes for the future

A role model

A favorite gift or possession

Why do we study the past?

Personal goals

Depending on the experience, ability, and access to background information of your students, independent writing prompts can be summaries, a narrative, or a description.

One way to present a topic is to write it on the board and read it aloud without elaborating. Alternatively, you can provide more explanation. For example, rather than simply asking students to write about "a role model," you could give them the following paragraph:

A role model is someone you admire for having qualities you would like to have. He or she is a person whose behavior or achievements you respect. Think about someone you consider a role model, and write about why that person is special to you. You may choose someone you know or someone you have read about. You may choose someone who is alive today or someone who is no longer here but has made a lasting impression on you.

Many other subjects could work well as prompts, and you as the teacher are the best judge of what your particular students are likely to be able to write about. A word of caution, though: try to avoid prompts that are apt to yield lists, such as "winning the lottery" or "my favorite things." Also avoid topics that provide a sentence starter. If the topic is "a great school trip," for example, many students will start the assignment with those four words. Simpler phrases such as "school trip" or "role model" make better topics.

Bring in a Text: Having Students Write in Response to What They've Read

You may decide you'd like to have your students write in response to a specific text rather than a general prompt. There are several reasons why teachers might prefer this approach—but there are also potential pitfalls.

Using a Text: The Pros

Having students write about a text simulates more closely the kind of writing students will be asked to do on state assessments toward the end of the school year. Generally, Common Core–aligned state writing tests give students a passage to read and ask them to write in response to it, citing evidence from the text. The tests may also ask students to read two different texts and compare them, or to watch a video and read a text on the same subject and draw on both in their answers. You may want to give students assessments that ask them to write in response to multiple sources, as they will need to do on state-mandated tests.

Another advantage of providing students with a text is that some may find it hard to come up with ideas in response to a vague prompt such as "friendship." They may have more to say if they're given a text to read first and then a prompt that is based on it.

Faculty members at one of our partner schools in Washington, DC—Truesdell Education Campus, a high-poverty school with many English language learners—devised their own text-based assessments. For kindergarteners and first-graders, teachers read aloud a book called *How Rocket Learned to Read* and then asked students to explain in writing how the main character—a dog—learned to read. They were allowed to draw a picture to go along with their writing.

Students in second grade and up were expected to read texts on their own—some borrowed from existing assessments—and then write in response to them. Second-graders, for example, got a text about blizzards from an interim assessment created by The Achievement Network.

The prompt asked them to "explain why people should stay inside during a blizzard" and to support their answers with two important details from the text. Seventh- and eighth-graders got texts taken from practice tests released by PARCC, one of the two consortia that have developed Common Core–aligned tests.

Using a Text: The Cons

It's important to understand that using texts as a basis for writing assessments brings its own potential problems. Students may have trouble decoding—the complex process of converting the alphabet into words in order to understand their meaning. A lack of background knowledge can also prevent students from understanding the text. If that's the case, the assessment will not be measuring your students' writing skills.

One way to guard against this problem is to use a text that students are already familiar with or perhaps a new text on a topic they have recently studied in depth. Alternatively—or in addition—you can read through the text with students and ensure they understand it before you ask them to write in response to it. You'll need to be careful, though, not to shape students' thinking and writing in a way that prevents you from getting a clear idea of what they can do independently.

The Mechanics: How to Administer an Independent Writing Assessment

Whether you choose to give students a free-standing prompt or a text-based one, the first thing you'll need to do is explain the purpose of the activity. Let your students know that the assessment will help you understand where they need help to further develop their writing skills. Remind them to do their best work, so you'll be able to see what they already know how to do and what they still need help with.

To get an accurate picture of what students can do independently, try not to give them any help during the assessment. If a student has difficulty spelling a word, for example, ask him to use his best guess and provide the correct spelling only if he's unable to continue. If a student can't get started, you might have to provide him with a topic sentence. If you do need to provide help as a last resort, be sure to note on the assessment exactly what was done with teacher support.

Your instructions must be explicit. First, make it clear that students should keep their writing samples brief. If you're teaching first-graders, you may want to tell them that it's fine to write just a sentence or two. Even with older Level 1 and some Level 2 students, it's best to limit the samples to a single paragraph. You'll be asking them to revise and edit their work later, and that may feel overwhelming if they've written at length.

If students have learned how to develop an SPO, be sure to remind them to complete one before writing, so that you can assess their outlining skills. If Level 2 students have been taught to develop Multiple-Paragraph Outlines (MPOs), you might allow them to write up to three paragraphs—after completing an outline, of course. Be sure that students' outlines are attached to their writing samples.

It's also important to let your students know how much time they will have to complete the assessment. You may want to limit younger students to half an hour, and even older students should never be allowed more than one class period. Many will finish in less time, so make sure you have some independent activities on hand for them.

To evaluate students' ability to revise and edit their work, hand the assessment samples back to them the next day. Tell them that the best writers often find ways to improve and correct their work and that it's important for you to see what they would like to change in their writing. It's not necessary to have students make final copies of the assessment, unless their revised and edited version is illegible.

When the allotted time for revision and editing is up, collect each student's sample and date it. After assessing it, put it in a folder dedicated to each student's work, so you can carefully monitor individual progress.

You probably won't want to use the same prompt for all three independent writing assessments at the beginning, middle, and end of the school year. Using the same prompt—as Yan Lin's teacher did for her first-grade class, with the word *school*—does provide the clearest basis for comparison. However, it's not realistic to expect students to come up with fresh ideas about most topics three times during the year.

When evaluating writing assessments, you have two options. The first is our Single Paragraph Checklist. It will tell you where each student stands and can be filled out fairly quickly.

The second option is our Independent Writing Rubric, which covers essentially the same criteria as the checklist but provides a numerical score for each student. The rubric allows for a maximum score of 16 points. These two tools can be found on our website, http://twr-resources .thewritingrevolution.org/

Another document, the Independent Writing Tracker, also online at http://twr-resources.thewritingrevolution.org/, provides a scoring row for each student in your class, along with three columns: one for the beginning of the year, one for the middle of the year, and one for the end.

The independent writing assessments, when combined with the checklist or the rubric and the tracker, will not only give you a record of each individual student's development but also an overview of your class's progress. The results will help you determine what your instructional goals should be for the next few months, for the class as a whole and for specific students.

Home in on the Details: Assessing Specific Strategies

Independent writing assessments will give you a general sense of how—or whether—your students are making progress in their writing and if they're using TWR strategies even when not specifically prompted to do so. But to get a clearer picture of how far they've come and how far they still have to go, you'll also need to give them assessments that show whether they've mastered the specific strategies you've taught them.

TWR has developed a set of diagnostic tools designed to be given two or three times a year. They test students' proficiency in a range of strategies, from sentence skills to outlining and revising, with some assessments intended for Level 1 students and others for Level 2. These diagnostic assessments will evaluate not only what you've taught your students over the preceding months but also their cumulative growth in using the strategies since they were first introduced to the method. The diagnostic assessments can be found online at http://twr-resources .thewritingrevolution.org/.

Some of our diagnostic tests, especially those for Level 2, ask students to write in response to a text. As with independent writing assessments based on a text, you won't be able to accurately assess students' writing skills unless they have sufficient decoding ability, background knowledge, and vocabulary to understand the texts and the associated prompts.

We have also developed rubrics that you can use to assess your students' performance on the diagnostic assessments. Those rubrics can be found online at http://twr-resources.thewritingrevolution.org/.

You'll need to decide which diagnostics to administer depending on the strategies you've chosen to teach and the objectives you have for your particular students. If your students have been introduced to the MPO, for example, use an assessment that focuses on their ability to plan introductions and conclusions, develop categories, and supply sufficient and appropriate details.

Stragglers and Speed Demons: Using Assessments to Differentiate Your Instruction

Inevitably, some of your students will be moving at a different pace from the majority—either faster or slower. Some may pick up certain skills easily but struggle with others. Assessing your students' progress frequently will help you identify those who are either lagging behind or coasting and enable you to differentiate your instruction so that you're providing each student with the support or challenge she needs.

Throughout this book, we've provided suggestions for ways to differentiate TWR activities. For example, if a student is having trouble combining sentences on her own, you can provide a suggestion, such as "use an appositive." If a few students have mastered creating an SPO while most are still struggling, you can provide a topic sentence for the majority but require those who are zooming ahead to come up with topic sentences on their own. As you become increasingly familiar with TWR strategies and activities, you'll no doubt devise other ways to adapt strategies to the needs of your individual students.

Looking Backward: Maintaining Student Portfolios

You'll want to keep a folder—or a portfolio, if you prefer—of samples of each student's work, including independent writing and diagnostic assessments, throughout the year. This collection of writing samples can provide a dramatic reminder of the progress a student has made—progress that otherwise might be overlooked.

For example, Erika, a student at a large urban high school, produced the writing sample in Exhibit 9.3 at the beginning of her ninth-grade year.

Erika spoke English as a second language and qualified for special education services. Obviously, her ability to express herself in writing was significantly below what we would expect from a ninth-grader. It's far from clear what she was trying to communicate in her response.

During her ninth-grade year, Erika was introduced to TWR strategies for the first time. Her teachers taught her how to construct coherent, complex sentences, how to use transition words to connect them, and how to plan and outline a paragraph before she wrote.

Toward the end of the school year, in May, Erika independently wrote the paragraph in Exhibit 9.4, after studying the Mongol Empire.

EXHIBIT 9.3

School: _____

Name: _Erika_____

Grade: _9_____

Date: _____

Writing Pre-Assessment

Directions: Respond to the task below in a complete paragraph containing a topic sentence, supporting detail sentences and a closing sentence.

Task: Explain why we study the past.

_____We study the past because it part of_

something that they will ask in for job

as teacher.

_____

_____

_____

_____

_____

_____

Source: Copyright © 2017 The Writing Revolution.

EXHIBIT 9.4

_____The Mongol Empire was a powerful empire_
that had a great impact. Genghis Khan, a
powerful leader, was the universal ruler.
Their military was successful and well trained
because they used the Mongol war machine and
many techique. In addition, the Mongol empire
expaned because they conquered China, India
and Russia. Obviously the mongol had many
achievement. For example, during the Pax
Mongolia there was safe trade and religious
freedom. Clearly they were magnificant empire.

Source: Copyright © 2017 The Writing Revolution.

Before Erika wrote this paragraph, she used an SPO to plan. Although her writing isn't perfect, she is now using appositives and transitions, and she's marshaling evidence in support of her claims. She has included topic and concluding sentences.

If Erika's teacher hadn't kept her writing from early in the year, it might not have been so apparent how much progress Erika had made. These samples served as a powerful motivator for both Erika and her teacher.

Erika's writing kept on improving, by the way. In her junior year she was able to achieve a grade of 81 on the American History and Government Regents test, a challenging New York State exam that is required for graduation.

TO SUM UP

- When assessing student writing, be aware of the factors that can interfere with an accurate picture—such as a student's difficulty decoding or understanding the text used as a prompt and the frequency of mechanical errors.

- Administer brief independent writing assessments in response to a prompt or a text three times a year to measure students' independent writing ability.

- Assess students' ability to develop outlines and to revise their work.

- Use the Single Paragraph Checklist, Independent Writing Rubric, or Independent Writing Tracker to record individual students' progress and that of the class as a whole.

- Administer diagnostic assessments two or three times a year to gauge whether students have mastered the specific strategies you've recently taught them.

- Use data from assessments to help set your objectives for the class as a whole and differentiate instruction to meet students' individual needs.

- Maintain a folder or portfolio of each student's work to track progress made over the year.

Notes

1. S. Graham, K. Harris, and M. Hebert, *Informing Writing: The Benefits of Formative Assessment. A Carnegie Corporation Time to Act Report* (Washington, DC: Alliance for Excellent Education, 2011).

2. Ibid., Foreword.

3. Ibid.

4. J. Langan, *English Skills, Instructor's Edition.* 6th ed. (Boston: McGraw-Hill, 1997).

CHAPTER 10

Putting the Revolution Into Practice

Combining Our Sequence With Your Judgment

After we've finished leading a course or a workshop, we're frequently surrounded by teachers who are brimming with questions. "How long should we keep teaching fragments?" they want to know. "When can we start the Single-Paragraph Outlines?" "Should I stay with sentence expansion until I think the students have mastered it?" "How do we know when to start writing introductions?"

We certainly understand that teachers want clear guidelines about the pacing of the strategies and at what point they should move on to the next one. We wish we could provide them with straightforward answers, but writing instruction doesn't work like that. There's no one-size-fits-all approach. You'll need to assess where your students are at the outset, what they need, and how fast they should proceed through the sequence of strategies.

First Things First: Background Knowledge and Mastery of Mechanics

When deciding how long to spend on any one TWR strategy or activity, you'll need to exercise your own judgment about your students' oral and written language abilities. Among the factors to consider are the following:

- How much background knowledge do your students have?

- How extensive or limited is their vocabulary?

- How familiar are they with the conventions of standard English grammar?

- Do they have a sense of what they need to include in their writing so that it's understandable to a reader?

In addition—as we noted in Chapter 3—writing, more than any other task, taxes a student's working memory and executive functions. Remember that there's a limit to how many things we can hold in our working memory. If your students are still struggling with the mechanics of writing—handwriting, spelling, usage, and so on—they won't have the space in working memory to simultaneously think about higher-level aspects such as purpose, meaning, audience, word choice, and syntax. Before they can address those considerations, their lower-level skills will need to have reached a point where the mechanics are not absorbing most of their attention.

Make the Most of It: Weaving Writing Instruction Into Content Instruction

Remember that, as a general rule, whatever writing activities you give your students should be embedded in the content you're teaching. The only exception is if you're introducing a new TWR concept, in which case you can use content that all your students are familiar with—topics such as holidays or the seasons. Otherwise, if you're teaching about the empire of Mali, for example, your writing activities, including sentence-level work, should be about the empire of Mali. You'll be adapting TWR activities and templates to your particular content, drawing on and reinforcing the material your students have been reading and discussing.

To teach writing skills, you don't need a separate writing block during which students may be producing a narrative about a trip they took or an argument piece on school uniforms. In fact, it's far more effective to weave writing into regular instruction and embed it in curricular content than to teach it in a separate block. Rather than having to transfer skills they've acquired while writing about an unrelated subject—a transfer that often doesn't happen—your students will be developing skills and content knowledge simultaneously. *Writing isn't just a skill, it's also a powerful method of teaching content.*

Keep in mind that the *content* of TWR activities is what drives their rigor: the same format can challenge students at different grade levels, depending on the content. For example, if you've been teaching kindergarteners about butterflies, you might have them do a *because, but,* and *so* activity orally on caterpillars and cocoons. If you're teaching an AP American history class, you can also give your high school students a *because, but,* and *so* activity—but you'll have them do it in written form and focus on the effectiveness of the New Deal. The form of the exercise is the same, but the latter activity would obviously be far beyond the capacities of the kindergarteners.

Similarly, the principles of organizing and planning Single-Paragraph Outlines (SPOs) and Multiple-Paragraph Outlines (MPOs) don't differ significantly from one grade level or ability level to another. It's the content that makes the task more challenging.

Leave No Strategy Behind: Bringing Activities Along as Students Progress

Throughout this book, we present TWR strategies in a linear fashion. In this chapter, we'll be describing a sequence of instruction, with one activity following the next. But when you teach, you'll progress through the strategies in a cumulative fashion rather than a linear one.

The idea is not to get all students to master a particular strategy and then move on, leaving that strategy behind. Because content and writing skills are so interconnected, "mastery" will depend as much on the content you're teaching as on any particular strategy. So you'll want to keep moving through your curricular sequence, bringing previous strategies into your instruction and using them alongside others as the content becomes more challenging. As we'll discuss in more detail, you can always modify strategies for students who are struggling.

Laying a Strong Foundation: Sentence-Level Activities

As we pointed out in the Introduction, sentences are the foundation for all writing. If students haven't learned to write a clear, coherent sentence, they'll never be able to write a clear, coherent paragraph or essay. And sentence-level activities can be just as challenging for students as lengthier writing assignments—sometimes even more challenging.

All students, regardless of their grade or ability level, need to practice crafting various kinds of sentences. Throughout this book, you've seen multiple examples of TWR sentence activities for all levels and in all subjects.

If you're teaching beginning writers, English language learners, and the many students who write the way they speak, the first step is to make sure they understand what a sentence is. It's not enough to get them to repeat an abstract definition, such as "a sentence expresses a complete thought." They will need ample practice in distinguishing between complete sentences and fragments—and turning fragments into complete sentences. They'll also need practice in correcting run-on sentences.

Even if your students are more proficient writers, you'll still want to introduce them to the whole range of TWR sentence strategies. The difference is that your pace can be faster. Level 2 students can also do much of their sentence-level work in the context of expanding unelaborated paragraphs and improving their own writing in response to your specific feedback. Give them sentence activities as comprehension checks on tests, quizzes, and exit slips.

Generally, all students should practice at least some sentence activities daily, orally and in writing, whether through the kinds of checks we just listed or through do-now activities, stop and jots, turn-and-talks, or homework. When students are ready to develop outlines, continue to include regular practice with sentences in your lessons. As students start converting their outlines into drafts, they can use what they've learned in the sentence activities as tools for revision.

Don't Skip Steps: Scaffolding an Outline

The same pacing advice is true for introducing the various TWR outlines. Don't skip any of the scaffolding steps; just change your rate for more able students. Make sure, for example, that your students have had practice identifying and constructing topic sentences before you ask them to create one for an SPO.

It's important to provide your students with plenty of practice and demonstrations to get them to the point where they'll be able to craft varied sentences; plan and develop cohesive, coherent paragraphs and compositions; and revise their writing effectively. Each activity and assignment needs clear objectives.

You may be tempted to let your students just plunge into a piece of writing without going through all these steps, figuring they can just plan and revise on the fly. After all, don't experienced writers do that? The answer is that some do and many don't. Especially for more analytical and longer forms of writing—books, for example—many accomplished writers find outlining to be essential, and all professional writers take time to revise.

Beyond that, mature, competent writers are able to juggle numerous factors simultaneously, so that composing becomes a recursive process. They may fine-tune their sentences as they go, replacing a word here and omitting a comma there. They may repeatedly shift the order of paragraphs and ideas. But these writers can draw on ample experience as well as deep knowledge of both written language and their topic. They may be equipped to draft, revise, and even plan their writing more or less simultaneously.

The great majority of the students we work with, however, lack that experience and level of knowledge. They need to approach the task one step at a time, while continuing to practice previously learned strategies, in order to produce an effective piece of writing. As with sentence activities, even after your students have become experienced at creating outlines, you'll want them to keep practicing the scaffolding activities that helped them arrive at that point. For example, you can have them write a topic sentence or thesis statement as a do-now, comprehension check, or exit slip.

One Topic, Many Strategies: Using Strategies Concurrently

One way to have students keep practicing strategies you've already taught is to bring in several different strategies while teaching a single book or topic. This is, in fact, the optimal way to use the strategies once your students have become familiar with several of them.

The following examples illustrate how to use this approach with Level 1 and Level 2 students. In both cases, the strategies help students develop their writing or prewriting skills while simultaneously deepening their understanding of content.

Level 1 /Elementary Example

If you're teaching kindergarten or first grade and you've read the book *Rocket Learns to Read* aloud to the class, you can give students a phrase—orally—and ask them if it's a sentence or a fragment. For example, you might say:

> "The yellow bird"... What does that tell us about the yellow bird? Does it tell us what it did?

When the students respond by saying "no," you can tell them that means it's not a complete sentence; it's a fragment. Then you can ask them to turn the fragment into a sentence. They might respond:

The yellow bird taught Rocket to read.

You can then have students complete sentence stems—again, orally. This activity will not only check students' comprehension but also develop their ability to provide extended responses. Make sure that students respond in complete sentences, not just with the phrase that follows the stem.

You'll want to start with *because,* which is usually the easiest of the three conjunctions for students to grasp. For example:

Rocket learned to read because _____.

Students might respond:

Rocket learned to read because *the bird taught him.*

You can then move on to the other conjunctions, one at a time:

Rocket learned to read, but *he didn't want to at first.*

Rocket learned to read, so *he felt very proud.*

Another strategy you can use to develop comprehension and language skills is to have the students ask questions about the story or the illustrations in the book. For example, students might say:

How did Rocket feel when the bird flew south?

Why did Rocket get interested in the story the bird read to him?

Level 2/Secondary Example

If your class has been studying Sumer, Babylon, and Hammurabi, you might give them the following *because, but,* and *so*—shown with possible student responses:

Hammurabi created a written code of laws because *he wanted to impose order on Babylon.*

Hammurabi created a written code of laws, but *most Babylonians couldn't read them.*

Hammurabi created a written code of laws, so *there was a decrease in crime.*

You could also have students develop test questions about the content using expository terms:

Explain the purpose of a written code of laws.

Enumerate the reasons why a code of laws was needed.

Describe how social class influenced punishments.

Next, you could give your students stems beginning with subordinating conjunctions and have them develop complete sentences, such as in the following examples:

If Hammurabi had not developed a written code of laws, *he would have failed to unite Babylonia.*

Although Sumer's city-states were defeated, *the Babylonian Empire adopted many of their ideas and practices.*

If students have been introduced to SPOs, give them a topic sentence and ask them to complete an SPO. More able students can go on to convert the outline into a paragraph.

T.S. Sumerians created one of the first civilizations.

1. *cuneiform = system of writing @2300 BC / maps scientific info / clay tablets*

2. *number system = basis today (60) for measuring time & geometry*

3. *architecture = arches / columns / ramps / pyramid shape*

4. *written code of laws*

C.S. *The contributions of Sumer had a great influence on later civilizations.*

Different Strokes for Different Students: How to Use TWR to Differentiate Your Instruction

Virtually every class encompasses a range of student ability—sometimes a wide range. One of the most challenging aspects of teaching is accommodating all of those levels without going over some students' heads while boring others.

Keep an Eye Out for Struggling Students

As we've demonstrated throughout this book, TWR activities easily lend themselves to differentiation. It's not necessary to come up with a completely different version of the activities or use different content for students of varying abilities—in fact, that approach risks leaving struggling students permanently behind. What's important is that you have a clear idea of what students are supposed to be learning and a good sense of whether all students have mastered it.[1]

Along with the formal assessment tools we described in Chapter 9, frequent comprehension checks—for example, in the form of sentence-level activities—will help you determine who is mastering what. Inevitably, some students will be struggling with the writing strategy the class is practicing or the content they're learning, or both. When that happens, it's crucial to provide prompt feedback and intervention to bring students up to speed as much as possible. That can be accomplished by following some of the suggestions in the next section.

How You Can Adapt the Same Strategy for Students at Different Levels

We've described how you can differentiate many of the strategies as we've introduced them. But to recap, here are some examples:

- *Sentence expansion.* Ask fewer question words of students who are having difficulty. For example, give all students a kernel such as "They rebelled," but ask some students *who, when, why,* and *where* while asking others only *who* and *when.*

- *Because, but,* and *so.* Give all students the same stem—for example, "The British invaded the colonies"—but ask some students to provide complete sentences for all three conjunctions while asking others to write a sentence for only one or two conjunctions.

- *Combining sentences.* Give all students the same group of short sentences to combine into one long one, but provide some students with hints that will help them construct the long sentence. You might ask them to use an appositive or insert a conjunction. (Be sure that you ask them to use only the strategies they've already learned.)

- *Appositives.* Ask all students to supply an appositive to describe a person, place, or thing, but give some students a list of words and phrases to choose from.

- *Revising unelaborated paragraphs.* Give all students the same bare-bones paragraph, but give some students fewer instructions on how to revise it. For example, you might give some students a list of six things to do and limit others to only one or two, such as "improve T.S. and C.S."

- *SPOs.* Have all students complete an SPO, but provide some students with the topic or the concluding sentence while asking others to come up with those sentences independently. You might also require some students to use only key words and phrases for their notes on the dotted lines, while others use abbreviations and symbols as well.

- *MPOs.* Have all students complete an MPO, but provide some students with the categories they'll need to organize their paragraphs while having others come up with their own categories. You can also provide some students with the thesis statement or the general or specific statements to include in their introduction and conclusion.

Sequence of TWR Strategies

We suggest you introduce TWR strategies in the sequence outlined in this section. The pace at which you move through this sequence will depend on the following factors:

- Grade level

- The particular abilities of your students

- Whether your students have been taught TWR strategies in prior grades

- The grade level at which TWR strategies were first introduced

The sequence assumes that students are being introduced to the method in first grade. If that's not the case for your students, you'll need to adjust accordingly. You don't want to assume that simply because a student is in 9th or 10th grade, she already understands the concept of a sentence or how to plan and construct an effective paragraph. We know from our experience that many high school students have yet to acquire these skills. All students who are being introduced to the method for the first time, no matter their grade level, should begin with sentence-level strategies and activities and proceed through the sequence in order.

It's also important to notice that the sequence is cumulative: The activities for each grade incorporate those introduced in all previous grades. So the activities that appear in the elementary grades in the following sequence should also be a regular part of instruction for all middle and high school students—for those who are old hands as well as for those who are new to the method. When they're embedded in the content of the curriculum, these activities not only teach writing but are also a powerful method of teaching subject matter.

The beginning-of-the-year independent writing assessment you administer will help you determine your instructional priorities and objectives. Although you'll probably find a range of skill levels, you'll need to focus on the skills the majority of your students need.

Grade 1

Sentence Activities

- Converting fragments to sentences*
- Sentence expansion (*when, where, why*)*
- Sentence completion with the words *because* and *but**
- Sentence types (statements and questions)*
- Ending punctuation
- SPOs and paragraphs as a class*

*Orally

Grade 2

All of the sentence activities for Grade 1 should be included in addition to the following activities.

Sentence Activities

- Converting fragments to sentences
- Correcting run-ons
- Scrambled sentences
- Sentence expansion (using all question words)
- All sentence types
- Sentence completion with the words *because, but,* and *so*
- Subordinating conjunctions to introduce dependent clauses at the beginning of a sentence (*after, before, when,* and *if*)
- Sentence combining (two or three sentences)

Outlining and Paragraph Activities

- Brainstorming or relating details (written as key words and phrases) for a given topic sentence and filling in an SPO as a class (narrative and expository text structures)
- Distinguishing topic sentences from supporting sentences

- Generating a topic sentence from given details written as key words and phrases, using the sentence-type strategy

- Selecting relevant details from a list to support a given topic sentence

- Using conclusion transitions and, in narratives, time-sequence transitions

Grade 3

All of the sentence activities for Grades 1–2 should be included in addition to the following activities.

Sentence Activities

- Subordinating conjunctions (to introduce dependent clauses at the beginning of a sentence); add *whenever, even though, although,* and *since*

- Transitions; add illustration transitions

- Sentence combining (two, three, and four sentences)

- Appositives

- Creating a new sentence that follows a given sentence, using a given transition (e.g., "The colonists struggled during the winters. For example, _____." "Global warming is causing the oceans to rise. As a result,_____.")

- Proofreading and editing for commas, capitalization, and punctuation

Outline and Paragraph Activities

- Developing topic sentences using all three strategies (sentence types, appositives, and subordinating conjunctions)

- Transforming key words, abbreviations, and symbols into sentences, and vice versa

- Using common abbreviations on detail lines of SPO

- Using symbols on detail lines (/, =, →, <, >, and +)

- Clustering details that have been derived from brainstorming, from relating a sequence of facts, or from a given list into categories or a logical or chronological order

- Improving given topic and concluding sentences

- Varying vocabulary

- Revising and editing an unelaborated paragraph, first as a class and then in pairs or small groups when given explicit instructions

- Outlining and then drafting and revising paragraphs that use narrative, compare-contrast, problem-solution, and opinion text structures

Grade 4

All of the activities for Grades 1–3 should be included in addition to the following activities.

Outline Activities

- Using additional symbols when appropriate for detail lines on outlines and for margin notes
- Converting a given paragraph into an SPO

Sentence and Paragraph Activities

- Subordinating conjunctions (to introduce dependent clauses at the beginning of a sentence); add *unless* and *while*
- Underlining key words and phrases in a given paragraph
- Creating SPOs for text structures introduced in third grade and adding descriptive, cause-effect, and separate pro-and-con SPOs
- Revising unelaborated paragraphs and students' own work, given specific instructions
- Practicing with all types of transitions
- Correcting errors in verb **tense** and **number agreement** in given sentences and paragraphs and then in their own writing
- Using all transitions (time-and-sequence, conclusion, illustration, change-of-direction, and emphasis) in sentence activities and inserted in paragraphs when appropriate
- Single-sentence and SPO summaries
- Transition Outlines or MPOs without thesis statements (book reports, biographies)

Grade 5

All of the activities for Grades 1–4 should be included in addition to the following activities.

Outline Activities

- Three- and four-paragraph MPOs for neutral pro-con compositions

- Developing thesis statements
- Completing segments of MPOs as a class (scaffolding activities)

Sentence and Paragraph Activities

- Citing evidence from text using illustration transitions
- Combined Outline summaries

Grade 6

All of the activities for Grades 1–5 should be included in addition to the following activities.

Outline Activities

- Transitions within and between paragraphs
- Developing main ideas for MPOs (biography, cause-effect, compare-contrast, problem-solution, pro-con)

Sentence, Paragraph, and Composition Activities

- Using the Revise and Edit Checklist to have students check their own work (see Appendix E)
- Developing various types of MPOs (e.g., compare-and-contrast, cause-and-effect, four-paragraph neutral pro-con)
- Modeling introductions and conclusions
- Introduction and conclusion scaffolding activities

Grade 7

All of the activities for Grades 1–6 should be included in addition to the following activities.

Outline Activities

- Developing a five-paragraph MPO that takes a position backed by evidence

Sentence, Paragraph, and Composition Activities

- Practicing introductions and conclusions for varied text structures
- Embedding and framing quotations
- Paraphrasing text

Grade 8

All of the activities for Grades 1–7 should be included in addition to the following activities.

Outline Activities

- Developing a thesis statement from a given topic
- Constructing an MPO independently from a given topic

Sentence, Paragraph, and Composition Activities

- Developing introductions and conclusions independently

Grades 9–10

All of the activities from Grades 1–8 should be included in addition to the following activities.

Outline, Sentence, Paragraph, and Composition Activities

- Given a debatable topic, researching both sides and developing a thesis statement for an argumentative essay
- Sequencing claims and counterclaims for argumentative essays
- Embedding quotations in a way that supports an argument
- Writing introductions and conclusions for argumentative essays
- Writing an argumentative essay on a given topic

Grades 11–12

All of the activities from Grades 1–10 should be included in addition to the following activities.

- Selecting a topic for an argument essay
- Researching the topic
- Writing an argumentative essay

Pacing Guides

The pacing guides for elementary, middle, and high school students demonstrate a general sense of when our partner schools introduce specific strategies. You'll find two sample pacing guides at the end of the book: Grade 3 (Appendix G) and Grades 7–12 (Appendix H). Both assume that this is the first year of TWR instruction. Guides for all grades—all of them assuming that TWR instruction is in its first year—can be found online at http://twr-resource.thewritingrevolution.org/.

Our pacing guides are fluid. You'll find that sometimes you'll quicken the pace, and at other times you'll need to backtrack. Bear in mind that your pace will be determined by your students' skill level, not their grade level. If you're teaching at the middle or high school level, you may be able to proceed through the sequence of strategies more rapidly than a teacher whose students are in the early elementary grades. But that may not be the case if your students are still learning English, have language-based learning disabilities, or face other challenges.

The pacing guides also don't address the content of the activities. As we noted previously, you should try to embed the activities as much as possible in the particular content that you're teaching. If you want to modify any of the pacing guides to fit your content, you can use the interactive versions available online.

More Than a Writing Method: Using TWR to Advance Your Students' Thinking

TWR isn't just a method of teaching writing—it's a method of teaching, period. It may be different from what you're used to, and it may take some adjustment. But teachers have told us that they quickly become comfortable with the method. Soon they integrate it into all of their instruction: presenting information, asking questions, checking comprehension, and setting goals. They use it routinely because they see it's producing dramatic improvements not only in their students' writing but also in their mastery of content, analytical abilities, and speaking skills.

Of course, you're more likely to see these results if other teachers in your school are implementing TWR's method at the same time, in as many subjects as possible. Ideally, you'll be collaborating with these other teachers, coordinating your pacing, and sharing observations and ideas.

But even if you're just working on your own, you can have a significant impact on your students' writing skills and their learning in general. If you provide your students with step-by-step strategies that improve their writing and thinking and expand their knowledge—and have them practice the strategies frequently and consistently—you'll be providing them with a precious gift that could well change the trajectory of their lives.

TO SUM UP

- To decide how long to spend on a particular TWR strategy or set of activities, you'll need to use your own judgment about your particular students' needs and abilities.

- By weaving TWR activities into regular instruction and embedding them in curricular content, you'll be able to use writing instruction as a powerful teaching tool.

- Continue using TWR strategies that you have already taught, alongside new ones that you are introducing.

- All students, regardless of grade or ability level, should begin with TWR sentence-level activities and practice all of the scaffolding steps that lead to creating outlines.

- Expect students to revise their own work and unelaborated paragraphs regularly. Give feedback that draws on the sentence strategies students have learned.

- Use several strategies concurrently while teaching a single book or topic.

- Differentiate TWR activities for students who are struggling or are racing ahead, without altering the basic form of the activity or using different content.

- Use TWR's pacing guides, in combination with beginning-of-the-year assessments, to determine goals for the year.

- Note that the pacing guide for each grade incorporates all TWR activities described as having been introduced in previous grades.

Note

1. Kim Marshall, "Rethinking Differentiation—Using Teachers' Time Most Effectively," *Kappan* (September 2016): 8–13.

Appendixes

A. Expository Writing Terms

Analyze

Tell about the main ideas or specific points, how they are related, and why they are important.

Comment

Discuss, criticize, or explain the subject.

Compare

Describe how things are alike.

Contrast

Describe how things are different.

Criticize

Evaluate on the basis of strengths and weaknesses.

Define

Give the meaning of a word or concept.

Describe

Present a word picture of a thing, person, situation, or series of events. Use sensory details that include seeing, hearing, smelling, touching, and tasting.

Discuss

Present ideas or opinions about or consider from various points of view.

Enumerate

Name or list specified points, such as main ideas or steps in a sequence, one by one.

Evaluate

Give your own judgment or expert opinion of how important an idea is; explain strengths and weaknesses, advantages, and limitations.

Explain

Make clear; interpret.

Illustrate

Explain by giving examples.

Interpret

Give the meaning by using examples or personal ideas.

Justify

Present good reasons why you think an idea is important; present facts to support a position.

Outline

Write main ideas and supporting details.

Relate

Describe how things are connected or how one thing can cause another.

State

Describe as clearly as possible.

Summarize

Sum up; present main points briefly.

Trace

Follow the progress or history of an idea.

B. Abbreviations and Symbols

Abbreviations

am or pm	before or after noon	lg	large
amt	amount	max	maximum
asap	as soon as possible	min	minimum
b/4	before	nat'l	national
b/c	because	p., pp.	page, pages
C.S.	concluding sentence	re:	regarding
ch	chapter	S	specific statement
cont'd	continued	sm	small
e.g. or ex.	for example	T	thesis statement
esp.	especially	T.S.	topic sentence
etc	et cetera: and so forth	vs	versus
G	general statement	w/	with
gov't	government	w/in	within
i.e.	in other words	w/o	without

addresses	(Ave., St.)	numbers	(four = 4)
days	(Mon., Tue., Wed., etc.)	states or countries	(NY, US)
measurements	(qt., ft., lb. tsp.)	titles	(Ms., Mrs., Mr., Dr.)
months	(Jan., Feb., Mar., etc.)		

Symbols

/	comma or period	< or >	less than or more than
=	means that	%	percent
+ or &	and	@	at
→	results in	$	money
*	important	↑ or ↓	increase or decrease
#	number	¶	paragraph

C. Listening Evaluation Checklist

E = Excellent   G =Good   F =Fair   NI =Needs Improvement

1. **Introduction**

   Brief/to the point/interesting to audience _____

2. **Topic sentence**

   Engages audience _____

   Clearly stated _____

3. **Supporting details**

   Sufficient _____

   Relevant _____

   Clear _____

4. **Vocabulary**

   Appropriate _____

   Varied _____

   Vivid _____

5. **Conclusion**

   Summary _____

   Refers back to main idea _____

   Emphasizes important point(s) _____

6. **Presentation**

   Waits for attention of audience

   Posture _____

   Relaxed _____

   Eye contact _____

   Voice loud enough _____

   Pauses effectively _____

D. Proofreading Symbols

∧	Insert
⊙	Insert period
⋏	Insert comma
⌄	Insert apostrophe
#	Insert space
¶	New paragraph
no ¶	No new paragraph
◡	Close up the space
b̲ cap	Capitalize
ℬ lc	Make lowercase (small letter)
ℓ	Delete
rwd.	Reword
←	Move according to arrow direction
ⓔⓘⓣⓇ	Transpose
[	Move to the left
]	Move to the right
ᶐ	Add a letter

E. Revise and Edit Checklist

Does Your Draft Follow Your Outline?

1. Is your topic sentence (or thesis statement) clearly stated? _____

2. Is your topic sentence interesting? _____

3. Are the supporting details in the best sequence? _____

4. Do the supporting details support your topic sentence? _____

5. Do your paragraphs support your thesis statement? _____

6. Is your conclusion clearly stated? _____

Can You Improve Your Sentences?

1. Did you use different types of sentences? _____

2. Are your sentences varied in length? _____

3. Are there sentences that should be combined? _____

4. Are there sentences that should be expanded? _____

5. Did you use transition words? _____

Can You Improve Your Style?

1. Are your words, phrases, and ideas repetitive? _____

2. Are your word choices vivid? _____

3. Are your word choices accurate? _____

Does Your Draft Contain Proofreading Errors?

1. Are there any run-on sentences? _____

2. Are there any sentence fragments? _____

3. Are there any spelling errors? _____

4. Is your punctuation correct? _____

5. Is your capitalization correct? _____

6. Do pronouns refer to the proper antecedents? _____

7. Have you checked tense agreement? _____

8. Have you checked number agreement? _____

F. Research Plan Time Sequence Sheet

Name: _____ Topic: _____

Steps	Date Due	Grade	Comments
Approval of topic			
Gather material			
Develop working thesis Develop categories for main ideas			
Preliminary bibliography			
Note cards due			
Develop MPO			
Write first draft (documentation and bibliography)			
Revise draft			
Revise draft			
Write final copy (one grade for content and one grade for mechanics)		C: M:	
Final Grade for Project			

G. Sample Pacing Guide (Grade 3)

September–October	November–December	January–February	March–April	May–June
• **Punctuation / Capitalization of First Word** – Capitalize first word, proper nouns; use commas in a list; and insert correct end punctuation. • **Sentences Versus Fragments** – Distinguish between a sentence and a fragment. – Correct fragments. – Identify and correct fragments and run-ons in paragraphs. • **Scrambled Sentences** – Rearrange sequences of words into sentences, adding correct capitalization and punctuation. • **Sentence Types** – Write a statement, question, exclamation, and command about a picture, topic, or text. – Write questions about a topic, picture, or text. • **Conjunctions (*because, but, so*)** – Complete sentence stems with *because, but, and so.* – Independently write sentences with *because, but, and so.*	**Continue previous sentence activities.** • **Sentence Expansion** – Expand kernel sentences with appropriate Q words: *who, what, when, where, why, and how.* – Determine whether a specified part of a sentence tells *who, what, when, where, why, and how.* • **Sentence Combining** – Combine sentences with compound subjects using pronouns, conjunctions (*and, but, because, and so*), and transitions when appropriate. • **Subordinating Conjunctions** – Complete sentences beginning with subordinating conjunctions *after, before, whenever, even though, since, and if.* – Practice writing T.S.s with subordinating conjunctions.	**Continue previous sentence activities.** • **Appositives** – Identify an appositive in a sentence. – Match appositives to noun phrases. • **Transition Words and Phrases** – Fill in correct transitions in paragraphs with blanks (time-sequence, illustration, change-of-direction, and conclusion). – Follow a given sentence with another one beginning with an illustration or cause-effect conclusion transition (*Colonists needed transportation for their goods. As a result,_____ Blacksmiths needed certain tools. Specifically,_____*	**Continue previous sentence activities.** • **Appositives** – Match an appositive to a noun or noun phrase. – Fill in blanks with appositives. – Given an appositive, write a sentence. – Given a topic, write a T.S. using an appositive. • **Transition Words and Phrases** – Insert transition words or phrases (time-sequence, illustration, change-of-direction, and conclusion) into given paragraphs. • **Single-Sentence Summary** – Given the subject, use question words without a kernel sentence to create a summary sentence.	**Continue previous sentence activities.** • **Sentence Combining** – Combine sentences using appositives, pronouns, and conjunctions.

Outline and Paragraph Skills

Single-Paragraph Outline – Brainstorm or relate details for a given topic sentence. – Generate SPOs and paragraphs as a class. – Distinguish a topic sentence from supporting details. – Given a topic, generate a T.S. – Select details from a list to support a given T.S., eliminating irrelevant details. **Note-Taking** – Introduce and model taking notes using key words and phrases.	**Continue previous paragraph activities.** **Note-Taking** – Convert sentences into key words and phrases. – Convert key words and phrases into sentences.	**Continue previous paragraph activities.** **Single-Paragraph Outline** – Use time-sequence and conclusion transitions. – Generate SPOs using key words and phrases. – Deconstruct a given paragraph into an SPO. **Note-Taking and Underlining Key Words and Phrases** – Introduce common abbreviations and symbols $(+, =, \rightarrow, /)$. – Model underlining key words in paragraphs. **Revise and Edit (Unelaborated Paragraphs)** – Revise unelaborated paragraphs as a class. – Revise with a peer with specific directions. – Put unelaborated paragraphs on board. Students suggest improvements. – Revise with peer without directions. – Have students improve their own work given specific directions.	**Continue previous paragraph activities.** **Revise and Edit** – Revise with peer without directions. – Have students improve their own work given specific directions.	**Continue previous paragraph activities.** **Single-Paragraph Outline** – Independently generate narrative or expository SPO and paragraph. – Practice developing T.S.s with appositives, subordinating conjunctions, and sentence types. – Practice outlining (SPOs) and writing drafts of compare-contrast, problem-solutions, and opinion text structures.

H. Sample Pacing Guide (Grades 7–12)

September–October	November–December	January–February	March–April
Sentence Strategies – Distinguish between fragments and sentences and correct fragments. – Rearrange words in scrambled sentences. – Identify and practice using the four sentence types. – Complete sentence stems with *because, but, so*. – Complete sentences beginning with subordinating conjunctions. – Identify appositives and match to noun phrases. **Single-Paragraph Outline** – Introduce key words and phrases, abbreviations, and symbols. – Practice scaffolding activities. – Construct SPOs as a whole-class activity.	**Continue previous activities.** • **Sentence Combining** • **Sentence Expansion** • **Single-Paragraph Outline** – Develop SPO and drafts independently. – Convert a paragraph into an SPO. – Write pro-and-con SPOs. • **Revision** – Improve topic and concluding sentences by using one of the sentence types, using an appositive, and beginning with a subordinating conjunction.	**Continue previous activities.** • **Revision** – Improve brief, unelaborated paragraphs (with no spelling, capitalization, or punctuation errors) following explicit directions such as expand, insert transition, combine, and improve T.S. and C.S. – Edit for mechanics, looking for errors in capitalization, spelling, grammar and usage, and internal and ending punctuation. • **Summarizing (Three Ways)** – Use a summary sentence. – Create an SPO. – Put them together to create a Combined Outline.	**Continue previous activities.** • **Multiple-Paragraph Outline** – Practice using key words and phrases, abbreviations, symbols. – Develop categories. – Select appropriate details. – Distinguish among general, specific, and thesis statements. – Write details for body paragraphs in note form.

May–June			
Continue previous activities. • **Multiple-Paragraph Outline** – Write general, specific, and thesis statements. – Write a complete body paragraph. – Practice text structures: compare-contrast, problem-solution, cause-effect, and pro-con.			

I. Single-Paragraph Outline

Name: _____ Date: _____

T.S. _____

_____

_____

1. ....

2. ....

3. ....

4. ....

C.S. _____

_____

_____

J. Summary Sentence

Name: _____ Date: _____

who/what: ....

(did/will do) what: ....

when: ....

where: ....

why: ....

how: ....

Summary Sentence

_____

_____

_____

_____

K. Combined Outline

Name: _____ Date: _____

Title: _____

who/what: ....

(did/will do) what: ....

when: ....

where: ....

why: ....

how: ....

T.S. (summary sentence): _____

_____

_____

Details:

1. ....

2. ....

3. ....

4. ....

C.S. _____

_____

_____

L. Transition Outline (2 Paragraphs)

Name: _____ Date: _____

Topic: _____

1st ¶ —T.S. _____

_____

1. ....

2. ....

3. ....

2nd ¶ —T.S. _____

_____

1. ....

2. ....

3. ....

C.S.: _____

_____

_____

M. Transition Outline (3 Paragraphs)

Name: _____ Date: _____

Topic: _____

1st ¶ —T.S. _____

_____

1. ....

2. ....

3. ....

2nd ¶ —T.S. _____

_____

1. ....

2. ....

3. ....

3rd ¶ —T.S. _____

_____

1. ....

2. ....

3. ....

C.S.: _____

_____

_____

N. Single-Paragraph Outline (Book Report)

Name: _____ Date: _____

T.S. (include title and author): _____

_____

_____

Book Summary:

1. ....

2. ....

3. ....

4. ....

C.S. (opinion and recommended audience): _____

_____

_____

O. Multiple-Paragraph Outline (3 Paragraphs)

Name: _____ Date: _____

Topic: _____

Thesis Statement: _____

_____

Main Idea	Details
Introduction ¶ 1	....
¶ 2	....
Conclusion ¶ 3	....

P. Multiple-Paragraph Outline (4 Paragraphs)

Name: _____ Date: _____

Topic: _____

Thesis Statement: _____

_____

Main Idea	Details
Introduction ¶ 1	....
¶ 2	....
¶ 3	....
Conclusion ¶ 4	....

Q. Multiple-Paragraph Outline (5 Paragraphs)

Name:_____ Date:_____

Topic: _____

Thesis Statement: _____

_____

Main Idea	Details
Introduction ¶ 1	....
  ¶ 2	....
  ¶ 3	....
  ¶ 4	....
Conclusion ¶ 5	....

R. Multiple-Paragraph Outline (Book Report)

Name: _____ Date: _____

Title of Book: _____

Thesis Statement: _____

_____

Main Idea	Details
Introduction ¶ 1	....
Book Summary ¶ 2	....
Opinion ¶ 3	....

Glossary

adjectives

Words that modify a noun or pronoun, making its meaning more exact.

> Sarah is a <u>fine young</u> lady.

appositive

A second noun, or a phrase or clause equivalent to a noun, that is placed beside another noun to explain it more fully.

> George Washington, <u>a great general,</u> was the first president of the United States.

argumentative writing

Writing that presents a claim (or claims) and supports it (or them) with evidence and examples, usually citing sources; it acknowledges and sometimes rebuts opposing views or counterclaims.

cause-and-effect

A text structure that shows a relationship between the cause (why something happened) and the effect (what happened).

claim

The writer's thesis; a statement of the writer's argument.

clauses

Groups of words that contain a subject and a predicate and are part of a sentence.

Jim saw the bird <u>as it fell from the sky.</u>

coherence

The quality of writing in which sentences and paragraphs are logically related to each other.

Combined Outline

A summary outline that combines sentence expansion with a Single Paragraph Outline.

compare-contrast

A text structure that shows how two or more things are alike and/or how they are different.

complex sentence

A sentence that consists of a main clause and one or more subordinate clauses.

Since it was raining, we decided to stay home.

Rachel decided to stay home even though Seth went out.

composition (essay)

A series of paragraphs united by a common theme.

conjunctions

Words that join other words, phrases, and clauses to one another. They help make writing clear and linguistically rich. *See also* coordinating conjunctions *and* subordinating conjunction.

coordinating conjunctions

Conjunctions that join two or more independent clauses, such as *and, but, or, yet, nor, for,* and *so.*

Terrell ate quickly, <u>yet</u> he was still late.

counterclaim

An opposing point of view; the position(s) refuting the claim.

declarative sentence (statement)

A sentence that makes a statement.

The show starts at eight o'clock.

dependent (subordinate) clause

A clause that does not express a complete thought and cannot stand alone as a sentence.

> <u>As soon as Carlita left,</u> it began to rain.

descriptive

A text structure that describes a topic, idea, person, place, or thing by its features, characteristics, or examples.

diagnostic worksheets

A type of assessment used to determine whether students have mastered specific strategies they have been taught and are ready to move on.

do-now activities

Brief activities that students do at the beginning of class.

editing

Correcting the mechanics of writing, including punctuation, capitalization, spelling, grammar, and usage.

essay

A series of paragraphs united by a common theme.

exclamatory sentence (exclamation)

A sentence that expresses strong or sudden feeling. It ends with an exclamation point.

> I need help this minute!

executive functions

Cognitive processes that affect all aspects of memory, attention, and language; they have a great impact on writing.

exit slips (tickets)

Brief writing tasks to be completed by students at the end of a class, using a specific sentence activity or one of the scaffolding activities leading up to a paragraph or composition. They reflect the content studied during the class period and assess comprehension.

expository terms

Words that require an explanatory or informative response, such as *discuss*, *justify*, or *describe*.

expository writing

Writing that explains or informs.

fragment

A group of words that is not a grammatically complete sentence. Usually a fragment lacks a subject, verb, or both or is a dependent clause that is not connected to an independent clause.

> Before I left the house

independent writing sample

Assessment given at the beginning, middle, and end of the school year, designed to provide an overall picture of students' independent writing, measure their progress, and highlight areas where they need more support.

imperative sentence (command)

A sentence that expresses a command; the subject is not always explicitly stated.

> Come here immediately.

independent (main) clause

A clause that expresses a complete thought and could stand alone as a sentence.

> Although Lisa has a Toyota, <u>Kevin has a Ford.</u>

interrogative sentence (question)

A sentence that asks a question. It ends with a question mark.

> Is Anthony coming?

kernel sentences

Simple, active, declarative sentences containing no modifiers or connectives that may be used in making more elaborate sentences.

> The children ran.

> Rob threw the ball.

main clause

See independent (main) clause.

Multiple-Paragraph Outline (MPO)

A plan for developing an essay.

narrative

A text structure that describes items or events in order or relates the steps necessary to do or make something.

noun

A word that names a person, place, thing, quality, action, or idea. *See also* proper noun.

> <u>Alice</u> has lovely <u>eyes.</u>

> <u>Hatred</u> is a destructive <u>emotion.</u>

number agreement

A singular subject must have a singular verb.

> This apple <u>is</u> very crisp.

A plural subject must have a plural verb.

> These apples <u>are</u> very crisp.

opinion writing

Writing that presents the author's opinion, giving reasons in support of it, but does not raise or rebut counterarguments. The reasons offered may be based on the author's personal experience rather than objective evidence.

outlines

Plans that help the writer identify the main points of a paragraph or essay and organize details in a way that effectively conveys information to a reader.

paragraph

A group of sentences that includes details supporting a specific point.

phrase

A group of related words that does not contain both a verb and its subject.

> Jan danced <u>without her shoes</u>.

> <u>Despite Rashida's directions</u>, I made a left turn.

plan of development

A summary of the main points the writer will discuss in an essay. It is often embedded in the thesis statement.

> The outcome of the Civil War had profound social, economic, and political effects.

predicate

One or more words, including a verb, that says something about the subject.

> The young boy <u>danced for hours.</u>

> The volcano <u>erupted.</u>

problem-solution

A text structure that describes a problem, sometimes explains why the problem exists, and then gives one or more possible solutions.

pro-con essay

A multiple-paragraph composition that presents two sides of an issue but does not take a position.

pronoun

A word used in place of a noun. The noun a pronoun replaces is called its *antecedent*.

> Akira went to the store because <u>it</u> was open all night.

proper noun

A specific person, place, or thing; it begins with a capital letter.

> Simon, New York, Monday

rebut

To refute an opposing point of view or counterclaim in an argumentative essay.

revising

Improving the content, organization, sentence structures, or word choice of a piece of writing.

run-on sentences

Written sequences of two or more main clauses that are not separated by a period or any other punctuation or joined by a conjunction.

> Rose defrosted the refrigerator the ice was an inch thick.

sentence

A set of words that expresses a complete thought, typically containing a subject and predicate and conveying a statement, question, exclamation, or command. Sentences generally consist of a main clause and sometimes one or more subordinate clauses. *See also* complex sentence, declarative sentence (statement), exclamatory sentence (exclamation), interrogative sentence (question), *and* imperative sentence (command).

sentence stem

An independent or a dependent clause beginning a sentence that the writer is expected to complete.

> Although the colonists settled near rivers, _____.
>
> The colonists settled near rivers, but _____.

Single-Paragraph Outline (SPO)

A plan for one paragraph.

stop and jot

A brief writing task, usually a sentence activity, that is assigned during a lesson and may be shared with the class. It serves as a comprehension check and can be a scaffolding activity for a paragraph.

subject

The part of a sentence that states who or what the sentence is about.

> The <u>plant</u> grew rapidly.
>
> <u>Joe</u> caught the ball

subordinate clause

See dependent clause.

subordinating conjunctions

Conjunctions that introduce an adverb clause and signal the relationship between that clause and the main idea. Some common subordinating conjunctions include *although, while, before, if, whenever,* and *unless.*

> <u>Although</u> the book sold well, it was not very good.

summary

A brief, concise restatement (not a retelling) of the main idea of a composition, lecture, or reading selection. It presents the main point of a body of material in condensed form.

summary sentence

A single sentence summarizing a specific text that could serve as the topic sentence of a paragraph.

syntax

The specific ways in which words are ordered to create logical, meaningful phrases, clauses, and sentences.

tense agreement

Consistency in verb tenses within one sentence and from one sentence to the next.

> Last Tuesday, as I <u>was driving</u> to school, a child <u>ran</u> in front of my car. I <u>swerved</u> to avoid hitting her.

text structures

The organization of a paragraph or essay. *See also* cause-and-effect, compare-contrast, narrative, and problem-solution.

thesis statement

A sentence stating the main theme of a composition. It is usually included as the last sentence in the introductory paragraph and rephrased as the first sentence in the conclusion.

topic sentence

A statement of the main idea of a paragraph.

transitions

Words and phrases that provide connections between ideas, sentences, and paragraphs and improve the flow and clarity of writing.

Transition Outline (TO)

An intermediate step, if needed, for students who are comfortable creating an SPO but not yet ready for the MPO. It can be used to plan a two- or three-paragraph essay.

turn-and-talks

In-class activities in which students turn to a partner to discuss a specific topic. This enables students to formulate and share ideas with their peers instead of always answering a teacher's questions.

unelaborated paragraph

Four to six related sentences that have no mechanical errors but are extremely simple and need to be revised and improved. Initially, specific instructions are given for revision. Later, students decide with each other and then on their own what revisions are needed to make the paragraph better.

verb

A word or group of words used to express physical or mental action, condition, or being.

working memory

The part of cognition that enables us to manipulate multiple inputs and process them simultaneously, drawing on the surrounding environment and on information stored in long-term memory. If students do not have the mechanical skills necessary for writing embedded in their long-term memory and therefore readily accessible, they will find it difficult to simultaneously keep those skills in their working memory along with higher-level considerations such as purpose, audience, meaning, word choice, and syntax.

Index

Page numbers in italics refer to exhibits and tables.

Notes

Notes

Notes

Notes

Notes

Notes